Hands-On Exploratory Data Analysis with Python

Perform EDA techniques to understand, summarize, and investigate your data

Suresh Kumar Mukhiya
Usman Ahmed

BIRMINGHAM - MUMBAI

Hands-On Exploratory Data Analysis with Python

Copyright © 2020 Packt Publishing

Commissioning Editor: Pravin Dhandre
Acquisition Editor: Ali Abidi
Content Development Editor: Nathanya Dias
Senior Editor: Ayaan Hoda
Technical Editor: Manikandan Kurup
Copy Editor: Safis Editing
Project Coordinator: Aishwarya Mohan
Proofreader: Safis Editing
Indexer: Rekha Nair
Production Designer: Deepika Naik

First published: March 2020

Production reference: 1270320

Published by Packt Publishing Ltd.
Livery Place
35 Livery Street
Birmingham
B3 2PB, UK.

ISBN 978-1-78953-725-3

www.packt.com

Packt.com

Subscribe to our online digital library for full access to over 7,000 books and videos, as well as industry leading tools to help you plan your personal development and advance your career. For more information, please visit our website.

Why subscribe?

- Spend less time learning and more time coding with practical eBooks and Videos from over 4,000 industry professionals

- Improve your learning with Skill Plans built especially for you

- Get a free eBook or video every month

- Fully searchable for easy access to vital information

- Copy and paste, print, and bookmark content

Did you know that Packt offers eBook versions of every book published, with PDF and ePub files available? You can upgrade to the eBook version at www.packt.com and as a print book customer, you are entitled to a discount on the eBook copy. Get in touch with us at customercare@packtpub.com for more details.

At www.packt.com, you can also read a collection of free technical articles, sign up for a range of free newsletters, and receive exclusive discounts and offers on Packt books and eBooks.

Contributors

About the authors

Suresh Kumar Mukhiya is a Ph.D. candidate currently affiliated with the Western Norway University of Applied Sciences (HVL). He is a big data enthusiast, specializing in information systems, model-driven software engineering, big data analysis, artificial intelligence, and frontend development. He has completed his Master's degree in information systems at the Norwegian University of Science and Technology (NTNU, Norway), along with a thesis in processing mining. He also holds a Bachelor's degree in computer science and information technology (BSc.CSIT) from Tribhuvan University, Nepal, where he was decorated with the Vice-Chancellor's Award for obtaining the highest score. He is a passionate photographer and a resilient traveler.

> *Special thanks go to the people who have helped in the creation of this book. We want to acknowledge the following contributors whose constructive feedback and ideas made this book possible: Asha Gaire (asha.gaire95@gmail.com), Bachelor in Computer Science and Information Technology, Nepal. She proofread the final draft and contributed to the major sections of the book especially Data Transformation, Grouping Dataset, and Correlation chapters. Anju Mukhiya (anjumukhiya@gmail.com) for reading an early draft and making many corrections and suggestions. Lilash Sah, (lilashsah2012@gmail.com) Master in Information Technology, King's Own Institute -Sydney, for reading and validating the codes used in this book.*

Usman Ahmed is a data scientist and Ph.D. candidate at the Western Norway University of Applied Sciences (HVL). He has rich experience in building and scaling high-performance systems based on data mining, natural language processing, and machine learning. Usman's research interests are sequential data mining, heterogeneous computing, natural language processing, recommendation systems, and machine learning. He has completed the Master of Science degree in computer science at Capital University of Science and Technology, Islamabad, Pakistan. Usman Ahmed was awarded a gold medal for his bachelor of computer science degree from Heavy Industries Taxila Education City.

About the reviewer

Jamshaid Sohail is passionate about data science, machine learning, computer vision, natural language processing, and big data, and has completed over 65 online courses in related fields. He has worked in a Silicon Valley-based start-up named Funnelbeam as a data scientist. He worked with the founders of Funnelbeam, who came from Stanford University, and he generated a lot of revenue by completing several projects and products. Currently, he is working as a data scientist at Fiverivers Technologies. He authored the course *Data Wrangling with Python 3.X* for Packt and has reviewed a number of books and courses.

Packt is searching for authors like you

If you're interested in becoming an author for Packt, please visit authors.packtpub.com and apply today. We have worked with thousands of developers and tech professionals, just like you, to help them share their insight with the global tech community. You can make a general application, apply for a specific hot topic that we are recruiting an author for, or submit your own idea.

Table of Contents

Section 2: Descriptive Statistics

Preface

Data is a collection of discrete objects, events, and facts in the form of numbers, text, pictures, videos, objects, audio, and other entities. Processing data provides a great deal of information. But the million-dollar question is—*how* do we get *meaningful* information from data? The answer to this question is **Exploratory Data Analysis** (**EDA**), which is the process of investigating datasets, elucidating subjects, and visualizing outcomes. EDA is an approach to data analysis that applies a variety of techniques to maximize specific insights into a dataset, reveal an underlying structure, extract significant variables, detect outliers and anomalies, test assumptions, develop models, and determine best parameters for future estimations. This book, *Hands-On Exploratory Data Analysis with Python*, aims to provide practical knowledge about the main pillars of EDA, including data cleansing, data preparation, data exploration, and data visualization. Why visualization? Well, several research studies have shown that portraying data in graphical form makes complex statistical data analyses and business intelligence more marketable.

You will get the opportunity to explore open source datasets including healthcare datasets, demographics datasets, a Titanic dataset, a wine quality dataset, automobile datasets, a Boston housing pricing dataset, and many others. Using these real-life datasets, you will get hands-on practice in understanding data, summarize data's characteristics, and visualizing data for business intelligence purposes. This book expects you to use pandas, a powerful library for working with data, and other core Python libraries including NumPy, scikit-learn, SciPy, StatsModels for regression, and Matplotlib for visualization.

Who this book is for

This book is for anyone who intends to analyze data, including students, teachers, managers, engineers, statisticians, data analysts, and data scientists. The practical concepts presented in this hands-on book are applicable to applications in various disciplines, including linguistics, sociology, astronomy, marketing, business, management, quality control, education, economics, medicine, psychology, engineering, biology, physics, computer science, geosciences, chemistry, and any other fields where data analysis and synthesis is required in order to improve knowledge and help in decision-making processes. Fundamental understanding of Python programming and some statistical concepts is all you need to get started with this book.

What this book covers

Chapter 1, *Exploratory Data Analysis Fundamentals*, will help us learn and revise the fundamental aspects of EDA. We will dig into the importance of EDA and the main data analysis tasks, and try to make sense out of data. In addition to that, we will use Python to explore different types of data, including numerical data, time-series data, geospatial data, categorical data, and others.

Chapter 2, *Visual Aids for EDA*, will help us gain proficiency with different tools for visualizing the information that we get from investigation and make analysis much clearer. We will figure out how to use data visualization tools such as box plots, histograms, multi-variate charts, and more. Notwithstanding that, we will get our hands dirty in plotting an enlightening visual graph using real databases. Finally, we will investigate the intuitive forms of these plots.

Chapter 3, *EDA with Personal Email*, will help us figure out how to import a dataset from your personal Gmail account and work on analyzing the extracted dataset. We will perform basic EDA techniques, including data loading, data cleansing, data preparation, data visualization, and data analysis, on the extracted dataset.

Chapter 4, *Data Transformation*, is where you will take your first steps in data wrangling. We will see how to merge database-style DataFrames, merge on the index, concatenate along an axis, combine data with overlaps, reshape with hierarchical indexing, and pivot from long to wide format. We will look at what needs to be done with a dataset before analysis takes place, such as removing duplicates, replacing values, renaming axis indexes, discretization and binning, and detecting and filtering outliers. We will work on transforming data using a function or mapping, permutation, and random sampling and computing indicators/dummy variables.

Chapter 5, *Descriptive Statistics*, will teach you about essential statistical measures for gaining insights about data that are not noticeable at the surface level. We will become familiar with the equations for computing the variance and standard deviation of datasets as well as figuring out percentiles and quartiles. Furthermore, we will envision those factual measures with visualization. We will use tools such as box plots to gain knowledge from statistics.

Chapter 6, *Grouping Datasets*, will cover the rudiments of grouping and how it can change our datasets in order to help us to analyze them better. We will look at different group-by mechanics that will amass our dataset into various classes in which we can perform aggregate activities. We will also figure out how to dissect categorical data with visualizations, utilizing pivot tables and cross-tabulations.

Chapter 7, *Correlation*, will help us to understand the correlation between different factors and to identify to what degree different factors are relevant. We will learn about the different kinds of examinations that we can carry out to discover the relationships between data, including univariate analysis, bivariate analysis, and multivariate analysis on the Titanic dataset, as well as looking at Simpson's paradox. We will observe how correlation does not always equal causation.

Chapter 8, *Time Series Analysis*, will help us to understand time-series data and how to perform EDA on it. We will use the open power system data for time series analysis.

Chapter 9, *Hypothesis Testing and Regression*, will help us learn about hypothesis testing and linear, non-linear, and multiple linear regression. We will build a basis for model development and evaluation. We will be using polynomial regression and pipelines for model evaluation.

Chapter 10, *Model Development and Evaluation*, will help us learn about a unified machine learning approach, discuss different types of machine learning algorithms and evaluation techniques. Moreover, in this chapter, we are going to perform the unsupervised learning task of clustering with text data. Furthermore, we will discuss model selection and model deployment techniques.

Chapter 11, *EDA on Wine Quality Data*, will teach us how to use all the techniques learned throughout the book to perform advanced EDA on a wine quality dataset. We will import the dataset, research the variables, slice the data based on different points of interest, and perform data analysis.

To get the most out of this book

All the EDA activities in this book are based on Python 3.x. So, the first and foremost requirement to run any code from this book is for you to have Python 3.x installed on your computer irrespective of the operating system. Python can be installed on your system by following the documentation on its official website: https://www.python.org/downloads/.

Here is the software that needs to be installed in order to execute the code:

Software/hardware covered in the book	OS requirements
Python 3.x	Windows, macOS, Linux, or any other OS
Python notebooks	There are several options: Local: Jupyter: `https://jupyter.org/` Local: `https://www.anaconda.com/distribution/` Online: `https://colab.research.google.com/`
Python libraries	NumPy, pandas, scikit-learn, Matplotlib, Seaborn, StatsModel

We primarily used Python notebooks to execute our code. One of the reasons for that is, with them, it is relatively easy to break code into a clear structure and see the output on the fly. It is always safer to install a notebook locally. The official website holds great information on how they can be installed. However, if you do not want the hassle and simply want to start learning immediately, then Google Colab provides a great platform where you can code and execute code using both Python 2.x and Python 3.x with support for **Graphics Processing Units (GPUs)** and **Tensor Processing Units (TPUs)**.

If you are using the digital version of this book, we advise you to type the code yourself or access the code via the GitHub repository (link available in the next section). Doing so will help you avoid any potential errors related to the copying and pasting of code.

Download the example code files

You can download the example code files for this book from your account at `www.packt.com`. If you purchased this book elsewhere, you can visit `www.packtpub.com/support` and register to have the files emailed directly to you.

You can download the code files by following these steps:

1. Log in or register at `www.packt.com`.
2. Select the **Support** tab.
3. Click on **Code Downloads**.
4. Enter the name of the book in the **Search** box and follow the onscreen instructions.

Once the file is downloaded, please make sure that you unzip or extract the folder using the latest version of:

- WinRAR/7-Zip for Windows
- Zipeg/iZip/UnRarX for Mac
- 7-Zip/PeaZip for Linux

The code bundle for the book is also hosted on GitHub at `https://github.com/PacktPublishing/hands-on-exploratory-data-analysis-with-python`. In case there's an update to the code, it will be updated on the existing GitHub repository.

We also have other code bundles from our rich catalog of books and videos available at `https://github.com/PacktPublishing/`. Check them out!

Download the color images

We also provide a PDF file that has color images of the screenshots/diagrams used in this book. You can download it here: `https://static.packt-cdn.com/downloads/9781789537253_ColorImages.pdf`.

Conventions used

There are a number of text conventions used throughout this book.

`CodeInText`: Indicates code words in the text, database table names, folder names, filenames, file extensions, pathnames, dummy URLs, user input, and Twitter handles. Here is an example: "we visualized a time series dataset using the `matplotlib` and `seaborn` libraries."

A block of code is set as follows:

```
import os
import numpy as np
%matplotlib inline from matplotlib
import pyplot as plt
import seaborn as sns
```

Any command-line input or output is written as follows:

```
> pip install virtualenv
> virtualenv Local_Version_Directory -p Python_System_Directory
```

Bold: Indicates a new term, an important word, or words that you see onscreen. For example, words in menus or dialog boxes appear in the text like this. Here is an example: "Time series data may contain a notable amount of **outliers**."

 Warnings or important notes appear like this.

 Tips and tricks appear like this.

Get in touch

Feedback from our readers is always welcome.

General feedback: If you have questions about any aspect of this book, mention the book title in the subject of your message and email us at customercare@packtpub.com.

Errata: Although we have taken every care to ensure the accuracy of our content, mistakes do happen. If you have found a mistake in this book, we would be grateful if you would report this to us. Please visit www.packtpub.com/support/errata, selecting your book, clicking on the Errata Submission Form link, and entering the details.

Piracy: If you come across any illegal copies of our works in any form on the Internet, we would be grateful if you would provide us with the location address or website name. Please contact us at copyright@packt.com with a link to the material.

If you are interested in becoming an author: If there is a topic that you have expertise in and you are interested in either writing or contributing to a book, please visit authors.packtpub.com.

Reviews

Please leave a review. Once you have read and used this book, why not leave a review on the site that you purchased it from? Potential readers can then see and use your unbiased opinion to make purchase decisions, we at Packt can understand what you think about our products, and our authors can see your feedback on their book. Thank you!

For more information about Packt, please visit packt.com.

Section 1: The Fundamentals of EDA

The main objective of this section is to cover the fundamentals of **Exploratory Data Analysis (EDA)** and understand different stages of the EDA process. We will also look at the key concepts of profiling, quality assessment, the main aspects of EDA, and the challenges and opportunities in EDA. In addition to this, we will be discovering different useful visualization techniques. Finally, we will be discussing essential data transformation techniques, including database-style dataframe merges, transformation techniques, and benefits of data transformation.

This section contains the following chapters:

- Chapter 1, *Exploratory Data Analysis Fundamentals*
- Chapter 2, *Visual Aids for EDA*
- Chapter 3, *EDA with Personal Email*
- Chapter 4, *Data Transformation*

1
Exploratory Data Analysis Fundamentals

The main objective of this introductory chapter is to revise the fundamentals of **Exploratory Data Analysis** (**EDA**), what it is, the key concepts of profiling and quality assessment, the main dimensions of EDA, and the main challenges and opportunities in EDA.

Data encompasses a collection of discrete objects, numbers, words, events, facts, measurements, observations, or even descriptions of things. Such data is collected and stored by every event or process occurring in several disciplines, including biology, economics, engineering, marketing, and others. Processing such data elicits useful *information* and processing such information generates useful knowledge. But an important question is: how can we generate meaningful and useful information from such data? An answer to this question is EDA. EDA is a process of examining the available dataset to discover patterns, spot anomalies, test hypotheses, and check assumptions using statistical measures. In this chapter, we are going to discuss the steps involved in performing top-notch exploratory data analysis and get our hands dirty using some open source databases.

As mentioned here and in several studies, the primary aim of EDA is to examine what data can tell us before actually going through formal modeling or hypothesis formulation. John Tuckey promoted EDA to statisticians to examine and discover the data and create newer hypotheses that could be used for the development of a newer approach in data collection and experimentations.

In this chapter, we are going to learn and revise the following topics:

- Understanding data science
- The significance of EDA
- Making sense of data
- Comparing EDA with classical and Bayesian analysis
- Software tools available for EDA
- Getting started with EDA

Understanding data science

Let's get this out of the way by pointing out that, if you have not heard about data science, then you should not be reading this book. Everyone right now is talking about data science in one way or another. Data science is at the peak of its hype and the skills for data scientists are changing. Now, data scientists are not only required to build a performant model, but it is essential for them to explain the results obtained and use the result for business intelligence. During my talks, seminars, and presentations, I find several people trying to ask me: *what type of skillset do I need to learn in order to become a top-notch data scientist? Do I need to get a Ph.D. in data science?* Well, one thing I could tell you straight away is you do not need a Ph.D. to be an expert in data science. But one thing that people generally agree on is that data science involves cross-disciplinary knowledge from computer science, data, statistics, and mathematics. There are several phases of data analysis, including data requirements, data collection, data processing, data cleaning, exploratory data analysis, modeling and algorithms, and data product and communication. These phases are similar to the **CRoss-Industry Standard Process for data mining** (**CRISP**) framework in data mining.

The main takeaway here is the stages of EDA, as it is an important aspect of data analysis and data mining. Let's understand in brief what these stages are:

- **Data requirements:** There can be various sources of data for an organization. It is important to comprehend what type of data is required for the organization to be collected, curated, and stored. For example, an application tracking the sleeping pattern of patients suffering from dementia requires several types of sensors' data storage, such as sleep data, heart rate from the patient, electro-dermal activities, and user activities pattern. All of these data points are required to correctly diagnose the mental state of the person. Hence, these are mandatory requirements for the application. In addition to this, it is required to categorize the data, numerical or categorical, and the format of storage and dissemination.
- **Data collection:** Data collected from several sources must be stored in the correct format and transferred to the right information technology personnel within a company. As mentioned previously, data can be collected from several objects on several events using different types of sensors and storage tools.
- **Data processing:** Preprocessing involves the process of pre-curating the dataset before actual analysis. Common tasks involve correctly exporting the dataset, placing them under the right tables, structuring them, and exporting them in the correct format.

- **Data cleaning:** Preprocessed data is still not ready for detailed analysis. It must be correctly transformed for an incompleteness check, duplicates check, error check, and missing value check. These tasks are performed in the data cleaning stage, which involves responsibilities such as matching the correct record, finding inaccuracies in the dataset, understanding the overall data quality, removing duplicate items, and filling in the missing values. However, how could we identify these anomalies on any dataset? Finding such data issues requires us to perform some analytical techniques. We will be learning several such analytical techniques in Chapter 4, *Data Transformation*. To understand briefly, data cleaning is dependent on the types of data under study. Hence, it is most essential for data scientists or EDA experts to comprehend different types of datasets. An example of data cleaning would be using outlier detection methods for quantitative data cleaning.

- **EDA:** Exploratory data analysis, as mentioned before, is the stage where we actually start to understand the message contained in the data. It should be noted that several types of data transformation techniques might be required during the process of exploration. We will cover descriptive statistics in-depth in *Section 2*, Chapter 5, *Descriptive Statistics*, to understand the mathematical foundation behind descriptive statistics. This entire book is dedicated to tasks involved in exploratory data analysis.

- **Modeling and algorithm**: From a data science perspective, generalized models or mathematical formulas can represent or exhibit relationships among different variables, such as correlation or causation. These models or equations involve one or more variables that depend on other variables to cause an event. For example, when buying, say, pens, the total price of *pens(Total) = price for one pen(UnitPrice) * the number of pens bought (Quantity)*. Hence, our model would be *Total = UnitPrice * Quantity*. Here, the total price is dependent on the unit price. Hence, the total price is referred to as the dependent variable and the unit price is referred to as an independent variable. In general, a model always describes the relationship between independent and dependent variables. Inferential statistics deals with quantifying relationships between particular variables.
The Judd model for describing the relationship between data, model, and error still holds true: *Data = Model + Error*. We will discuss in detail model development in *Section 3*, Chapter 10, *Model Evaluation*. An example of inferential statistics would be regression analysis. We will discuss regression analysis in Chapter 9, *Regression*.

- **Data Product:** Any computer software that uses data as inputs, produces outputs, and provides feedback based on the output to control the environment is referred to as a data product. A data product is generally based on a model developed during data analysis, for example, a recommendation model that inputs user purchase history and recommends a related item that the user is highly likely to buy.
- **Communication:** This stage deals with disseminating the results to end stakeholders to use the result for *business intelligence*. One of the most notable steps in this stage is data visualization. Visualization deals with information relay techniques such as tables, charts, summary diagrams, and bar charts to show the analyzed result. We will outline several visualization techniques in `Chapter 2`, *Visual Aids for EDA*, with different types of data.

The significance of EDA

Different fields of science, economics, engineering, and marketing accumulate and store data primarily in electronic databases. Appropriate and well-established decisions should be made using the data collected. It is practically impossible to make sense of datasets containing more than a handful of data points without the help of computer programs. To be certain of the insights that the collected data provides and to make further decisions, data mining is performed where we go through distinctive analysis processes. Exploratory data analysis is key, and usually the first exercise in data mining. It allows us to visualize data to understand it as well as to create hypotheses for further analysis. The exploratory analysis centers around creating a synopsis of data or insights for the next steps in a data mining project.

EDA actually reveals ground truth about the content without making any underlying assumptions. This is the fact that data scientists use this process to actually understand what type of modeling and hypotheses can be created. Key components of exploratory data analysis include summarizing data, statistical analysis, and visualization of data. Python provides expert tools for exploratory analysis, with `pandas` for summarizing; `scipy`, along with others, for statistical analysis; and `matplotlib` and `plotly` for visualizations.

That makes sense, right? Of course it does. That is one of the reasons why you are going through this book. After understanding the significance of EDA, let's discover what are the most generic steps involved in EDA in the next section.

Steps in EDA

Having understood what EDA is, and its significance, let's understand the various steps involved in data analysis. Basically, it involves four different steps. Let's go through each of them to get a brief understanding of each step:

- **Problem definition:** Before trying to extract useful insight from the data, it is essential to define the business problem to be solved. The problem definition works as the driving force for a data analysis plan execution. The main tasks involved in problem definition are defining the main objective of the analysis, defining the main deliverables, outlining the main roles and responsibilities, obtaining the current status of the data, defining the timetable, and performing cost/benefit analysis. Based on such a problem definition, an execution plan can be created.

- **Data preparation**: This step involves methods for preparing the dataset before actual analysis. In this step, we define the sources of data, define data schemas and tables, understand the main characteristics of the data, clean the dataset, delete non-relevant datasets, transform the data, and divide the data into required chunks for analysis.

- **Data analysis:** This is one of the most crucial steps that deals with descriptive statistics and analysis of the data. The main tasks involve summarizing the data, finding the hidden correlation and relationships among the data, developing predictive models, evaluating the models, and calculating the accuracies. Some of the techniques used for data summarization are summary tables, graphs, descriptive statistics, inferential statistics, correlation statistics, searching, grouping, and mathematical models.

- **Development and representation of the results:** This step involves presenting the dataset to the target audience in the form of graphs, summary tables, maps, and diagrams. This is also an essential step as the result analyzed from the dataset should be interpretable by the business stakeholders, which is one of the major goals of EDA. Most of the graphical analysis techniques include scattering plots, character plots, histograms, box plots, residual plots, mean plots, and others. We will explore several types of graphical representation in Chapter 2, *Visual Aids for EDA*.

Making sense of data

It is crucial to identify the type of data under analysis. In this section, we are going to learn about different types of data that you can encounter during analysis. Different disciplines store different kinds of data for different purposes. For example, medical researchers store patients' data, universities store students' and teachers' data, and real estate industries storehouse and building datasets. A dataset contains many observations about a particular object. For instance, a dataset about patients in a hospital can contain many observations. A patient can be described by a *patient identifier (ID), name, address, weight, date of birth, address, email,* and *gender*. Each of these features that describes a patient is a variable. Each observation can have a specific value for each of these variables. For example, a patient can have the following:

```
PATIENT_ID = 1001
Name = Yoshmi Mukhiya
Address = Mannsverk 61, 5094, Bergen, Norway
Date of birth = 10th July 2018
Email = yoshmimukhiya@gmail.com
Weight = 10
Gender = Female
```

These datasets are stored in hospitals and are presented for analysis. Most of this data is stored in some sort of database management system in tables/schema. An example of a table for storing patient information is shown here:

PATIENT_ID	NAME	ADDRESS	DOB	EMAIL	Gender	WEIGHT
001	Suresh Kumar Mukhiya	Mannsverk, 61	30.12.1989	skmu@hvl.no	Male	68
002	Yoshmi Mukhiya	Mannsverk 61, 5094, Bergen	10.07.2018	yoshmimukhiya@gmail.com	Female	1
003	Anju Mukhiya	Mannsverk 61, 5094, Bergen	10.12.1997	anjumukhiya@gmail.com	Female	24
004	Asha Gaire	Butwal, Nepal	30.11.1990	aasha.gaire@gmail.com	Female	23
005	Ola Nordmann	Danmark, Sweden	12.12.1789	ola@gmail.com	Male	75

To summarize the preceding table, there are four observations (001, 002, 003, 004, 005). Each observation describes variables (`PatientID`, `name`, `address`, `dob`, `email`, `gender`, and `weight`). Most of the dataset broadly falls into two groups—numerical data and categorical data.

Numerical data

This data has a sense of measurement involved in it; for example, a person's age, height, weight, blood pressure, heart rate, temperature, number of teeth, number of bones, and the number of family members. This data is often referred to as **quantitative data** in statistics. The numerical dataset can be either discrete or continuous types.

Discrete data

This is data that is countable and its values can be listed out. For example, if we flip a coin, the number of heads in 200 coin flips can take values from 0 to 200 (finite) cases. A variable that represents a discrete dataset is referred to as a discrete variable. The discrete variable takes a fixed number of distinct values. For example, the `Country` variable can have values such as Nepal, India, Norway, and Japan. It is fixed. The `Rank` variable of a student in a classroom can take values from 1, 2, 3, 4, 5, and so on.

Continuous data

A variable that can have an infinite number of numerical values within a specific range is classified as continuous data. A variable describing continuous data is a continuous variable. For example, what is the temperature of your city today? Can we be finite? Similarly, the `weight` variable in the previous section is a continuous variable. We are going to use a car dataset in `Chapter 5`, *Descriptive Statistics*, to perform EDA.

A section of the table is shown in the following table:

Model	Year	Engine Fuel Type	Engine HP	Engine Cylinders	Transmission Type	Driven_Wheels	Number of Doors	Market Category	Vehicle Size	Vehicle Style	highway MPG	city mpg	Popularity	MSRP
1 Series M	2011	premium unleaded (required)	335.0	6.0	MANUAL	rear wheel drive	2.0	Factory Tuner,Luxury,High-Performance	Compact	Coupe	26	19	3916	46135
1 Series	2011	premium unleaded (required)	300.0	6.0	MANUAL	rear wheel drive	2.0	Luxury,Performance	Compact	Convertible	28	19	3916	40650
1 Series	2011	premium unleaded (required)	300.0	6.0	MANUAL	rear wheel drive	2.0	Luxury,High-Performance	Compact	Coupe	28	20	3916	36350
1 Series	2011	premium unleaded (required)	230.0	6.0	MANUAL	rear wheel drive	2.0	Luxury,Performance	Compact	Coupe	28	18	3916	29450
1 Series	2011	premium unleaded (required)	230.0	6.0	MANUAL	rear wheel drive	2.0	Luxury	Compact	Convertible	28	18	3916	34500
1 Series	2012	premium unleaded (required)	230.0	6.0	MANUAL	rear wheel drive	2.0	Luxury,Performance	Compact	Coupe	28	18	3916	31200
1 Series	2012	premium unleaded (required)	300.0	6.0	MANUAL	rear wheel drive	2.0	Luxury,Performance	Compact	Convertible	26	17	3916	44100
1 Series	2012	premium unleaded (required)	300.0	6.0	MANUAL	rear wheel drive	2.0	Luxury,High-Performance	Compact	Coupe	28	20	3916	39300

Check the preceding table and determine which of the variables are discrete and which of the variables are continuous. Can you justify your claim? Continuous data can follow an interval measure of scale or ratio measure of scale. We will go into more detail in the *Measurement scales* section in this chapter.

Categorical data

This type of data represents the characteristics of an object; for example, gender, marital status, type of address, or categories of the movies. This data is often referred to as **qualitative datasets** in statistics. To understand clearly, here are some of the most common types of categorical data you can find in data:

- Gender (Male, Female, Other, or Unknown)
- Marital Status (Annulled, Divorced, Interlocutory, Legally Separated, Married, Polygamous, Never Married, Domestic Partner, Unmarried, Widowed, or Unknown)
- Movie genres (Action, Adventure, Comedy, Crime, Drama, Fantasy, Historical, Horror, Mystery, Philosophical, Political, Romance, Saga, Satire, Science Fiction, Social, Thriller, Urban, or Western)

- Blood type (A, B, AB, or O)
- Types of drugs (Stimulants, Depressants, Hallucinogens, Dissociatives, Opioids, Inhalants, or Cannabis)

A variable describing categorical data is referred to as a **categorical variable**. These types of variables can have one of a limited number of values. It is easier for computer science students to understand categorical values as enumerated types or enumerations of variables. There are different types of categorical variables:

- A binary categorical variable can take exactly two values and is also referred to as a **dichotomous variable**. For example, when you create an experiment, the result is either success or failure. Hence, results can be understood as a **binary categorical variable**.
- **Polytomous variables** are categorical variables that can take more than two possible values. For example, marital status can have several values, such as annulled, divorced, interlocutory, legally separated, married, polygamous, never married, domestic partners, unmarried, widowed, domestic partner, and unknown. Since marital status can take more than two possible values, it is a **polytomous variable.**

Most of the categorical dataset follows either nominal or ordinal measurement scales. Let's understand what is a nominal or ordinal scale in the next section.

Measurement scales

There are four different types of measurement scales described in statistics: nominal, ordinal, interval, and ratio. These scales are used more in academic industries. Let's understand each of them with some examples.

Nominal

These are practiced for labeling variables without any quantitative value. The scales are generally referred to as **labels**. And these scales are mutually exclusive and do not carry any numerical importance. Let's see some examples:

- What is your gender?
  - Male
  - Female
  - Third gender/Non-binary

- • I prefer not to answer
- • Other
- • Other examples include the following:
  - • The languages that are spoken in a particular country
  - • Biological species
  - • Parts of speech in grammar (noun, pronoun, adjective, and so on)
  - • Taxonomic ranks in biology (Archea, Bacteria, and Eukarya)

Nominal scales are considered qualitative scales and the measurements that are taken using qualitative scales are considered **qualitative data**. However, the advancement in qualitative research has created confusion to be definitely considered as qualitative. If, for example, someone uses numbers as labels in the nominal measurement sense, they have no concrete numerical value or meaning. No form of arithmetic calculation can be made on nominal measures.

You might be thinking *why should you care about whether data is nominal or ordinal? Should we not just start loading the data and begin our analysis?* Well, we could. But think about this: you have a dataset, and you want to analyze it. How will you decide whether you can make a pie chart, bar chart, or histogram? Are you getting my point?

Well, for example, in the case of a nominal dataset, you can certainly know the following:

- • **Frequency** is the rate at which a label occurs over a period of time within the dataset.
- • **Proportion** can be calculated by dividing the frequency by the total number of events.
- • Then, you could compute the **percentage** of each proportion.
- • And to **visualize** the nominal dataset, you can use either a pie chart or a bar chart.

If you know your data follows nominal scales, you can use a pie chart or bar chart. That's one less thing to worry about, right? My point is, understanding the type of data is relevant in understanding what type of computation you can perform, what type of model you should fit on the dataset, and what type of visualization you can generate.

Ordinal

The main difference in the ordinal and nominal scale is the order. In ordinal scales, the order of the values is a significant factor. An easy tip to remember the ordinal scale is that it sounds like an *order*. Have you heard about the **Likert scale**, which uses a variation of an ordinal scale? Let's check an example of ordinal scale using the Likert scale: *WordPress is making content managers' lives easier. How do you feel about this statement?* The following diagram shows the Likert scale:

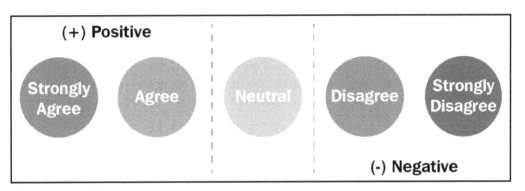

As depicted in the preceding diagram, the answer to the question of *WordPress is making content managers' lives easier* is scaled down to five different ordinal values, **Strongly Agree**, **Agree**, **Neutral**, **Disagree**, and **Strongly Disagree**. Scales like these are referred to as the Likert scale. Similarly, the following diagram shows more examples of the Likert scale:

How do you feel today?	How satisfied are you with our service?
● 1 - Very Unhappy	● 1 - Very Unsatisfied
○ 2 - Unhappy	○ 2 - Somewhat Unsatisfied
○ 3 - OK	○ 3 - Neutral
○ 4 - Happy	○ 4 - Somewhat Satisfied
○ 5 - Very Happy	○ 5 - Very Satisfied

To make it easier, consider ordinal scales as an order of ranking (1st, 2nd, 3rd, 4th, and so on). The **median** item is allowed as the measure of central tendency; however, the **average** is not permitted.

Interval

In interval scales, both the order and exact differences between the values are significant. Interval scales are widely used in statistics, for example, in the *measure of central tendencies—mean, median, mode, and standard deviations.* Examples include location in Cartesian coordinates and direction measured in degrees from magnetic north. The mean, median, and mode are allowed on interval data.

Ratio

Ratio scales contain order, exact values, and absolute zero, which makes it possible to be used in descriptive and inferential statistics. These scales provide numerous possibilities for statistical analysis. Mathematical operations, the measure of central tendencies, and the **measure of dispersion** and **coefficient of variation** can also be computed from such scales.

Examples include a measure of energy, mass, length, duration, electrical energy, plan angle, and volume. The following table gives a summary of the data types and scale measures:

Provides:	Nominal	Ordinal	Interval	Ratio
The "order"of values is known		✔	✔	✔
"Counts," aka "Frequency of Distribution"	✔	✔	✔	✔
Mode	✔	✔	✔	✔
Median		✔	✔	✔
Mean			✔	✔
Can quantify the difference between each value			✔	✔
Can add or subtract values			✔	✔
Can multiple and divide values				✔
Has "true zero"				✔

In the next section, we will compare EDA with classical and Bayesian analysis.

Comparing EDA with classical and Bayesian analysis

There are several approaches to data analysis. The most popular ones that are relevant to this book are the following:

- **Classical data analysis:** For the classical data analysis approach, the problem definition and data collection step are followed by model development, which is followed by analysis and result communication.

- **Exploratory data analysis approach**: For the EDA approach, it follows the same approach as classical data analysis except the model imposition and the data analysis steps are swapped. The main focus is on the data, its structure, outliers, models, and visualizations. Generally, in EDA, we do not impose any deterministic or probabilistic models on the data.

- **Bayesian data analysis approach:** The Bayesian approach incorporates prior probability distribution knowledge into the analysis steps as shown in the following diagram. Well, simply put, prior probability distribution of any quantity expresses the belief about that particular quantity before considering some evidence. Are you still lost with the term prior probability distribution? Andrew Gelman has a very descriptive paper about *prior probability distribution*. The following diagram shows three different approaches for data analysis illustrating the difference in their execution steps:

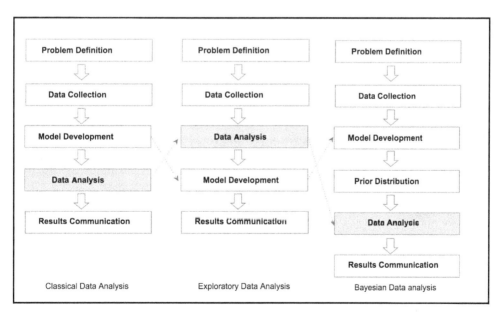

Data analysts and data scientists freely mix steps mentioned in the preceding approaches to get meaningful insights from the data. In addition to that, it is essentially difficult to judge or estimate which model is best for data analysis. All of them have their paradigms and are suitable for different types of data analysis.

Software tools available for EDA

There are several software tools that are available to facilitate EDA. Here, we are going to outline some of the open source tools:

- **Python**: This is an open source programming language widely used in data analysis, data mining, and data science (`https://www.python.org/`). For this book, we will be using Python.
- **R programming language**: R is an open source programming language that is widely utilized in statistical computation and graphical data analysis (`https://www.r-project.org`).
- **Weka**: This is an open source data mining package that involves several EDA tools and algorithms (`https://www.cs.waikato.ac.nz/ml/weka/`).
- **KNIME**: This is an open source tool for data analysis and is based on Eclipse (`https://www.knime.com/`).

Getting started with EDA

As mentioned earlier, we are going to use Python as the main tool for data analysis. Yay! Well, if you ask me why, Python has been consistently ranked among the top 10 programming languages and is widely adopted for data analysis and data mining by data science experts. In this book, we assume you have a working knowledge of Python. If you are not familiar with Python, it's probably too early to get started with data analysis. I assume you are familiar with the following Python tools and packages:

Python programming	Fundamental concepts of variables, string, and data types Conditionals and functions Sequences, collections, and iterations Working with files Object-oriented programming

NumPy	Create arrays with NumPy, copy arrays, and divide arrays Perform different operations on NumPy arrays Understand array selections, advanced indexing, and expanding Working with multi-dimensional arrays Linear algebraic functions and built-in NumPy functions
pandas	Understand and create `DataFrame` objects Subsetting data and indexing data Arithmetic functions, and mapping with pandas Managing index Building style for visual analysis
Matplotlib	Loading linear datasets Adjusting axes, grids, labels, titles, and legends Saving plots
SciPy	Importing the package Using statistical packages from SciPy Performing descriptive statistics Inference and data analysis

Before diving into details about analysis, we need to make sure we are on the same page. Let's go through the checklist and verify that you meet all of the prerequisites to get the best out of this book:

Setting up a virtual environment	``` > pip install virtualenv > virtualenv Local_Version_Directory -p Python_System_Directory ```

Reading/writing to files	```
	filename = "datamining.txt"
	file = open(filename, mode="r", encoding='utf-8')
	for line in file:
	 lines = file.readlines()
	print(lines)
	file.close()
	``

Error handling	```
	try:
	   Value = int(input("Type a number between 47 and 100:"))
	except ValueError:
	   print("You must type a number between 47 and 100!")
	else:
	   if (Value > 47) and (Value <= 100):
	       print("You typed: ", Value)
	   else:
	       print("The value you typed is incorrect!")
	``

Object-oriented concept	```
	class Disease:
	   def __init__(self, disease = 'Depression'):
	     self.type = disease
	   def getName(self):
	     print("Mental Health Diseases: {0}".format(self.type))
	
	d1 = Disease('Social Anxiety Disorder')
	d1.getName()
	``

Next, let's look at the basic operations of EDA using the NumPy library.

NumPy

In this section, we are going to revise the basic operations of EDA using the NumPy library. If you are familiar with these operations, feel free to jump to the next section. It might feel obvious when going through the code, but it is essential to make sure you understand these concepts before digging into EDA operations. When I started learning data science approaches, I followed a lot of blogs where they just reshaped an array or matrix. When I ran their code, it worked fine, but I never understood how I was able to add two matrices of different dimensions. In this section, I have tried to explicitly point out some of the basic numpy operations:

- For importing numpy, we will use the following code:

```
import numpy as np
```

- For creating different types of numpy arrays, we will use the following code:

```
# importing numpy
import numpy as np

# Defining 1D array
my1DArray = np.array([1, 8, 27, 64])
print(my1DArray)

# Defining and printing 2D array
my2DArray = np.array([[1, 2, 3, 4], [2, 4, 9, 16], [4, 8, 18, 32]])
print(my2DArray)

#Defining and printing 3D array
my3Darray = np.array([[[ 1, 2 , 3 , 4],[ 5 , 6 , 7 ,8]], [[ 1, 2, 3, 4],[ 9, 10, 11, 12]]])
print(my3Darray)
```

- For displaying basic information, such as the data type, shape, size, and strides of a NumPy array, we will use the following code:

```
# Print out memory address
print(my2DArray.data)

# Print the shape of array
print(my2DArray.shape)

# Print out the data type of the array
print(my2DArray.dtype)

# Print the stride of the array.
print(my2DArray.strides)
```

- For creating an array using built-in NumPy functions, we will use the following code:

```
# Array of ones
ones = np.ones((3,4))
print(ones)

# Array of zeros
zeros = np.zeros((2,3,4),dtype=np.int16)
print(zeros)

# Array with random values
np.random.random((2,2))

# Empty array
emptyArray = np.empty((3,2))
print(emptyArray)

# Full array
fullArray = np.full((2,2),7)
print(fullArray)

# Array of evenly-spaced values
evenSpacedArray = np.arange(10,25,5)
print(evenSpacedArray)

# Array of evenly-spaced values
evenSpacedArray2 = np.linspace(0,2,9)
print(evenSpacedArray2)
```

- For NumPy arrays and file operations, we will use the following code:

```
# Save a numpy array into file
x = np.arange(0.0,50.0,1.0)
np.savetxt('data.out', x, delimiter=',')

# Loading numpy array from text
z = np.loadtxt('data.out', unpack=True)
print(z)

# Loading numpy array using genfromtxt method
my_array2 = np.genfromtxt('data.out',
                          skip_header=1,
                          filling_values=-999)
print(my_array2)
```

- For inspecting NumPy arrays, we will use the following code:

```
# Print the number of `my2DArray`'s dimensions
print(my2DArray.ndim)

# Print the number of `my2DArray`'s elements
print(my2DArray.size)

# Print information about `my2DArray`'s memory layout
print(my2DArray.flags)

# Print the length of one array element in bytes
print(my2DArray.itemsize)

# Print the total consumed bytes by `my2DArray`'s elements
print(my2DArray.nbytes)
```

- Broadcasting is a mechanism that permits NumPy to operate with arrays of different shapes when performing arithmetic operations:

```
# Rule 1: Two dimensions are operatable if they are equal
# Create an array of two dimension
A =np.ones((6, 8))

# Shape of A
print(A.shape)

# Create another array
B = np.random.random((6,8))

# Shape of B
print(B.shape)

# Sum of A and B, here the shape of both the matrix is same.
print(A + B)
```

Secondly, two dimensions are also compatible when one of the dimensions of the array is 1. Check the example given here:

```
# Rule 2: Two dimensions are also compatible when one of them is 1
# Initialize `x`
x = np.ones((3,4))
print(x)

# Check shape of `x`
print(x.shape)

# Initialize `y`
y = np.arange(4)
print(y)

# Check shape of `y`
print(y.shape)

# Subtract `x` and `y`
print(x - y)
```

Lastly, there is a third rule that says two arrays can be broadcast together if they are compatible in all of the dimensions. Check the example given here:

```
# Rule 3: Arrays can be broadcast together if they are compatible
in all dimensions
x = np.ones((6,8))
y = np.random.random((10, 1, 8))
print(x + y)
```

The dimensions of *x(6,8)* and *y(10,1,8)* are different. However, it is possible to add them. Why is that? Also, change *y(10,2,8)* or *y(10,1,4)* and it will give `ValueError`. Can you find out why? (**Hint**: check rule 1).

- For seeing NumPy mathematics at work, we will use the following example:

```
# Basic operations (+, -, *, /, %)
x = np.array([[1, 2, 3], [2, 3, 4]])
y = np.array([[1, 4, 9], [2, 3, -2]])

# Add two array
add = np.add(x, y)
print(add)

# Subtract two array
sub = np.subtract(x, y)
print(sub)

# Multiply two array
mul = np.multiply(x, y)
print(mul)

# Divide x, y
div = np.divide(x,y)
print(div)

# Calculated the remainder of x and y
rem = np.remainder(x, y)
print(rem)
```

- Let's now see how we can create a subset and slice an array using an index:

```
x = np.array([10, 20, 30, 40, 50])

# Select items at index 0 and 1
print(x[0:2])

# Select item at row 0 and 1 and column 1 from 2D array
y = np.array([[ 1, 2, 3, 4], [ 9, 10, 11 ,12]])
print(y[0:2, 1])

# Specifying conditions
biggerThan2 = (y >= 2)
print(y[biggerThan2])
```

Next, we will use the `pandas` library to gain insights from data.

Pandas

Wes McKinney open sourced the `pandas` library (`https://github.com/wesm`) that has been widely used in data science. We will be utilizing this library to get meaningful insight from the data. Before delving in detail into this section, we are going to revisit some of the most fundamental techniques in pandas that you should be familiar with so as to be able to follow upcoming chapters. If these things are new to you, feel free to check one of the further reading sections for additional resources. Perform the following steps:

1. Use the following to set default parameters:

```
import numpy as np
import pandas as pd
print("Pandas Version:", pd.__version__)

pd.set_option('display.max_columns', 500)
pd.set_option('display.max_rows', 500)
```

2. In pandas, we can create data structures in two ways: series and dataframes. Check the following snippet to understand how we can create a dataframe from series, dictionary, and n-dimensional arrays.

The following code snippet shows how we can create a dataframe from a series:

```
series = pd.Series([2, 3, 7, 11, 13, 17, 19, 23])
print(series)

# Creating dataframe from Series
series_df = pd.DataFrame({
    'A': range(1, 5),
    'B': pd.Timestamp('20190526'),
    'C': pd.Series(5, index=list(range(4)), dtype='float64'),
    'D': np.array([3] * 4, dtype='int64'),
    'E': pd.Categorical(["Depression", "Social Anxiety", "Bipolar
Disorder", "Eating Disorder"]),
    'F': 'Mental health',
    'G': 'is challenging'
})
print(series_df)
```

The following code snippet shows how to create a dataframe for a dictionary:

```
# Creating dataframe from Dictionary
dict_df = [{'A': 'Apple', 'B': 'Ball'},{'A': 'Aeroplane', 'B':
'Bat', 'C': 'Cat'}]
dict_df = pd.DataFrame(dict_df)
print(dict_df)
```

The following code snippet shows how to create a dataframe from n-dimensional arrays:

```
# Creating a dataframe from ndarrays
sdf = {
    'County':['Østfold', 'Hordaland', 'Oslo', 'Hedmark', 'Oppland',
'Buskerud'],
    'ISO-Code':[1,2,3,4,5,6],
    'Area': [4180.69, 4917.94, 454.07, 27397.76, 25192.10,
14910.94],
    'Administrative centre': ["Sarpsborg", "Oslo", "City of Oslo",
"Hamar", "Lillehammer", "Drammen"]
    }
sdf = pd.DataFrame(sdf)
print(sdf)
```

3. Now, let's load a dataset from an external source into a pandas `DataFrame`. After that, let's see the first 10 entries:

```
columns = ['age', 'workclass', 'fnlwgt', 'education',
'education_num',
    'marital_status', 'occupation', 'relationship', 'ethnicity',
'gender','capital_gain','capital_loss','hours_per_week','country_of
_origin','income']
df =
pd.read_csv('http://archive.ics.uci.edu/ml/machine-learning-databas
es/adult/adult.data',names=columns)
df.head(10)
```

If you run the preceding cell, you should get an output similar to the following screenshot:

	age	workclass	fnlwgt	education	education_num	marital_status	occupation	relationship	ethnicity	gender	capital_gain	capital_loss	hours_per_week
0	39	State-gov	77516	Bachelors	13	Never-married	Adm-clerical	Not-in-family	White	Male	2174	0	40
1	50	Self-emp-not-inc	83311	Bachelors	13	Married-civ-spouse	Exec-managerial	Husband	White	Male	0	0	13
2	38	Private	215646	HS-grad	9	Divorced	Handlers-cleaners	Not-in-family	White	Male	0	0	40
3	53	Private	234721	11th	7	Married-civ-spouse	Handlers-cleaners	Husband	Black	Male	0	0	40
4	28	Private	338409	Bachelors	13	Married-civ-spouse	Prof-specialty	Wife	Black	Female	0	0	40
5	37	Private	284582	Masters	14	Married-civ-spouse	Exec-managerial	Wife	White	Female	0	0	40
6	49	Private	160187	9th	5	Married-spouse-absent	Other-service	Not-in-family	Black	Female	0	0	16
7	52	Self-emp-not-inc	209642	HS-grad	9	Married-civ-spouse	Exec-managerial	Husband	White	Male	0	0	45
8	31	Private	45781	Masters	14	Never-married	Prof-specialty	Not-in-family	White	Female	14084	0	50
9	42	Private	159449	Bachelors	13	Married-civ-spouse	Exec-managerial	Husband	White	Male	5178	0	40

4. The following code displays the rows, columns, data types, and memory used by the dataframe:

```
df.info()
```

The output of the preceding code snippet should be similar to the following:

```
# Output:
<class 'pandas.core.frame.DataFrame'>
RangeIndex: 32561 entries, 0 to 32560
Data columns (total 15 columns):
age 32561 non-null int64
workclass 32561 non-null object
fnlwgt 32561 non-null int64
education 32561 non-null object
education_num 32561 non-null int64
marital_status 32561 non-null object
occupation 32561 non-null object
relationship 32561 non-null object
ethnicity 32561 non-null object
gender 32561 non-null object
capital_gain 32561 non-null int64
capital_loss 32561 non-null int64
hours_per_week 32561 non-null int64
country_of_origin 32561 non-null object
income 32561 non-null object
dtypes: int64(6), object(9)
memory usage: 3.7+ MB
```

5. Let's now see how we can select rows and columns in any dataframe:

```
# Selects a row
df.iloc[10]

# Selects 10 rows
df.iloc[0:10]

# Selects a range of rows
df.iloc[10:15]

 # Selects the last 2 rows
df.iloc[-2:]

# Selects every other row in columns 3-5
df.iloc[::2, 3:5].head()
```

6. Let's combine NumPy and pandas to create a dataframe as follows:

```
import pandas as pd
import numpy as np

np.random.seed(24)
dFrame = pd.DataFrame({'F': np.linspace(1, 10, 10)})
dFrame = pd.concat([df, pd.DataFrame(np.random.randn(10, 5),
columns=list('EDCBA'))],
                 axis=1)
dFrame.iloc[0, 2] = np.nan
dFrame
```

It should produce a dataframe table similar to the following screenshot:

	F	E	D	C	B	A
0	1.0	1.329212	NaN	-0.316280	-0.990810	-1.070816
1	2.0	-1.438713	0.564417	0.295722	-1.626404	0.219565
2	3.0	0.678805	1.889273	0.961538	0.104011	-0.481165
3	4.0	0.850229	1.453425	1.057737	0.165562	0.515018
4	5.0	-1.336936	0.562861	1.392855	-0.063328	0.121668
5	6.0	1.207603	-0.002040	1.627796	0.354493	1.037528
6	7.0	-0.385684	0.519818	1.686583	-1.325963	1.428984
7	8.0	-2.089354	-0.129820	0.631523	-0.586538	0.290720
8	9.0	1.264103	0.290035	-1.970288	0.803906	1.030550
9	10.0	0.118098	-0.021853	0.046841	-1.628753	-0.392361

7. Let's style this table using a custom rule. If the values are greater than zero, we change the color to black (the default color); if the value is less than zero, we change the color to red; and finally, everything else would be colored green. Let's define a Python function to accomplish that:

```
# Define a function that should color the values that are less than
0
def colorNegativeValueToRed(value):
  if value < 0:
    color = 'red'
  elif value > 0:
    color = 'black'
```

```
else:
    color = 'green'

return 'color: %s' % color
```

8. Now, let's pass this function to the dataframe. We can do this by using the `style` method provided by pandas inside the dataframe:

```
s = df.style.applymap(colorNegativeValueToRed,
subset=['A','B','C','D','E'])
s
```

It should display a colored dataframe as shown in the following screenshot:

	F	E	D	C	B	A
0	1	1.32921	nan	-0.31628	-0.99081	-1.07082
1	2	-1.43871	0.564417	0.295722	-1.6264	0.219565
2	3	0.678805	1.88927	0.961538	0.104011	-0.481165
3	4	0.850229	1.45342	1.05774	0.165562	0.515018
4	5	-1.33694	0.562861	1.39285	-0.063328	0.121668
5	6	1.2076	-0.00204021	1.6278	0.354493	1.03753
6	7	-0.385684	0.519818	1.68658	-1.32596	1.42898
7	8	-2.08935	-0.12982	0.631523	-0.586538	0.29072
8	9	1.2641	0.290035	-1.97029	0.803906	1.03055
9	10	0.118098	-0.0218533	0.0468407	-1.62875	-0.392361

It should be noted that the `applymap` and `apply` methods are computationally expensive as they apply to each value inside the dataframe. Hence, it will take some time to execute. Have patience and await execution.

9. Now, let's go one step deeper. We want to scan each column and highlight the maximum value and the minimum value in that column:

```
def highlightMax(s):
    isMax = s == s.max()
    return ['background-color: orange' if v else '' for v in isMax]

def highlightMin(s):
    isMin = s == s.min()
    return ['background-color: green' if v else '' for v in isMin]
```

We apply these two functions to the dataframe as follows:

```
df.style.apply(highlightMax).apply(highlightMin).highlight_null(nul
l_color='red')
```

The output should be similar to the following screenshot:

	F	E	D	C	B	A
0	1	1.32921	nan	-0.31628	-0.99081	-1.07082
1	2	-1.43871	0.564417	0.295722	-1.6264	0.219565
2	3	0.678805	1.88927	0.961538	0.104011	-0.481165
3	4	0.850229	1.45342	1.05774	0.165562	0.515018
4	5	-1.33694	0.562861	1.39285	-0.063328	0.121668
5	6	1.2076	-0.00204021	1.6278	0.354493	1.03753
6	7	-0.385684	0.519818	1.68658	-1.32596	1.42898
7	8	-2.08935	-0.12982	0.631523	-0.586538	0.29072
8	9	1.2641	0.290035	-1.97029	0.803906	1.03055
9	10	0.118098	-0.0218533	0.0468407	-1.62875	-0.392361

10. Are you still not happy with your visualization? Let's try to use another Python library called `seaborn` and provide a gradient to the table:

```
import seaborn as sns

colorMap = sns.light_palette("pink", as_cmap=True)

styled = df.style.background_gradient(cmap=colorMap)
styled
```

The dataframe should have an orange gradient applied to it:

	F	E	D	C	B	A
0	1	1.32921	nan	-0.31628	-0.99081	-1.07082
1	2	-1.43871	0.564417	0.295722	-1.6264	0.219565
2	3	0.678805	1.88927	0.961538	0.104011	-0.481165
3	4	0.850229	1.45342	1.05774	0.165562	0.515018
4	5	-1.33694	0.562861	1.39285	-0.063328	0.121668
5	6	1.2076	-0.00204021	1.6278	0.354493	1.03753
6	7	-0.385684	0.519818	1.68658	-1.32596	1.42898
7	8	-2.08935	-0.12982	0.631523	-0.586538	0.29072
8	9	1.2641	0.290035	-1.97029	0.803906	1.03055
9	10	0.118098	-0.0218533	0.0468407	-1.62875	-0.392361

There are endless possibilities. How you present your result depends on you. Keep in mind that when you present your results to end stakeholders (your managers, boss, or non-technical persons), no matter how intelligently written your code is, it is worthless to them if they cannot make sense of your program. It is widely accepted that better-visualized results are easy to market.

SciPy

SciPy is a scientific library for Python and is open source. We are going to use this library in the upcoming chapters. This library depends on the NumPy library, which provides an efficient n-dimensional array manipulation function. We are going to learn more about these libraries in the upcoming chapters. My intention here is just to inform you to get prepared to face other libraries apart from NumPy and pandas. If you want to get started early, check for `scipy.stats` from the SciPy library.

Matplotlib

Matplotlib provides a huge library of customizable plots, along with a comprehensive set of backends. It can be utilized to create professional reporting applications, interactive analytical applications, complex dashboard applications, web/GUI applications, embedded views, and many more. We are going to explore Matplotlib in detail in `Chapter 2`, *Visual Aids for EDA*.

Summary

In this chapter, we revisited the most fundamental theory behind data analysis and exploratory data analysis. EDA is one of the most prominent steps in data analysis and involves steps such as data requirements, data collection, data processing, data cleaning, exploratory data analysis, modeling and algorithms, data production, and communication. It is crucial to identify the type of data under analysis. Different disciplines store different kinds of data for different purposes. For example, medical researchers store patients' data, universities store students' and teachers' data, real estate industries store house and building datasets, and many more. A dataset contains many observations about a particular object. Most of the datasets can be divided into numerical data and categorical datasets. There are four types of data measurement scales: nominal, ordinal, interval, and ratio.

We are going to use several Python libraries, including NumPy, pandas, SciPy, and Matplotlib, in this book for performing simple to complex exploratory data analysis. In the next chapter, we are going to learn about various types of visualization aids for exploratory data analysis.

Further reading

- Myatt, Glenn J. (2006). *Making Sense of Data: A Practical Guide to Exploratory Data Analysis and Data Mining.* Print ISBN:9780470074718 | Online ISBN:9780470101025 | DOI:10.1002/0470101024
- Chatfield, C. (1995). *Problem Solving: A Statistician's Guide* (2nd ed.). Chapman and Hall. ISBN 978-0412606304.
- *Prior distribution*, Andrew Gelman Volume 3, pp 1634–1637, http://www.stat.columbia.edu/~gelman/research/published/p039-_o.pdf
- Shearer, C. (2000). *The CRISP-DM model: the new blueprint for data mining.* J Data Warehousing; 5:13—22.
- Judd, Charles and McCleland, Gary (1989). *Data Analysis.* Harcourt Brace Jovanovich. ISBN 0-15-516765-0.
- Carifio, James and Perla, Rocco J. (2007). *Ten Common Misunderstandings, Misconceptions, Persistent Myths, and Urban Legends about Likert Scales and Likert Response Formats and Their Antidotes. Journal of Social Sciences.* 3 (3): 106–116. DOI:10.3844/jssp.2007.106.116

Visual Aids for EDA 2

As data scientists, two important goals in our work would be to extract knowledge from the data and to present the data to stakeholders. Presenting results to stakeholders is very complex in the sense that our audience may not have enough technical know-how to understand programming jargon and other technicalities. Hence, visual aids are very useful tools. In this chapter, we will focus on different types of visual aids that can be used with our datasets. We are going to learn about different types of techniques that can be used in the visualization of data.

In this chapter, we will cover the following topics:

- Line chart
- Bar chart
- Scatter plot
- Area plot and stacked plot
- Pie chart
- Table chart
- Polar chart
- Histogram
- Lollipop chart
- Choosing the best chart
- Other libraries to explore

Technical requirements

You can find the code for this chapter on GitHub: `https://github.com/PacktPublishing/ hands-on-exploratory-data-analysis-with-python`. In order to get the best out of this chapter, ensure the following:

- Make sure you have Python 3.X installed on your computer. It is recommended to use a Python notebook such as Anaconda.
- You must have Python libraries such as `pandas`, `seaborn`, and `matplotlib` installed.

Line chart

Do you remember what a continuous variable is and what a discrete variable is? If not, have a quick look at `Chapter 1`, *Exploratory Data Analysis Fundamentals*. Back to the main topic, a line chart is used to illustrate the relationship between two or more continuous variables.

We are going to use the `matplotlib` library and the stock price data to plot time series lines. First of all, let's understand the dataset. We have created a function using the `faker` Python library to generate the dataset. It is the simplest possible dataset you can imagine, with just two columns. The first column is `Date` and the second column is `Price`, indicating the stock price on that date.

Let's generate the dataset by calling the helper method. In addition to this, we have saved the CSV file. You can optionally load the CSV file using the `pandas` (`read_csv`) library and proceed with visualization.

My `generateData` function is defined here:

```
import datetime
import math
import pandas as pd
import random
import radar
from faker import Faker
fake = Faker()

def generateData(n):
  listdata = []
  start = datetime.datetime(2019, 8, 1)
  end = datetime.datetime(2019, 8, 30)
```

```
    delta = end - start
    for _ in range(n):
        date = radar.random_datetime(start='2019-08-1',
  stop='2019-08-30').strftime("%Y-%m-%d")
        price = round(random.uniform(900, 1000), 4)
        listdata.append([date, price])
    df = pd.DataFrame(listdata, columns = ['Date', 'Price'])
    df['Date'] = pd.to_datetime(df['Date'], format='%Y-%m-%d')
    df = df.groupby(by='Date').mean()

    return df
```

Having defined the method to generate data, let's get the data into a pandas dataframe and check the first 10 entries:

```
df = generateData(50)
df.head(10)
```

The output of the preceding code is shown in the following screenshot:

	Price
Date	
2019-08-01	999.598900
2019-08-02	957.870150
2019-08-04	978.674200
2019-08-05	963.380375
2019-08-06	978.092900
2019-08-07	987.847700
2019-08-08	952.669900
2019-08-10	973.929400
2019-08-13	971.485600
2019-08-14	977.036200

Let's create the line chart in the next section.

Steps involved

Let's look at the process of creating the line chart:

1. Load and prepare the dataset. We will learn more about how to prepare data in `Chapter 4`, *Data Transformation*. For this exercise, all the data is preprocessed.

2. Import the `matplotlib` library. It can be done with this command:

   ```
   import matplotlib.pyplot as plt
   ```

3. Plot the graph:

   ```
   plt.plot(df)
   ```

4. Display it on the screen:

   ```
   plt.show()
   ```

Here is the code if we put it all together:

```
import matplotlib.pyplot as plt

plt.rcParams['figure.figsize'] = (14, 10)
plt.plot(df)
```

And the plotted graph looks something like this:

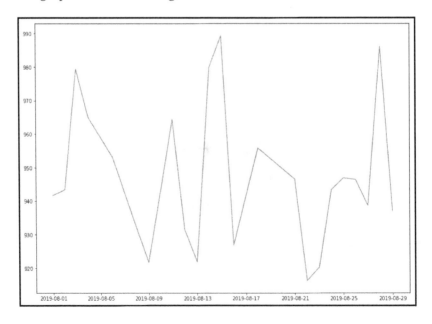

In the preceding example, we assume the data is available in the CSV format. In real-life scenarios, the data is mostly available in CSV, JSON, Excel, or XML formats and is mostly disseminated through some standard API. For this series, we assume you are already familiar with pandas and how to read different types of files. If not, it's time to revise pandas. Refer to the pandas documentation for further details: `https://pandas-datareader.readthedocs.io/en/latest/`.

Bar charts

This is one of the most common types of visualization that almost everyone must have encountered. Bars can be drawn horizontally or vertically to represent **categorical variables**.

Bar charts are frequently used to distinguish objects between distinct collections in order to track variations over time. In most cases, bar charts are very convenient when the changes are large. In order to learn about bar charts, let's assume a pharmacy in Norway keeps track of the amount of **Zoloft** sold every month. Zoloft is a medicine prescribed to patients suffering from depression. We can use the `calendar` Python library to keep track of the months of the year (1 to 12) corresponding to January to December:

1. Let's import the required libraries:

```
import numpy as np
import calendar
import matplotlib.pyplot as plt
```

2. Set up the data. Remember, the `range` stopping parameter is exclusive, meaning if you generate range from `(1, 13)`, the last item, `13`, is not included:

```
months = list(range(1, 13))
sold_quantity = [round(random.uniform(100, 200)) for x in range(1,
13)]
```

3. Specify the layout of the figure and allocate space:

```
figure, axis = plt.subplots()
```

4. In the *x* axis, we would like to display the names of the months:

```
plt.xticks(months, calendar.month_name[1:13], rotation=20)
```

5. Plot the graph:

```
plot = axis.bar(months, sold_quantity)
```

6. This step is optional depending upon whether you are interested in displaying the data value on the head of the bar. It visually gives more meaning to show an actual number of sold items on the bar itself:

```
for rectangle in plot:
height = rectangle.get_height()
axis.text(rectangle.get_x() + rectangle.get_width() /2., 1.002 *
height, '%d' % int(height), ha='center', va = 'bottom')
```

7. Display the graph on the screen:

```
plt.show()
```

The bar chart is as follows:

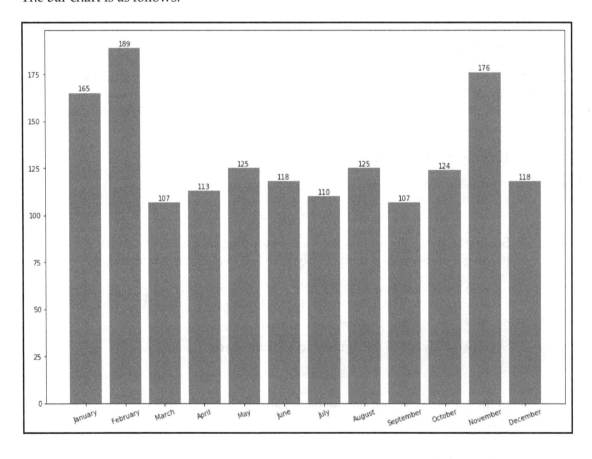

Here are important observations from the preceding visualizations:

- `months` and `sold_quantity` are Python lists representing the amount of Zoloft sold every month.
- We are using the `subplots()` method in the preceding code. Why? Well, it provides a way to define the layout of the figure in terms of the number of graphs and provides ways to organize them. Still confused? Don't worry, we will be using subplots plenty of times in this chapter. Moreover, if you need a quick reference, Packt has several books explaining `matplotlib`. Some of the most interesting reads have been mentioned in the *Further reading* section of this chapter.
- In *step 3*, we use the `plt.xticks()` function, which allows us to change the *x* axis tickers from 1 to 12, whereas `calender.months[1:13]` changes this numerical format into corresponding months from the `calendar` Python library.
- *Step 4* actually prints the bar with months and quantity sold.
- `ax.text()` within the `for` loop annotates each bar with its corresponding values. How it does this might be interesting. We plotted these values by getting the x and y coordinates and then adding `bar_width/2` to the x coordinates with a height of `1.002`, which is the y coordinate. Then, using the `va` and `ha` arguments, we align the text centrally over the bar.
- *Step 6* actually displays the graph on the screen.

As mentioned in the introduction to this section, we said that bars can be either horizontal or vertical. Let's change to a horizontal format. All the code remains the same, except `plt.xticks` changes to `plt.yticks()` and `plt.bar()` changes to `plt.barh()`. We assume it is self-explanatory.

In addition to this, placing the exact data values is a bit tricky and requires a few iterations of trial and error to place them perfectly. But let's see them in action:

```
months = list(range(1, 13))
sold_quantity = [round(random.uniform(100, 200)) for x in range(1, 13)]

figure, axis = plt.subplots()

plt.yticks(months, calendar.month_name[1:13], rotation=20)

plot = axis.barh(months, sold_quantity)

for rectangle in plot:
    width = rectangle.get_width()
    axis.text(width + 2.5, rectangle.get_y() + 0.38, '%d' % int(width),
ha='center', va = 'bottom')

plt.show()
```

And the graph it generates is as follows:

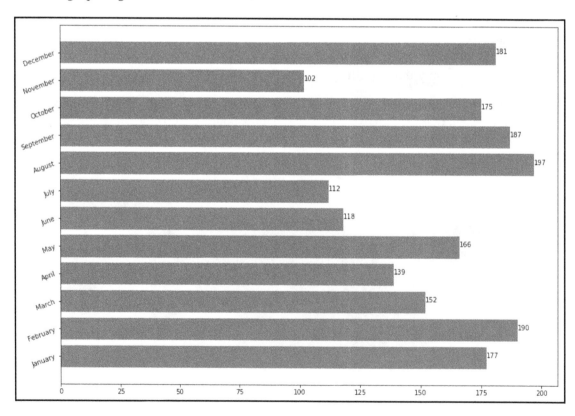

Well, that's all about the bar chart in this chapter. We are certainly going to use several other attributes in the subsequent chapters. Next, we are going to visualize data using a scatter plot.

Scatter plot

Scatter plots are also called scatter graphs, scatter charts, scattergrams, and scatter diagrams. They use a **Cartesian coordinates system** to display values of typically two variables for a set of data.

When should we use a scatter plot? Scatter plots can be constructed in the following two situations:

- When one continuous variable is dependent on another variable, which is under the control of the observer
- When both continuous variables are independent

There are two important concepts—**independent variable** and **dependent variable**. In statistical modeling or mathematical modeling, the values of dependent variables rely on the values of independent variables. The dependent variable is the outcome variable being studied. The independent variables are also referred to as **regressors**. The takeaway message here is that scatter plots are used when we need to show the relationship between two variables, and hence are sometimes referred to as correlation plots. We will dig into more details about correlation in Chapter 7, *Correlation.*

You are either an expert data scientist or a beginner computer science student, and no doubt you have encountered a form of scatter plot before. These plots are powerful tools for visualization, despite their simplicity. The main reasons are that they have a lot of options, representational powers, and design choices, and are flexible enough to represent a graph in attractive ways.

Some examples in which scatter plots are suitable are as follows:

- Research studies have successfully established that the number of hours of sleep required by a person depends on the age of the person.
- The average income for adults is based on the number of years of education.

Let's take the first case. The dataset can be found in the form of a CSV file in the GitHub repository:

```
headers_cols = ['age','min_recommended', 'max_recommended',
'may_be_appropriate_min', 'may_be_appropriate_max', 'min_not_recommended',
'max_not_recommended']

sleepDf =
pd.read_csv('https://raw.githubusercontent.com/PacktPublishing/hands-on-exp
loratory-data-analysis-with-python/master/Chapter%202/sleep_vs_age.csv',
columns=headers_cols)
sleepDf.head(10)
```

Having imported the dataset correctly, let's display a scatter plot. We start by importing the required libraries and then plotting the actual graph. Next, we display the x-label and the y-label. The code is given in the following code block:

```
import seaborn as sns
import matplotlib.pyplot as plt
sns.set()

# A regular scatter plot
plt.scatter(x=sleepDf["age"]/12., y=sleepDf["min_recommended"])
plt.scatter(x=sleepDf["age"]/12., y=sleepDf['max_recommended'])
plt.xlabel('Age of person in Years')
plt.ylabel('Total hours of sleep required')
plt.show()
```

The scatter plot generated by the preceding code is as follows:

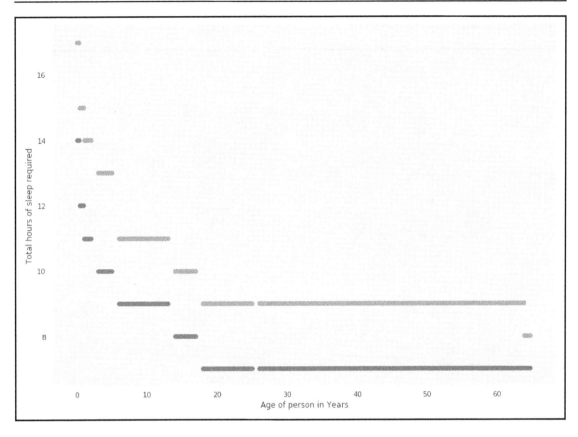

That was not so difficult, was it? Let's see if we can interpret the graph. You can explicitly see that the total number of hours of sleep required by a person is high initially and gradually decreases as age increases. The resulting graph is interpretable, but due to the lack of a continuous line, the results are not self-explanatory. Let's fit a line to it and see if that explains the results in a more obvious way:

```
# Line plot
plt.plot(sleepDf['age']/12., sleepDf['min_recommended'], 'g--')
plt.plot(sleepDf['age']/12., sleepDf['max_recommended'], 'r--')
plt.xlabel('Age of person in Years')
plt.ylabel('Total hours of sleep required')
plt.show()
```

A line chart of the same data is as follows:

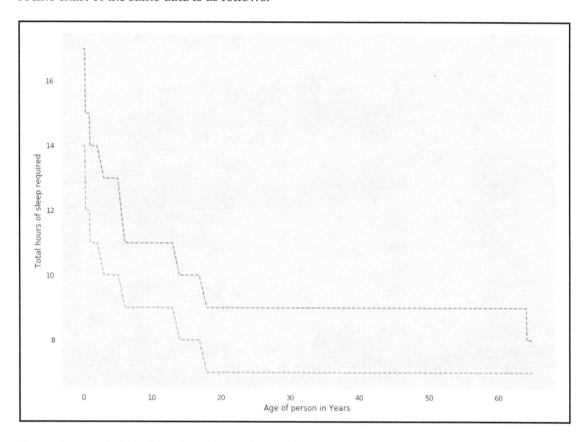

From the graph, it is clear that the two lines decline as the age increases. It shows that newborns between 0 and 3 months require at least 14-17 hours of sleep every day. Meanwhile, adults and the elderly require 7-9 hours of sleep every day. Is your sleeping pattern within this range?

Let's take another example of a scatter plot using the most popular dataset used in data science—the Iris dataset. The dataset was introduced by Ronald Fisher in 1936 and is widely adopted by bloggers, books, articles, and research papers to demonstrate various aspects of data science and data mining. The dataset holds 50 examples each of three different species of Iris, named setosa, virginica, and versicolor. Each example has four different attributes: `petal_length`, `petal_width`, `sepal_length`, and `sepal_width`. The dataset can be loaded in several ways.

Here, we are using `seaborn` to load the dataset:

1. Import `seaborn` and set some default parameters of `matplotlib`:

```
import seaborn as sns
import matplotlib.pyplot as plt

plt.rcParams['figure.figsize'] = (8, 6)
plt.rcParams['figure.dpi'] = 150
```

2. Use style from `seaborn`. Try to comment on the next line and see the difference in the graph:

```
sns.set()
```

3. Load the Iris dataset:

```
df = sns.load_dataset('iris')

df['species'] = df['species'].map({'setosa': 0, "versicolor": 1,
"virginica": 2})
```

4. Create a regular scatter plot:

```
plt.scatter(x=df["sepal_length"], y=df["sepal_width"], c =
df.species)
```

5. Create the labels for the axes:

```
plt.xlabel('Septal Length')
plt.ylabel('Petal length')
```

6. Display the plot on the screen:

```
plt.show()
```

The scatter plot generated by the preceding code is as follows:

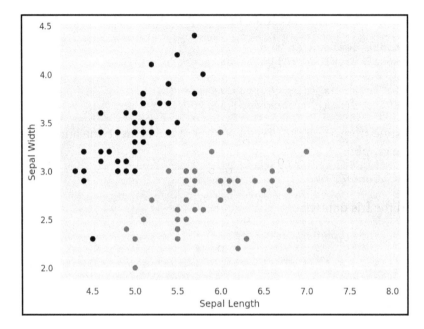

Do you find this graph informative? We would assume that most of you agree that you can clearly see three different types of points and that there are three different clusters. However, it is not clear which color represents which species of Iris. Thus, we are going to learn how to create legends in the *Scatter plot using seaborn* section.

Bubble chart

A bubble plot is a manifestation of the scatter plot where each data point on the graph is shown as a bubble. Each bubble can be illustrated with a different color, size, and appearance.

Let 's continue using the Iris dataset to get a bubble plot. Here, the important thing to note is that we are still going to use the `plt.scatter` method to draw a bubble chart:

```
# Load the Iris dataset
df = sns.load_dataset('iris')

df['species'] = df['species'].map({'setosa': 0, "versicolor": 1,
"virginica": 2})

# Create bubble plot
```

```
plt.scatter(df.petal_length, df.petal_width,
            s=50*df.petal_length*df.petal_width,
            c=df.species,
            alpha=0.3
            )

# Create labels for axises
plt.xlabel('Septal Length')
plt.ylabel('Petal length')
plt.show()
```

The bubble chart generated by the preceding code is as follows:

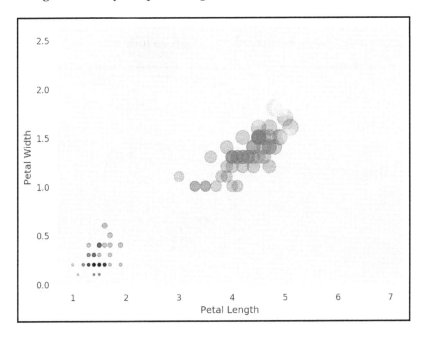

Can you interpret the results? Well, it is not clear from the graph which color represents which species of Iris. But we can clearly see three different *clusters*, which clearly indicates for each specific species or cluster there is a relationship between **Petal Length** and **Petal Width**.

Scatter plot using seaborn

A scatter plot can also be generated using the seaborn library. Seaborn makes the graph visually better. We can illustrate the relationship between x and y for distinct subsets of the data by utilizing the size, style, and hue parameters of the scatter plot in seaborn.

Get more detailed information about the parameters from seaborn's documentation website: `https://seaborn.pydata.org/generated/seaborn.scatterplot.html`.

Now, let's load the Iris dataset:

```
df = sns.load_dataset('iris')

df['species'] = df['species'].map({'setosa': 0, "versicolor": 1,
"virginica": 2})
sns.scatterplot(x=df["sepal_length"], y=df["sepal_width"], hue=df.species,
data=df)
```

The scatter plot generated from the preceding code is as follows:

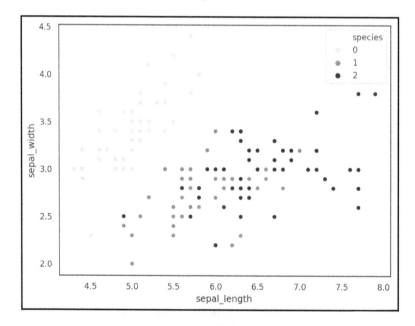

In the preceding plot, we can clearly see there are three species of flowers indicated by three distinct colors. It is more clear from the diagram how different specifies of flowers vary in terms of the sepal width and the length.

Area plot and stacked plot

The stacked plot owes its name to the fact that it represents the area under a line plot and that several such plots can be stacked on top of one another, giving the feeling of a stack. The stacked plot can be useful when we want to visualize the **cumulative effect** of multiple variables being plotted on the *y* axis.

In order to simplify this, think of an area plot as a line plot that shows the area covered by filling it with a color. Enough talk. Let's dive into the code base. First of all, let's define the dataset:

```
# House loan Mortgage cost per month for a year
houseLoanMortgage = [9000, 9000, 8000, 9000,
                     8000, 9000, 9000, 9000,
                     9000, 8000, 9000, 9000]

# Utilities Bills for a year
utilitiesBills = [4218, 4218, 4218, 4218,
                  4218, 4218, 4219, 2218,
                  3218, 4233, 3000, 3000]
# Transportation bill for a year
transportation = [782, 900, 732, 892,
                  334, 222, 300, 800,
                  900, 582, 596, 222]

# Car mortgage cost for one year
carMortgage = [700, 701, 702, 703,
               704, 705, 706, 707,
               708, 709, 710, 711]
```

Now, let's import the required libraries and plot stacked charts:

```
import matplotlib.pyplot as plt
import seaborn as sns
sns.set()

months= [x for x in range(1,13)]

# Create placeholders for plot and add required color
plt.plot([],[], color='sandybrown', label='houseLoanMortgage')
plt.plot([],[], color='tan', label='utilitiesBills')
plt.plot([],[], color='bisque', label='transportation')
plt.plot([],[], color='darkcyan', label='carMortgage')

# Add stacks to the plot
plt.stackplot(months, houseLoanMortgage, utilitiesBills, transportation,
carMortgage, colors=['sandybrown', 'tan', 'bisque', 'darkcyan'])
```

```
plt.legend()

# Add Labels
plt.title('Household Expenses')
plt.xlabel('Months of the year')
plt.ylabel('Cost')

# Display on the screen
plt.show()
```

In the preceding snippet, first, we imported `matplotlib` and `seaborn`. Nothing new, right? Then we added stacks with legends. Finally, we added labels to the axes and displayed the plot on the screen. Easy and straightforward. Now you know how to create an area plot or stacked plot. The area plot generated by the preceding code is as follows:

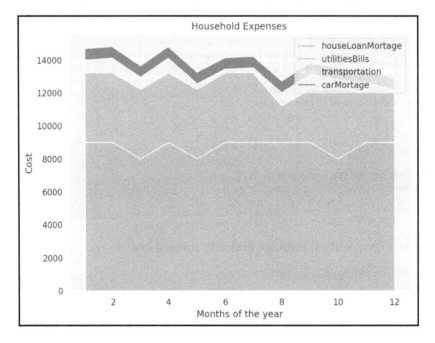

Now the most important part is the ability to interpret the graph. In the preceding graph, it is clear that the house mortgage loan is the largest expense since the area under the curve for the house mortgage loan is the largest. Secondly, the area of utility bills stack covers the second-largest area, and so on. The graph clearly disseminates meaningful information to the targeted audience. Labels, legends, and colors are important aspects of creating a meaningful visualization.

Pie chart

This is one of the more interesting types of data visualization graphs. We say interesting not because it has a higher preference or higher illustrative capacity, but because it is one of the most argued-about types of visualization in research.

A paper by Ian Spence in 2005, *No Humble Pie: The Origins and Usage of a Statistical Chart*, argues that the pie chart fails to appeal to most experts. Despite similar studies, people have still chosen to use pie charts. There are several arguments given by communities for not adhering to the pie chart. One of the arguments is that human beings are naturally poor at distinguishing differences in slices of a circle at a glance. Another argument is that people tend to overestimate the size of obtuse angles. Similarly, people seem to underestimate the size of acute angles.

Having looked at the criticism, let's also have some positivity. One counterargument is this: if the pie chart is not communicative, why does it persist? The main reason is that people love circles. Moreover, the purpose of the pie chart is to communicate proportions and it is widely accepted. Enough said; let's use the Pokemon dataset to draw a pie chart. There are two ways in which you can load the data: first, directly from the GitHub URL; or you can download the dataset from the GitHub and reference it from your local machine by providing the correct path. In either case, you can use the `read_csv` method from the `pandas` library. Check out the following snippet:

```
# Create URL to JSON file (alternatively this can be a filepath)
url =
'https://raw.githubusercontent.com/hmcuesta/PDA_Book/master/Chapter3/pokemo
nByType.csv'

# Load the first sheet of the JSON file into a data frame
pokemon = pd.read_csv(url, index_col='type')

pokemon
```

The preceding code snippet should display the dataframe as follows:

type	amount
Bug	45
Dark	16
Dragon	12
Electric	7
Fighting	3
Fire	14
Ghost	10
Grass	31
Ground	17
Ice	11
Normal	29
Poison	11
Psychic	9
Rock	24
Steel	13
Water	45

Next, we attempt to plot the pie chart:

```
import matplotlib.pyplot as plt

plt.pie(pokemon['amount'], labels=pokemon.index, shadow=False,
startangle=90, autopct='%1.1f%%',)
plt.axis('equal')
plt.show()
```

We should get the following pie chart from the preceding code:

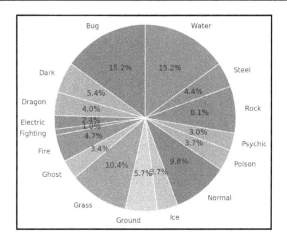

Do you know you can directly use the `pandas` library to create a pie chart? Checkout the following one-liner:

```
pokemon.plot.pie(y="amount", figsize=(20, 10))
```

The pie chart generated is as follows:

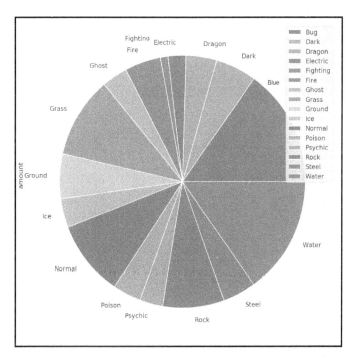

We generated a nice pie chart with a legend using one line of code. This is why Python is said to be a comedian. Do you know why? Because it has a lot of one-liners. Pretty true, right?

Table chart

A table chart combines a bar chart and a table. In order to understand the table chart, let's consider the following dataset. Consider standard LED bulbs that come in different wattages. The standard Philips LED bulb can be 4.5 Watts, 6 Watts, 7 Watts, 8.5 Watts, 9.5 Watts, 13.5 Watts, and 15 Watts. Let's assume there are two categorical variables, the year and the wattage, and a numeric variable, which is the number of units sold in a particular year.

Now, let's declare variables to hold the years and the available wattage data. It can be done as shown in the following snippet:

```
# Years under consideration
years = ["2010", "2011", "2012", "2013", "2014"]

# Available watt
columns = ['4.5W', '6.0W', '7.0W','8.5W','9.5W','13.5W','15W']
unitsSold = [
            [65, 141, 88, 111, 104, 71, 99],
            [85, 142, 89, 112, 103, 73, 98],
            [75, 143, 90, 113, 89, 75, 93],
            [65, 144, 91, 114, 90, 77, 92],
            [55, 145, 92, 115, 88, 79, 93],
            ]

# Define the range and scale for the y axis
values = np.arange(0, 600, 100)
```

We have now prepared the dataset. Let's now try to draw a table chart using the following code block:

```
colors = plt.cm.OrRd(np.linspace(0, 0.7, len(years)))
index = np.arange(len(columns)) + 0.3
bar_width = 0.7

y_offset = np.zeros(len(columns))
fig, ax = plt.subplots()

cell_text = []

n_rows = len(unitsSold)
```

```
for row in range(n_rows):
    plot = plt.bar(index, unitsSold[row], bar_width, bottom=y_offset,
                color=colors[row])
    y_offset = y_offset + unitsSold[row]
    cell_text.append(['%1.1f' % (x) for x in y_offset])
    i=0
# Each iteration of this for loop, labels each bar with corresponding value
for the given year
    for rect in plot:
        height = rect.get_height()
        ax.text(rect.get_x() + rect.get_width()/2, y_offset[i],'%d'
                % int(y_offset[i]),
            ha='center', va='bottom')
        i = i+1
```

Finally, let's add the table to the bottom of the chart:

```
# Add a table to the bottom of the axes
the_table = plt.table(cellText=cell_text, rowLabels=years,
            rowColours=colors, colLabels=columns, loc='bottom')
plt.ylabel("Units Sold")
plt.xticks([])
plt.title('Number of LED Bulb Sold/Year')
plt.show()
```

The preceding code snippets generate a nice table chart, as follows:

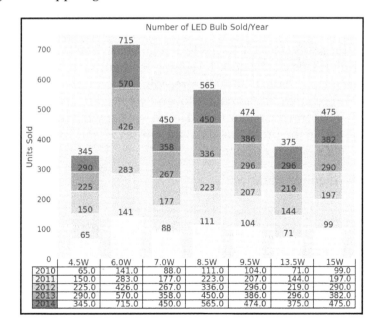

Look at the preceding table chart. Do you think it can be easily interpreted? It is pretty clear, right? You can see, for example, in the year **2014**, **345** units of the 4.5-Watt bulb were sold. Similarly, the same information can be deduced from the preceding table plot.

Polar chart

Do you remember the polar axis from mathematics class? Well, a polar chart is a diagram that is plotted on a polar axis. Its coordinates are angle and radius, as opposed to the Cartesian system of x and y coordinates. Sometimes, it is also referred to as a spider web plot. Let's see how we can plot an example of a polar chart.

First, let's create the dataset:

1. Let's assume you have five courses in your academic year:

   ```
   subjects = ["C programming", "Numerical methods", "Operating
   system", "DBMS", "Computer Networks"]
   ```

2. And you planned to obtain the following grades in each subject:

   ```
   plannedGrade = [90, 95, 92, 68, 68, 90]
   ```

3. However, after your final examination, these are the grades you got:

   ```
   actualGrade = [75, 89, 89, 80, 80, 75]
   ```

Now that the dataset is ready, let's try to create a polar chart. The first significant step is to initialize the spider plot. This can be done by setting the figure size and polar projection. This should be clear by now. Note that in the preceding dataset, the list of grades contains an extra entry. This is because it is a circular plot and we need to connect the first point and the last point together to form a circular flow. Hence, we copy the first entry from each list and append it to the list. In the preceding data, the entries 90 and 75 are the first entries of the list respectively. Let's look at each step:

1. Import the required libraries:

   ```
   import numpy as np
   import matplotlib.pyplot as plt
   ```

2. Prepare the dataset and set up theta:

   ```
   theta = np.linspace(0, 2 * np.pi, len(plannedGrade))
   ```

3. Initialize the plot with the figure size and polar projection:

```
plt.figure(figsize = (10,6))
plt.subplot(polar=True)
```

4. Get the grid lines to align with each of the subject names:

```
(lines,labels) = plt.thetagrids(range(0,360,
int(360/len(subjects))),
  (subjects))
```

5. Use the `plt.plot` method to plot the graph and fill the area under it:

```
plt.plot(theta, plannedGrade)
plt.fill(theta, plannedGrade, 'b', alpha=0.2)
```

6. Now, we plot the actual grades obtained:

```
plt.plot(theta, actualGrade)
```

7. We add a legend and a nice comprehensible title to the plot:

```
plt.legend(labels=('Planned Grades','Actual Grades'),loc=1)
plt.title("Plan vs Actual grades by Subject")
```

8. Finally, we show the plot on the screen:

```
plt.show()
```

The generated polar chart is shown in the following screenshot:

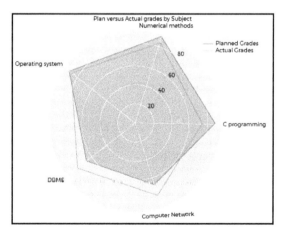

As illustrated in the preceding output, the planned and actual grades by subject can easily be distinguished. The legend makes it clear which line indicates the planned grades (the blue line in the screenshot) and which line indicates actual grades (the orange line in the screenshot). This gives a clear indication of the difference between the predicted and actual grades of a student to the target audience.

Histogram

Histogram plots are used to depict the distribution of any continuous variable. These types of plots are very popular in statistical analysis.

Consider the following use cases. A survey created in vocational training sessions of developers had 100 participants. They had several years of Python programming experience ranging from 0 to 20.

Let's import the required libraries and create the dataset:

```
import numpy as np
import matplotlib.pyplot as plt

#Create data set
yearsOfExperience = np.array([10, 16, 14, 5, 10, 11, 16, 14, 3, 14, 13, 19,
2, 5, 7, 3, 20,
        11, 11, 14, 2, 20, 15, 11, 1, 15, 15, 15, 2, 9, 18, 1, 17, 18,
        13, 9, 20, 13, 17, 13, 15, 17, 10, 2, 11, 8, 5, 19, 2, 4, 9,
        17, 16, 13, 18, 5, 7, 18, 15, 20, 2, 7, 0, 4, 14, 1, 14, 18,
        8, 11, 12, 2, 9, 7, 11, 2, 6, 15, 2, 14, 13, 4, 6, 15, 3,
        6, 10, 2, 11, 0, 18, 0, 13, 16, 18, 5, 14, 7, 14, 18])
yearsOfExperience
```

In order to plot the histogram chart, execute the following steps:

1. Plot the distribution of group experience:

```
nbins = 20
n, bins, patches = plt.hist(yearsOfExperience, bins=nbins)
```

2. Add labels to the axes and a title:

```
plt.xlabel("Years of experience with Python Programming")
plt.ylabel("Frequency")
plt.title("Distribution of Python programming experience in the
vocational training session")
```

3. Draw a green vertical line in the graph at the average experience:

```
plt.axvline(x=yearsOfExperience.mean(), linewidth=3, color = 'g')
```

4. Display the plot:

```
plt.show()
```

The preceding code generates the following histogram:

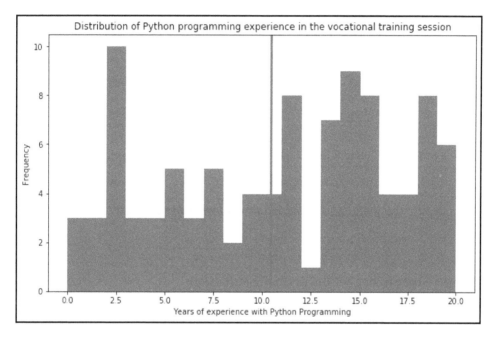

Much better, right? Now, from the graph, we can say that the average experience of the participants is around 10 years. Can we improve the graph for better readability? How about we try to plot the percentage of the sum of all the entries in yearsOfExperience? In addition to that, we can also plot a normal distribution using the mean and standard deviation of this data to see the distribution pattern. If you're not sure what a normal distribution is, we suggest you go through the references in Chapter 1, *Exploratory Data Analysis Fundamentals*. In a nutshell, the normal distribution is also referred to as the Gaussian distribution. The term indicates a probability distribution that is symmetrical about the mean, illustrating that data near the average (mean) is more frequent than data far from the mean. Enough theory; let's dive into the practice.

To plot the distribution, we can add a `density=1` parameter in the `plot.hist` function. Let's go through the code. Note that there are changes in *steps 1, 4, 5,* and *6.* The rest of the code is the same as the preceding example:

1. Plot the distribution of group experience:

    ```
    plt.figure(figsize = (10,6))

    nbins = 20
    n, bins, patches = plt.hist(yearsOfExperience, bins=nbins,
    density=1)
    ```

2. Add labels to the axes and a title:

    ```
    plt.xlabel("Years of experience with Python Programming")
    plt.ylabel("Frequency")
    plt.title("Distribution of Python programming experience in the
    vocational training session")
    ```

3. Draw a green vertical line in the graph at the average experience:

    ```
    plt.axvline(x=yearsOfExperience.mean(), linewidth=3, color = 'g')
    ```

4. Compute the mean and standard deviation of the dataset:

    ```
    mu = yearsOfExperience.mean()
    sigma = yearsOfExperience.std()
    ```

5. Add a best-fit line for the normal distribution:

    ```
    y = ((1 / (np.sqrt(2 * np.pi) * sigma)) * np.exp(-0.5 * (1 / sigma
    * (bins - mu))**2))
    ```

6. Plot the normal distribution:

    ```
    plt.plot(bins, y, '--')
    ```

7. Display the plot:

    ```
    plt.show()
    ```

And the generated histogram with the normal distribution is as follows:

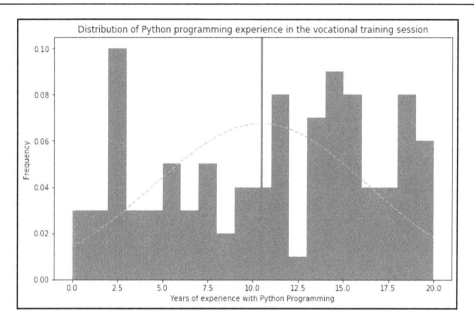

The preceding plot illustrates clearly that it is not following a normal distribution. There are many vertical bars that are above and below the best-fit curve for a normal distribution. Perhaps you are wondering where we got the formula to compute step 6 in the preceding code. Well, there is a little theory involved here. When we mentioned the normal distribution, we can compute the probability density function using the Gaussian distribution function given by `((1 / (np.sqrt(2 * np.pi) * sigma)) * np.exp(-0.5 * (1 / sigma * (bins - mu))**2))`.

Lollipop chart

A lollipop chart can be used to display ranking in the data. It is similar to an ordered bar chart.

Let's consider the `carDF` dataset. It can be found in the GitHub repository for chapter 2. Alternatively, it can be used from the GitHub link directly, as mention in the following code:

1. Load the dataset:

```
#Read the dataset

carDF =
pd.read_csv('https://raw.githubusercontent.com/PacktPublishing/hand
```

```
s-on-exploratory-data-analysis-with-
python/master/Chapter%202/cardata.csv')
```

2. Group the dataset by `manufacturer`. For now, if it does not make sense, just remember that the following snippet groups the entries by a particular field (we will go through `groupby` functions in detail in `Chapter 4, Data Transformation`):

```
#Group by manufacturer and take average mileage
processedDF =
carDF[['cty','manufacturer']].groupby('manufacturer').apply(lambda
x: x.mean())
```

3. Sort the values by `cty` and reset the `index` (again, we will go through sorting and how we reset the index in `Chapter 4, Data Transformation`):

```
#Sort the values by cty and reset index
processedDF.sort_values('cty', inplace=True)
processedDF.reset_index(inplace=True)
```

4. Plot the graph:

```
#Plot the graph
fig, ax = plt.subplots(figsize=(16,10), dpi= 80)
ax.vlines(x=processedDF.index, ymin=0, ymax=processedDF.cty,
color='firebrick', alpha=0.7, linewidth=2)
ax.scatter(x=processedDF.index, y=processedDF.cty, s=75,
color='firebrick', alpha=0.7)
```

5. Annotate the title:

```
#Annotate Title
ax.set_title('Lollipop Chart for Highway Mileage using car
dataset', fontdict={'size':22})
```

6. Annotate labels, `xticks`, and `ylims`:

```
ax.set_ylabel('Miles Per Gallon')
ax.set_xticks(processedDF.index)
ax.set_xticklabels(processedDF.manufacturer.str.upper(),
rotation=65, fontdict={'horizontalalignment': 'right', 'size':12})
ax.set_ylim(0, 30)
```

7. Write the actual mean values in the plot, and display the plot:

```
#Write the values in the plot
for row in processedDF.itertuples():
    ax.text(row.Index, row.cty+.5, s=round(row.cty, 2),
```

```
horizontalalignment= 'center', verticalalignment='bottom',
fontsize=14)

#Display the plot on the screen
plt.show()
```

The lollipop chart generated by the preceding snippet is as follows:

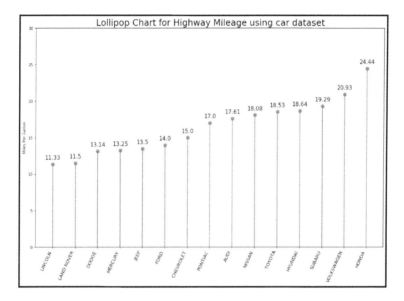

Having seen the preceding output, you now know why it is called a lollipop chart, don't you? The line and the circle on the top gives a nice illustration of different types of cars and their associated miles per gallon consumption. Now, the data makes more sense, doesn't it?

Choosing the best chart

There is no standard that defines which chart you should choose to visualize your data. However, there are some guidelines that can help you. Here are some of them:

- As mentioned with each of the preceding charts that we have seen, it is important to understand what type of data you have. If you have continuous variables, then a histogram would be a good choice. Similarly, if you want to show ranking, an ordered bar chart would be a good choice.
- Choose the chart that effectively conveys the right and relevant meaning of the data without actually distorting the facts.

- Simplicity is best. It is considered better to draw a simple chart that is comprehensible than to draw sophisticated ones that require several reports and texts in order to understand them.
- Choose a diagram that does not overload the audience with information. Our purpose should be to illustrate abstract information in a clear way.

Having said that, let's see if we can generalize some categories of charts based on various purposes.

The following table shows the different types of charts based on the purposes:

Purpose	Charts
Show correlation	Scatter plot Correlogram Pairwise plot Jittering with strip plot Counts plot Marginal histogram Scatter plot with a line of best fit Bubble plot with circling
Show deviation	Area chart Diverging bars Diverging texts Diverging dot plot Diverging lollipop plot with markers
Show distribution	Histogram for continuous variable Histogram for categorical variable Density plot Categorical plots Density curves with histogram Population pyramid Violin plot Joy plot Distributed dot plot Box plot
Show composition	Waffle chart Pie chart Treemap Bar chart

| Show change | Time series plot
Time series with peaks and troughs annotated
Autocorrelation plot
Cross-correlation plot
Multiple time series
Plotting with different scales using the secondary y axis
Stacked area chart
Seasonal plot
Calendar heat map
Area chart unstacked |
|---|---|
| Show groups | Dendrogram
Cluster plot
Andrews curve
Parallel coordinates |
| Show ranking | Ordered bar chart
Lollipop chart
Dot plot
Slope plot
Dumbbell plot |

Note that going through each and every type of plot mentioned in the table is beyond the scope of this book. However, we have tried to cover most of them in this chapter. A few of them will be used in the upcoming chapters; we will use these graphs in more contextual ways and with advanced settings.

Other libraries to explore

So far, we have seen different types of 2D and 3D visualization techniques using `matplotlib` and `seaborn`. Apart from these widely used Python libraries, there are other libraries that you can explore:

- `Ploty` (`https://plot.ly/python/`): This is a web-application-based toolkit for visualization. Its API for Jupyter Notebook and other applications makes it very powerful to represent 2D and 3D charts.
- `Ggplot` (`http://ggplot.yhathq.com/`): This is a Python implementation based on the *Grammar of Graphics* library from the R programming language.
- `Altair` (`https://altair-viz.github.io/`): This is built on the top of the powerful Vega-Lite visualization grammar and follows very declarative statistical visualization library techniques. In addition to that, it has a very descriptive and simple API.

Summary

Portraying any data, events, concepts, information, processes, or methods graphically has been always perceived with a high degree of comprehension on one hand and is easily marketable on the other. Presenting results to stakeholders is very complex in the sense that our audience may not be technical enough to understand programming jargon and technicalities. Hence, visual aids are widely used. In this chapter, we discussed how to use such data visualization tools.

In the next chapter, we are going to get started with exploratory data analysis in a very simple way. We will try to analyze our mailbox and analyze what type of emails we send and receive.

Further reading

- *Matplotlib 3.0 Cookbook, Srinivasa Rao Poladi, Packt Publishing,* October 22, 2018
- *Matplotlib Plotting Cookbook, Alexandre Devert, Packt Publishing,* March 26, 2014
- *Data Visualization with Python, Mario Döbler, Tim Großmann, Packt Publishing,* February 28, 2019
- *No Humble Pie: The Origins and Usage of a Statistical Chart, Ian Spence, University of Toronto,* 2005.

3
EDA with Personal Email

The exploration of useful insights from a dataset requires a great deal of thought and a high level of experience and practice. The more you deal with different types of datasets, the more experience you gain in understanding the types of insights that can be mined. For example, if you have worked with text datasets, you will discover that you can mine a lot of keywords, patterns, and phrases. Similarly, if you have worked with time-series datasets, then you will understand that you can mine patterns relevant to weeks, months, and seasons. The point here is that the more you practice, the better you become at understanding the types of insights that can be pulled and the types of visualizations that can be done. Having said that, in this chapter, we are going to use one of our own email datasets and perform **exploratory data analysis (EDA)**.

You will learn about how to export all your emails as a dataset, how to use import them inside a pandas dataframe, how to visualize them, and the different types of insights you can gain.

In this chapter, we will cover the following topics:

- Loading the dataset
- Data transformation
- Data analysis
- Further reading recommendations

Technical requirements

The code for this chapter can found inside the GitHub repository shared with this book inside the `Chapter 3` folder. This dataset consists of email data taken from my personal Gmail account. Due to privacy issues, the dataset cannot be shared with you. However, in this chapter, we will guide you on how you can download your own emails from Gmail to perform initial data analysis.

Here are the steps to follow:

1. Log in to your personal Gmail account.
2. Go to the following link: `https://takeout.google.com/settings/takeout`.
3. Deselect all the items but Gmail, as shown in the following screenshot:

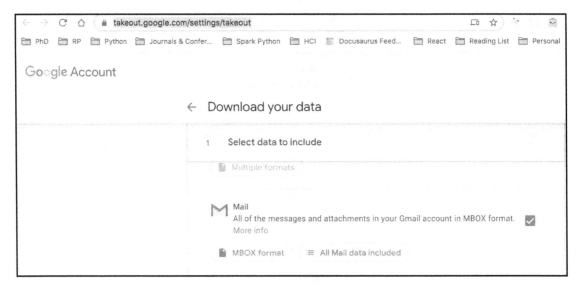

4. Select the archive format, as shown in the following screenshot:

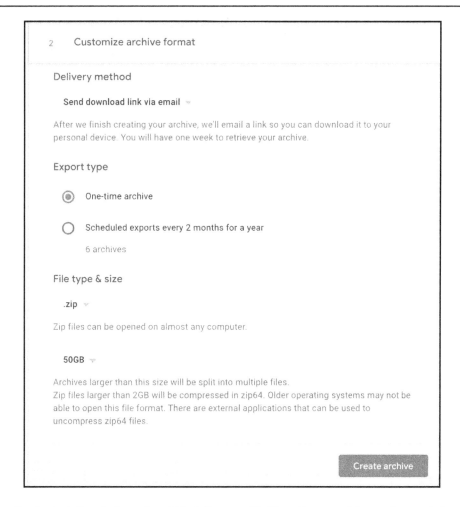

Note that I selected **Send download link by email**, **One-time archive**, **.zip**, and the maximum allowed size. You can customize the format. Once done, hit **Create archive**.

You will get an email archive that is ready for download. You can use the path to the `mbox` file for further analysis, which will be discussed in this chapter.

Now let's load the dataset.

Loading the dataset

First of all, it is essential to download the dataset. Follow the preceding steps from the *Technical requirements* section and download the data. Gmail (https://takeout.google.com/settings/takeout) provides data in mbox format. For this chapter, I loaded my own personal email from Google Mail. For privacy reasons, I cannot share the dataset. However, I will show you different EDA operations that you can perform to analyze several aspects of your email behavior:

1. Let's load the required libraries:

    ```
    import numpy as np
    import pandas as pd
    import matplotlib.pyplot as plt
    ```

 Note that for this analysis, we need to have the `mailbox` package installed. If it is not installed on your system, it can be added to your Python build using the `pip install mailbox` instruction.

2. When you have loaded the libraries, load the dataset:

    ```
    import mailbox

    mboxfile = "PATH TO DOWNLOADED MBOX FIL"
    mbox = mailbox.mbox(mboxfile)
    mbox
    ```

    Note that it is essential that you replace the mbox file path with your own path.

    The output of the preceding code is as follows:

    ```
    <mailbox.mbox at 0x7f124763f5c0>
    ```

    The output indicates that the mailbox has been successfully created.

3. Next, let's see the list of available keys:

    ```
    for key in mbox[0].keys():
      print(key)
    ```

The output of the preceding code is as follows:

```
X-GM-THRID
X-Gmail-Labels
Delivered-To
Received
X-Google-Smtp-Source
X-Received
ARC-Seal
ARC-Message-Signature
ARC-Authentication-Results
Return-Path
Received
Received-SPF
Authentication-Results
DKIM-Signature
DKIM-Signature
Subject
From
To
Reply-To
Date
MIME-Version
Content-Type
X-Mailer
X-Complaints-To
X-Feedback-ID
List-Unsubscribe
Message-ID
```

The preceding output shows the list of keys that are present in the extracted dataset.

Data transformation

Although there are a lot of objects returned by the extracted data, we do not need all the items. We will only extract the required fields. Data cleansing is one of the essential steps in the data analysis phase. For our analysis, all we need is data for the following: *subject, from, date, to, label,* and *thread*.

Let's look at all the steps involved in data transformation in the following sections.

Data cleansing

Let's create a CSV file with only the required fields. Let's start with the following steps:

1. Import the `csv` package:

```
import csv
```

2. Create a CSV file with only the required attributes:

```
with open('mailbox.csv', 'w') as outputfile:
 writer = csv.writer(outputfile)
  writer.writerow(['subject','from','date','to','label','thread'])
  for message in mbox:
    writer.writerow([
      message['subject'],
      message['from'],
      message['date'],
      message['to'],
      message['X-Gmail-Labels'],
      message['X-GM-THRID']
    ]
  )
```

The preceding output is a `csv` file named `mailbox.csv`. Next, instead of loading the mbox file, we can use the CSV file for loading, which will be smaller than the original dataset.

Loading the CSV file

We will load the CSV file. Refer to the following code block:

```
dfs = pd.read_csv('mailbox.csv', names=['subject', 'from', 'date', 'to',
'label', 'thread'])
```

The preceding code will generate a pandas dataframe with only the required fields stored in the CSV file.

Converting the date

Next, we will convert the date.

Check the datatypes of each column as shown here:

```
dfs.dtypes
```

The output of the preceding code is as follows:

```
subject object
from object
date object
to object
label object
thread float64
dtype: object
```

Note that a date field is an object. So, we need to convert it into a DateTime argument. In the next step, we are going to convert the date field into an actual DateTime argument. We can do this by using the pandas `to_datetime()` method. See the following code:

```
dfs['date'] = dfs['date'].apply(lambda x: pd.to_datetime(x,
errors='coerce', utc=True))
```

Let's move onto the next step, that is, removing NaN values from the fields.

Removing NaN values

Next, we are going to remove NaN values from the field.

We can do this as follows:

```
dfs = dfs[dfs['date'].notna()]
```

Next, it is good to save the preprocessed file into a separate CSV file in case we need it again. We can save the dataframe into a separate CSV file as follows:

```
dfs.to_csv('gmail.csv')
```

Great! Having done that, let's do some descriptive statistics.

Applying descriptive statistics

Having preprocessed the dataset, let's do some sanity checking using descriptive statistics techniques.

We can implement this as shown here:

```
dfs.info()
```

The output of the preceding code is as follows:

```
<class 'pandas.core.frame.DataFrame'>
Int64Index: 37554 entries, 1 to 78442
Data columns (total 6 columns):
subject 37367 non-null object
from 37554 non-null object
date 37554 non-null datetime64[ns, UTC]
to 36882 non-null object
label 36962 non-null object
thread 37554 non-null object
dtypes: datetime64[ns, UTC](1), object(5)
memory usage: 2.0+ MB
```

We will learn more about descriptive statistics in `Chapter 5`, *Descriptive Statistics*. Note that there are 37,554 emails, with each email containing six columns—subject, from, date, to, label, and thread. Let's check the first few entries of the email dataset:

```
dfs.head(10)
```

The output of the preceding code is as follows:

	subject	from	date	to	label	thread
0	New Books: The Python Journeyman + Understandi...	"James @ SitePoint" <james@sitepoint.com>	2019-09-20 14:07:05+00:00	"Suresh KUMAR Mukhiya" <itsmeskm99@gmail.com>	Inbox,Category Promotions,Unread	1.645217e+18
1	iPhone 11 Pro og iPhone 11 er her	Apple <News_Europe@InsideApple.Apple.com>	2019-09-20 10:33:27+00:00	itsmeskm99@gmail.com	Inbox,Category Promotions,Unread	1.645190e+18
2	=?utf-8?Q? Save=20on=20Burlap=20Bags=20Today=21...	=?utf-8?Q?Tote=20Bag=20Factory?= <support@tote...	2019-09-20 15:32:31+00:00	<itsmeskm99@gmail.com>	Inbox,Category Promotions,Unread	1.645210e+18
3	Hi there, looking for the best Dashain deals? ...	=?ISO-8859-1?B?RGFyYXogTlA=?= <info@email.dara...	2019-09-17 06:19:10+00:00	itsmeskm99@gmail.com	Inbox,Category Promotions,Unread	1.644916e+18
4	The file =?UTF-8?B? J0JyYW5kX0Jvb2sgGVzdC5wZGY...	"Box Updates" <noreply@box.com>	2019-09-20 19:04:16+00:00	itsmeskm99@gmail.com	Inbox,Opened,Category Updates	1.645222e+18
5	We miss you on Google Maps	Google Local Guides <noreply-local-guides@goog...	2019-09-20 11:19:56+00:00	itsmeskm99@gmail.com	Important,Trash,Category Updates,Unread	1.645193e+18
6	=?utf-8?B? VGFrZSB5b3VyIHNraWxscyB0byB0aGUGUgbmV4V4...	edX <news@edx.org>	2019-09-17 13:32:49+00:00	itsmeskm99@gmail.com	Inbox,Opened,Category Promotions	1.644930e+18
7	Freelancing 101: How to Market a Small Business	"Shopify Partner Blog" <partners@email.shopify...	2019-09-17 14:10:12+00:00	<itsmeskm99@gmail.com>	Inbox,Category Promotions,Unread	1.644932e+18
8	Suresh KUMAR, your profile is getting hits	=?UTF-8?B?TGlua2VkSW4=?= <linkedin@e.linkedin....	2019-09-17 17:29:38+00:00	itsmeskm99@gmail.com	Inbox,Opened,Category Social	1.644956e+18
9	=?UTF-8?Q? Forget_FOMO._=E2=80=93_you_can_go_bac...	Flatiron School <info@flatironschool.com>	2019-09-19 18:01:13+00:00	itsmeskm99@gmail.com	Inbox,Category Promotions,Unread	1.645128e+18

Note that our dataframe so far contains six different columns. Take a look at the `from` field: it contains both the name and the email. For our analysis, we only need an email address. We can use a regular expression to refactor the column.

Data refactoring

We noticed that the `from` field contains more information than we need. We just need to extract an email address from that field. Let's do some refactoring:

1. First of all, import the regular expression package:

   ```
   import re
   ```

2. Next, let's create a function that takes an entire string from any column and extracts an email address:

   ```
   def extract_email_ID(string):
     email = re.findall(r'<(.+?)>', string)
     if not email:
       email = list(filter(lambda y: '@' in y, string.split()))
     return email[0] if email else np.nan
   ```

   The preceding function is pretty straightforward, right? We have used a regular expression to find an email address. If there is no email address, we populate the field with `NaN`. Well, if you are not sure about regular expressions, don't worry. Just read the *Appendix*.

3. Next, let's apply the function to the `from` column:

   ```
   dfs['from'] = dfs['from'].apply(lambda x: extract_email_ID(x))
   ```

   We used the lambda function to apply the function to each and every value in the column.

4. Next, we are going to refactor the `label` field. The logic is simple. If an email is from your email address, then it is the *sent* email. Otherwise, it is a received email, that is, an inbox email:

   ```
   myemail = 'itsmeskm99@gmail.com'
   dfs['label'] = dfs['from'].apply(lambda x: 'sent' if x==myemail
   else 'inbox')
   ```

   The preceding code is self-explanatory.

Dropping columns

Let's drop a column:

1. Note that the `to` column only contains your own email. So, we can drop this irrelevant column:

```
dfs.drop(columns='to', inplace=True)
```

2. This drops the `to` column from the dataframe. Let's display the first 10 entries now:

```
dfs.head(10)
```

The output of the preceding code is as follows:

	subject	from	date	label	thread
0	New Books: The Python Journeyman + Understandi...	james@sitepoint.com	2019-09-20 14:07:05+00:00	inbox	1.645217e+18
1	iPhone 11 Pro og iPhone 11 er her	News_Europe@InsideApple.Apple.com	2019-09-20 10:33:27+00:00	inbox	1.645190e+18
2	=?utf-8?Q?Save=20on=20Burlap=20Bags=20Today=21...	support@totebagfactory.com	2019-09-20 15:32:31+00:00	inbox	1.645210e+18
3	Hi there, looking for the best Dashain deals? ...	info@email.daraz.com.np	2019-09-17 06:19:10+00:00	inbox	1.644916e+18
4	The file =?UTF-8?B?J0JyYW5kY0X0Jvb2gsgdGVzdC5wZGY...	noreply@box.com	2019-09-20 19:04:16+00:00	inbox	1.645222e+18
5	We miss you on Google Maps	noreply-local-guides@google.com	2019-09-20 11:19:56+00:00	inbox	1.645193e+18
6	=?utf-8?B?VGFrZSB5b3VyIHNraWxscyByb0byB0aGUgbmV4V4...	news@edx.org	2019-09-17 13:32:49+00:00	inbox	1.644930e+18
7	Freelancing 101: How to Market a Small Business	partners@email.shopify.com	2019-09-17 14:10:12+00:00	inbox	1.644932e+18
8	Suresh KUMAR, your profile is getting hits	linkedin@e.linkedin.com	2019-09-17 17:29:38+00:00	inbox	1.644956e+18
9	=?UTF-8?Q?Forget_FOMO_=E2=80=93_you_can_go_bac...	info@flatironschool.com	2019-09-19 18:01:13+00:00	inbox	1.645128e+18

Check the preceding output. The fields are cleaned. The data is transformed into the correct format.

Refactoring timezones

Next, we want to refactor the timezone based on our timezone:

1. We can refactor timezones by using the method given here:

```
import datetime
import pytz

def refactor_timezone(x):
    est = pytz.timezone('US/Eastern')
    return x.astimezone(est)
```

Note that in the preceding code, I converted the timezone into the US/Eastern timezone. You can choose whatever timezone you like.

2. Now that our function is created, let's call it:

```
dfs['date'] = dfs['date'].apply(lambda x: refactor_timezone(x))
```

3. Next, we want to convert the day of the week variable into the name of the day, as in, `Saturday`, `Sunday`, and so on. We can do that as shown here:

```
dfs['dayofweek'] = dfs['date'].apply(lambda x: x.weekday_name)
dfs['dayofweek'] = pd.Categorical(dfs['dayofweek'], categories=[
    'Monday', 'Tuesday', 'Wednesday', 'Thursday', 'Friday',
    'Saturday', 'Sunday'], ordered=True)
```

4. Great! Next, we do the same process for the time of the day. See the snippet given here:

```
dfs['timeofday'] = dfs['date'].apply(lambda x: x.hour + x.minute/60
+ x.second/3600)
```

5. Next, we refactor the hour, the year integer, and the year fraction, respectively. First, refactor the hour as shown here:

```
dfs['hour'] = dfs['date'].apply(lambda x: x.hour)
```

6. Refactor the year integer as shown here:

```
dfs['year_int'] = dfs['date'].apply(lambda x: x.year)
```

7. Lastly, refactor the year fraction as shown here:

```
dfs['year'] = dfs['date'].apply(lambda x: x.year +
x.dayofyear/365.25)
```

8. Having done that, we can set the date to `index` and we will no longer require the original `date` field. So, we can remove that:

```
dfs.index = dfs['date']
del dfs['date']
```

Great! Good work so far. We have successfully executed our data transformation steps. If some of the steps were not clear, don't worry—we are going to deal with each of these phases in detail in upcoming chapters.

Data analysis

This is the most important part of EDA. This is the part where we gain insights from the data that we have.

Let's answer the following questions one by one:

1. How many emails did I send during a given timeframe?
2. At what times of the day do I send and receive emails with Gmail?
3. What is the average number of emails per day?
4. What is the average number of emails per hour?
5. Whom do I communicate with most frequently?
6. What are the most active emailing days?
7. What am I mostly emailing about?

In the following sections, we will answer the preceding questions.

Number of emails

The answer to the first question, "How many emails did I send during a given timeframe?", can be answered as shown here:

```
print(dfs.index.min().strftime('%a, %d %b %Y %I:%M %p'))
print(dfs.index.max().strftime('%a, %d %b %Y %I:%M %p'))

print(dfs['label'].value_counts())
```

The output of the preceding code is given here:

```
Tue, 24 May 2011 11:04 AM
Fri, 20 Sep 2019 03:04 PM
inbox 32952
sent 4602
Name: label, dtype: int64
```

If you analyze the output, you'll see that we analyzed emails from Tue, 24 May 2011 11:04 AM, to Fri, 20 Sep 2019 03:04 PM. There were 32,952 emails received and 4,602 emails sent during this timeframe. That is a pretty good insight, right? Now, let's jump into the next question.

Time of day

To answer the next question, *At what times of the day do I send and receive emails with Gmail?* let's create a graph. We'll take a look at sent emails and received emails:

1. Let's create two sub-dataframe—one for sent emails and another for received emails:

```
sent = dfs[dfs['label']=='sent']
received = dfs[dfs['label']=='inbox']
```

It is pretty obvious, right? Remember, we set a couple of labels, `sent` and `inbox`, earlier. Now, let's create a plot.

2. First, let's import the required libraries:

```
import matplotlib.pyplot as plt
from matplotlib.ticker import MaxNLocator
from scipy import ndimage
import matplotlib.gridspec as gridspec
import matplotlib.patches as mpatches
```

3. Now, let's create a function that takes a dataframe as an input and creates a plot. See the following function:

```
def plot_todo_vs_year(df, ax, color='C0', s=0.5, title=''):
    ind = np.zeros(len(df), dtype='bool')
    est = pytz.timezone('US/Eastern')
    df[~ind].plot.scatter('year', 'timeofday', s=s, alpha=0.6, ax=ax,
color=color)
    ax.set_ylim(0, 24)
    ax.yaxis.set_major_locator(MaxNLocator(8))
    ax.set_yticklabels([datetime.datetime.strptime(str(int(np.mod(ts,
24))), "%H").strftime("%I %p") for ts in ax.get_yticks()]);

    ax.set_xlabel('')
    ax.set_ylabel('')
    ax.set_title(title)
    ax.grid(ls=':', color='k')

    return ax
```

By now, you should be familiar with how to create a scatter plot. We discussed doing so in detail in Chapter 2, *Visual Aids for EDA*. If you are confused about some terms, it is suggested that you revisit that chapter.

4. Now, let's plot both received and sent emails. Check out the code given here:

```
fig, ax = plt.subplots(nrows=1, ncols=2, figsize=(15, 4))

plot_todo_vs_year(sent, ax[0], title='Sent')
plot_todo_vs_year(received, ax[1], title='Received')
```

The output of the preceding code is as follows:

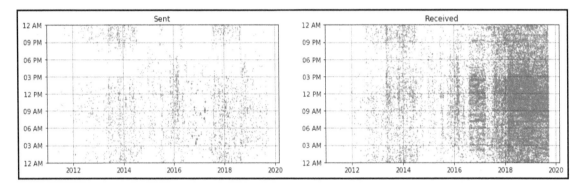

Check out the preceding graph. The higher the density of the graph data points, the higher the number of emails. Note that the number of sent emails is less than the number of received emails. I received more emails than I sent from 2018 to 2020. Note that I received most of the emails between 03:00 PM and 09:00 AM. This graph gives a nice overview of the time of day of email activity. This answers the second question.

Average emails per day and hour

Let's answer the rest of the questions, taking a look at the average number of emails per day and per hour:

1. To do so, we will create two functions, one that counts the total number of emails per day and one that plots the average number of emails per hour:

```
def plot_number_perday_per_year(df, ax, label=None, dt=0.3,
**plot_kwargs):
    year = df[df['year'].notna()]['year'].values
    T = year.max() - year.min()
    bins = int(T / dt)
```

```
    weights = 1 / (np.ones_like(year) * dt * 365.25)
    ax.hist(year, bins=bins, weights=weights, label=label,
**plot_kwargs);
    ax.grid(ls=':', color='k')
```

The preceding code creates a function that plots the average number of emails per day. Similarly, let's create a function that plots the average number of emails per hour:

```
def plot_number_perdhour_per_year(df, ax, label=None, dt=1,
smooth=False,
                        weight_fun=None, **plot_kwargs):

    tod = df[df['timeofday'].notna()]['timeofday'].values
    year = df[df['year'].notna()]['year'].values
    Ty = year.max() - year.min()
    T = tod.max() - tod.min()
    bins = int(T / dt)
    if weight_fun is None:
        weights = 1 / (np.ones_like(tod) * Ty * 365.25 / dt)
    else:
        weights = weight_fun(df)
    if smooth:
        hst, xedges = np.histogram(tod, bins=bins,
weights=weights);
        x = np.delete(xedges, -1) + 0.5*(xedges[1] - xedges[0])
        hst = ndimage.gaussian_filter(hst, sigma=0.75)
        f = interp1d(x, hst, kind='cubic')
        x = np.linspace(x.min(), x.max(), 10000)
        hst = f(x)
        ax.plot(x, hst, label=label, **plot_kwargs)
    else:
        ax.hist(tod, bins=bins, weights=weights, label=label,
**plot_kwargs);


    ax.grid(ls=':', color='k')
    orientation = plot_kwargs.get('orientation')
    if orientation is None or orientation == 'vertical':
        ax.set_xlim(0, 24)
        ax.xaxis.set_major_locator(MaxNLocator(8))
ax.set_xticklabels([datetime.datetime.strptime(str(int(np.mod(ts,
24))), "%H").strftime("%I %p")
                        for ts in ax.get_xticks()]);
    elif orientation == 'horizontal':
        ax.set_ylim(0, 24)
        ax.yaxis.set_major_locator(MaxNLocator(8))
ax.set_yticklabels([datetime.datetime.strptime(str(int(np.mod(ts,
```

```
24))), "%H").strftime("%I %p")
                            for ts in ax.get_yticks()]);
```

Now, let's create a class that plots the time of the day versus year for all the emails within the given timeframe:

```
class TriplePlot:
  def __init__(self):
    gs = gridspec.GridSpec(6, 6)
    self.ax1 = plt.subplot(gs[2:6, :4])
    self.ax2 = plt.subplot(gs[2:6, 4:6], sharey=self.ax1)
    plt.setp(self.ax2.get_yticklabels(), visible=False);
    self.ax3 = plt.subplot(gs[:2, :4])
    plt.setp(self.ax3.get_xticklabels(), visible=False);

  def plot(self, df, color='darkblue', alpha=0.8, markersize=0.5,
yr_bin=0.1, hr_bin=0.5):
    plot_todo_vs_year(df, self.ax1, color=color, s=markersize)
    plot_number_perdhour_per_year(df, self.ax2, dt=hr_bin,
color=color, alpha=alpha, orientation='horizontal')
    self.ax2.set_xlabel('Average emails per hour')
    plot_number_perday_per_year(df, self.ax3, dt=yr_bin,
color=color, alpha=alpha)
    self.ax3.set_ylabel('Average emails per day')
```

Now, finally, let's instantiate the class to plot the graph:

```
import matplotlib.gridspec as gridspec
import matplotlib.patches as mpatches

plt.figure(figsize=(12,12));
tpl = TriplePlot()

tpl.plot(received, color='C0', alpha=0.5)
tpl.plot(sent, color='C1', alpha=0.5)
p1 = mpatches.Patch(color='C0', label='Incoming', alpha=0.5)
p2 = mpatches.Patch(color='C1', label='Outgoing', alpha=0.5)
plt.legend(handles=[p1, p2], bbox_to_anchor=[1.45, 0.7],
fontsize=14, shadow=True);
```

The output of the preceding code is as follows:

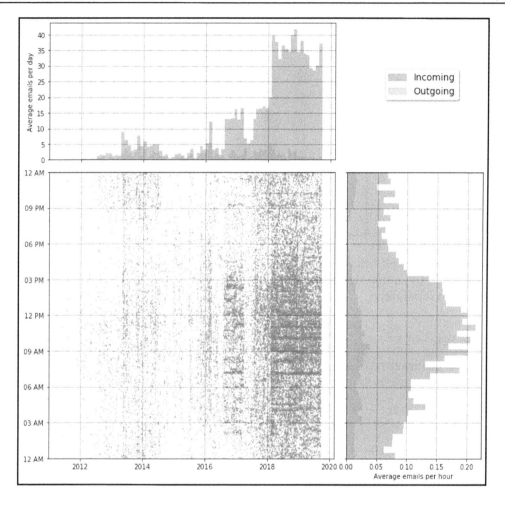

The average emails per hour and per graph is illustrated by the preceding graph. In my case, most email communication happened between 2018 and 2020.

Number of emails per day

Let's find the busiest day of the week in terms of emails:

```
counts = dfs.dayofweek.value_counts(sort=False)
counts.plot(kind='bar')
```

The output of the preceding code is as follows:

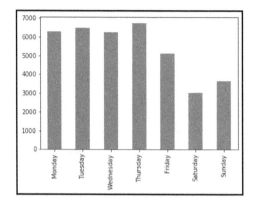

The preceding output shows that my busiest day is Thursday. I receive most of my emails on Thursdays. Let's go one step further and see the most active days for receiving and sending emails separately:

```
sdw = sent.groupby('dayofweek').size() / len(sent)
rdw = received.groupby('dayofweek').size() / len(received)

df_tmp = pd.DataFrame(data={'Outgoing Email': sdw, 'Incoming Email':rdw})
df_tmp.plot(kind='bar', rot=45, figsize=(8,5), alpha=0.5)
plt.xlabel('');
plt.ylabel('Fraction of weekly emails');
plt.grid(ls=':', color='k', alpha=0.5)
```

The output of the preceding code is as follows:

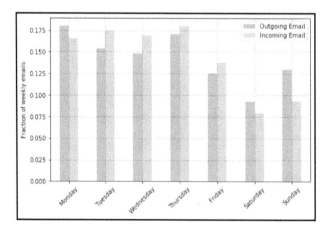

The output shown in the screenshot is pretty nice, right? Now, anyone can easily understand that my most active email communication days are Thursday for incoming emails and Monday for sending emails. That makes sense. I usually don't work on weekends, so, on Mondays, I always reply to my emails before starting the day. That is why on Monday, the analysis shows, I have more outgoing emails.

We can even go one level further. Let's find the most active time of day for email communication. We can do that easily. See the following code:

```
import scipy.ndimage
from scipy.interpolate import interp1d

plt.figure(figsize=(8,5))
ax = plt.subplot(111)
for ct, dow in enumerate(dfs.dayofweek.cat.categories):
    df_r = received[received['dayofweek']==dow]
    weights = np.ones(len(df_r)) / len(received)
    wfun = lambda x: weights
    plot_number_perdhour_per_year(df_r, ax, dt=1, smooth=True,
color=f'C{ct}',
                    alpha=0.8, lw=3, label=dow, weight_fun=wfun)

    df_s = sent[sent['dayofweek']==dow]
    weights = np.ones(len(df_s)) / len(sent)
    wfun = lambda x: weights
    plot_number_perdhour_per_year(df_s, ax, dt=1, smooth=True,
color=f'C{ct}',
                    alpha=0.8, lw=2, label=dow, ls='--', weight_fun=wfun)
ax.set_ylabel('Fraction of weekly emails per hour')
plt.legend(loc='upper left')
```

The output of the preceding code is as follows:

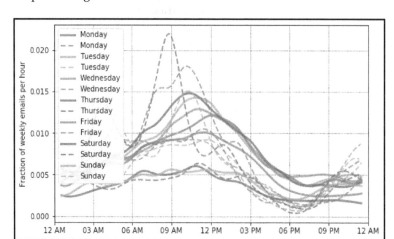

Sweet. The graph is a bit complex but still intuitive. From the previous graph, we noticed that my most active days were Monday (for outgoing emails) and Thursdays (for receiving emails). This graph shows that on Mondays, my active duration is between 09:00 AM and 12:00 PM. On Thursdays, my active duration is also between 9:00 AM and 12:00 PM. What are your most active hours based on your graph?

 If you encounter any error, please check the number of sent emails and the number of received emails. The number of emails, in either case, should be greater than one. If you have less or equal to one email, in either case, make sure you comment out the appropriate line to remove the error.

Most frequently used words

One of the easiest things to analyze about your emails is the most frequently used words. We can create a word cloud to see the most frequently used words. Let's first remove the archived emails:

```
from wordcloud import WordCloud

df_no_arxiv = dfs[dfs['from'] != 'no-reply@arXiv.org']
text = ' '.join(map(str, sent['subject'].values))
```

Next, let's plot the word cloud:

```
stopwords = ['Re', 'Fwd', '3A_']
wrd = WordCloud(width=700, height=480, margin=0, collocations=False)
for sw in stopwords:
    wrd.stopwords.add(sw)
wordcloud = wrd.generate(text)

plt.figure(figsize=(25,15))
plt.imshow(wordcloud, interpolation='bilinear')
plt.axis("off")
plt.margins(x=0, y=0)
```

I added some extra stop words to filter out from the graph. The output for me is as follows:

This tells me what I mostly communicate about. From the analysis of emails from 2011 to 2019, the most frequently used words are new, site, project, Data, WordPress, and website. This is really good, right? What is presented in this chapter is just a starting point. You can take this further in several other directions.

Summary

In this chapter, we imported data from our own Gmail accounts in mbox format. Then, we loaded the dataset and performed some primitive EDA techniques, including data loading, data transformation, and data analysis. We also tried to answer some basic questions about email communication.

In the next chapter, we are going to discuss data transformation. Data transformation is one of the most important steps of data analysis, because the more qualitative your data is, the better your results.

Further reading

- *Pandas Cookbook: Recipes for Scientific Computing, Time Series Analysis and Data Visualization using Python 1st Edition,* by *Theodore Petrou, Packt Publishing, 2017*
- *Mastering pandas – Second Edition,* by *Ashish Kumar, Packt Publishing,* October 25, 2019
- *Learning pandas – Second Edition,* by *Michael Heydt, Packt Publishing,* June 29, 2017

4

Data Transformation

One of the fundamental steps of **Exploratory Data Analysis** (**EDA**) is data wrangling. In this chapter, we will learn how to merge database-style dataframes, merging on the index, concatenating along an axis, combining data with overlap, reshaping with hierarchical indexing, and pivoting long to wide format. We will come to understand the work that must be completed before transferring our information for further examination, including, removing duplicates, replacing values, renaming axis indexes, discretization and binning, and detecting and filtering outliers. We will work on transforming data using a function, mapping, permutation and random sampling, and computing indicators/dummy variables.

This chapter will cover the following topics:

- Background
- Merging database-style dataframes
- Transformation techniques
- Benefits of data transformation

Technical requirements

The code for this chapter can be found in the GitHub repo inside `Chapter 4`, `https://github.com/PacktPublishing/hands-on-exploratory-data-analysis-with-python`.

We will be using the following Python libraries:

- Pandas
- NumPy
- Seaborn
- Matplotlib

Background

Data transformation is a set of techniques used to convert data from one format or structure to another format or structure. The following are some examples of transformation activities:

- *Data deduplication* involves the identification of duplicates and their removal.
- *Key restructuring* involves transforming any keys with built-in meanings to the generic keys.
- *Data cleansing* involves extracting words and deleting out-of-date, inaccurate, and incomplete information from the source language without extracting the meaning or information to enhance the accuracy of the source data.
- *Data validation* is a process of formulating rules or algorithms that help in validating different types of data against some known issues.
- *Format revisioning* involves converting from one format to another.
- *Data derivation* consists of creating a set of rules to generate more information from the data source.
- *Data aggregation* involves searching, extracting, summarizing, and preserving important information in different types of reporting systems.
- *Data integration* involves converting different data types and merging them into a common structure or schema.
- *Data filtering* involves identifying information relevant to any particular user.
- *Data joining* involves establishing a relationship between two or more tables.

The main reason for transforming the data is to get a better representation such that the transformed data is compatible with other data. In addition to this, interoperability in a system can be achieved by following a common data structure and format.

Having said that, let's start looking at data transformation techniques with data integration in the next section.

Merging database-style dataframes

Many beginner developers get confused when working with pandas dataframes, especially regarding when to use append, concat, merge, or join. In this section, we are going to check out the separate use cases for each of these.

Let's assume that you are working at a university as a professor teaching a *Software Engineering* course and an *Introduction to Machine Learning* course, and there are enough students to split into two classes. The examination for each class was done in two separate buildings and graded by two different professors. They gave you two different dataframes. In the first example, let's only consider one subject— the *Software Engineering* course.

Check out the following screenshot:

StudentID	ScoreSE		StudentID	ScoreSE
1	89		2	98
3	39		4	93
5	50		6	44
7	97		8	77
9	20		10	69
...	...		...	...
...	...		...	...
27	73		28	56
29	92		30	27

In the preceding dataset, the first column contains information about student identifiers and the second column contains their respective scores in any subject. The structure of the dataframes is the same in both cases. In this case, we would need to concatenate them.

We can do that by using the pandas concat() method:

```
dataframe = pd.concat([dataFrame1, dataFrame2], ignore_index=True)
dataframe
```

The output of the preceding code is a single dataframe combining both of the tables. These tables would be merged into a single one as shown in the following screenshot:

StudentID	ScoreSE
1	89
3	39
5	50
7	97
9	20
...	...
...	...
27	73
29	92
2	98
4	93
6	44
8	77
10	69
...	...
...	...
28	56
30	27

The ignore_index argument creates a new index; in its absence, we'd keep the original indices. Note that we combined the dataframes along axis=0, that is to say, we combined them together in the same direction. What if we want to combine them side by side? Then we have to specify axis=1.

See the difference using the following code:

```
pd.concat([dataFrame1, dataFrame2], axis=1)
```

The output of the preceding code is shown in the following screenshot:

	StudentID	Score	StudentID	Score
0	1	89	2	98
1	3	39	4	93
2	5	50	6	44
3	7	97	8	77
4	9	22	10	69
5	11	66	12	56
6	13	31	14	31
7	15	51	16	53
8	17	71	18	78
9	19	91	20	93
10	21	56	22	56
11	23	32	24	77
12	25	52	26	33
13	27	73	28	56
14	29	92	30	27

Note the difference in the output. When we specify `axis=1`, the concatenation happens on a side-by-side basis.

Let's continue using the same case we discussed in the preceding code. In the first example, you received two dataframe files for the same subject. Now, consider another use case where you are teaching two courses: *Software Engineering* and *Introduction to Machine Learning*. You will get two dataframes from each subject:

- Two for the *Software Engineering* course
- Another two for the *Introduction to Machine Learning* course

Check the following dataframes:

StudentID	ScoreSE
9	22
11	66
13	31
15	51
17	71
...	...
...	...
27	73
29	92

StudentID	ScoreSE
2	98
4	93
6	44
8	77
10	69
...	...
...	...
28	56
30	27

StudentID	ScoreML
1	39
3	49
5	55
7	77
9	52
...	...
...	...
27	23
29	49

StudentID	ScoreML
2	98
4	93
6	44
8	77
10	69
...	...
...	...
28	56
30	27

In case you missed it, there are important details you need to note in the preceding dataframes:

- There are some students who are not taking the software engineering exam.
- There are some students who are not taking the machine learning exam.
- There are students who appeared in both courses.

Now, assume your head of department walked up to your desk and started bombarding you with a series of questions:

- How many students appeared for the exams in total?
- How many students only appeared for the *Software Engineering* course?
- How many students only appeared for the *Machine Learning* course?

There are several ways in which you can answer these questions. Using the EDA technique is one of them. In this section, we are going to use the pandas library to answer the preceding questions.

Let's check the dataframes for both subjects:

```
import pandas as pd

df1SE = pd.DataFrame({ 'StudentID': [9, 11, 13, 15, 17, 19, 21, 23, 25, 27,
29], 'ScoreSE' : [22, 66, 31, 51, 71, 91, 56, 32, 52, 73, 92]})
df2SE = pd.DataFrame({'StudentID': [2, 4, 6, 8, 10, 12, 14, 16, 18, 20, 22,
24, 26, 28, 30], 'ScoreSE': [98, 93, 44, 77, 69, 56, 31, 53, 78, 93, 56,
77, 33, 56, 27]})

df1ML = pd.DataFrame({ 'StudentID': [1, 3, 5, 7, 9, 11, 13, 15, 17, 19, 21,
23, 25, 27, 29], 'ScoreML' : [39, 49, 55, 77, 52, 86, 41, 77, 73, 51, 86,
82, 92, 23, 49]})
df2ML = pd.DataFrame({'StudentID': [2, 4, 6, 8, 10, 12, 14, 16, 18, 20],
'ScoreML': [93, 44, 78, 97, 87, 89, 39, 43, 88, 78]})`
```

As you can see in the preceding dataset, you have two dataframes for each subject. So, the first task is to concatenate these two subjects into one. Secondly, these students have taken the *Introduction to Machine Learning* course as well as the *Software Engineering* course. So, we need to merge these scores into the same dataframes. There are several ways to do this. Let's explore some options.

Concatenating along with an axis

This is the first option. We'll use the `pd.concat()` method from the `pandas` library.

The code for combining the dataframes is as follows:

```
# Option 1
dfSE = pd.concat([df1SE, df2SE], ignore_index=True)
dfML = pd.concat([df1ML, df2ML], ignore_index=True)

df = pd.concat([dfML, dfSE], axis=1)
df
```

The code should be self-explanatory by now. We first concatenated the dataframes from the *Software Engineering* course and the *Machine Learning* course. Then, we concatenated the dataframes with `axis=1` to place them side by side.

The output of the preceding code is as follows:

	StudentID	ScoreML	StudentID	ScoreSE
0	1.0	39.0	9	22
1	3.0	49.0	11	66
2	5.0	55.0	13	31
3	7.0	77.0	15	51
4	9.0	52.0	17	71
5	11.0	86.0	19	91
6	13.0	41.0	21	56
7	15.0	77.0	23	32
8	17.0	73.0	25	52
9	19.0	51.0	27	73
10	21.0	86.0	29	92
11	23.0	82.0	2	98
12	25.0	92.0	4	93
13	27.0	23.0	6	44
14	29.0	49.0	8	77
15	2.0	93.0	10	69
16	4.0	44.0	12	56

You probably noticed that the StudentID field is repeated. One hack that could be done afterward is to delete the repeated field. However, let's see the other alternatives.

Using df.merge with an inner join

This is the second option. Let's now use the df.merge() method from the pandas library. The idea is simple. First of all, we concatenate the individual dataframes from each of the subjects, and then we use df.merge() methods.

Check the following code:

```
dfSE = pd.concat([df1SE, df2SE], ignore_index=True)
dfML = pd.concat([df1ML, df2ML], ignore_index=True)

df = dfSE.merge(dfML, how='inner')
df
```

Here, you performed an inner join on each dataframe. That is to say, if an item exists in both dataframes, it will be included in the new dataframe. This means we will get a list of students who appeared in both the courses.

The output of the preceding code is shown in the following screenshot:

	StudentID	ScoreSE	ScoreML
0	9	22	52
1	11	66	86
2	13	31	41
3	15	51	77
4	17	71	73
5	19	91	51
6	21	56	86
7	23	32	82
8	25	52	92
9	27	73	23
10	29	92	49
11	2	98	93
12	4	93	44
13	6	44	78
14	8	77	97
15	10	69	87
16	12	56	89
17	14	31	39
18	16	53	43
19	18	78	88
20	20	93	78

Note that this should answer one of the questions mentioned earlier: we now know there are 21 students who took both the courses.

Using the pd.merge() method with a left join

The third option is to use the `pd.merge()` method with the left join technique. By now, you should have understood the concept of a merge. The argument of the `pd.merge()` method allows us to use different types of joins.

These are the following types of joins:

- The `inner` join takes the intersection from two or more dataframes. It corresponds to the `INNER JOIN` in **Structured Query Language (SQL)**.
- The `outer` join takes the union from two or more dataframes. It corresponds to the `FULL OUTER JOIN` in SQL.
- The `left` join uses the keys from the left-hand dataframe only. It corresponds to the `LEFT OUTER JOIN` in SQL.
- The `right` join uses the keys from the right-hand dataframe only. It corresponds to the `RIGHT OUTER JOIN` in SQL.

Let's see how we can use the left outer join:

```
dfSE = pd.concat([df1SE, df2SE], ignore_index=True)
dfML = pd.concat([df1ML, df2ML], ignore_index=True)

df = dfSE.merge(dfML, how='left')
df
```

The output of the preceding code is as follows:

	StudentID	ScoreSE	ScoreML
0	9	22	52.0
1	11	66	86.0
2	13	31	41.0
3	15	51	77.0
4	17	71	73.0
5	19	91	51.0
6	21	56	86.0
7	23	32	82.0
8	25	52	92.0
9	27	73	23.0
10	29	92	49.0
11	2	98	93.0
12	4	93	44.0
13	6	44	78.0
14	8	77	97.0
15	10	69	87.0
16	12	56	89.0
17	14	31	39.0
18	16	53	43.0
19	18	78	88.0
20	20	93	78.0
21	22	56	NaN
22	24	77	NaN
23	26	33	NaN
24	28	56	NaN
25	30	27	NaN

If you look at the preceding screenshot, you can correctly answer how many students only appeared for the *Software Engineering* course. The total number would be 26. Note that these students did not appear for the *Machine Learning* exam and hence their scores are marked as NaN.

Using the pd.merge() method with a right join

This is the fourth option. Similarly to those options we've already looked at, we can use the right join to get a list of all the students who appeared in the *Machine Learning* course.

The code for doing it is as follows:

```
dfSE = pd.concat([df1SE, df2SE], ignore_index=True)
dfML = pd.concat([df1ML, df2ML], ignore_index=True)

df = dfSE.merge(dfML, how='right')
df
```

The output of this snippet is left as part of an exercise for you to complete. Check which columns have NaN values.

Using pd.merge() methods with outer join

This is the fifth option. Finally, we want to know the total number of students appearing for at least one course. This can be done using an outer join:

```
dfSE = pd.concat([df1SE, df2SE], ignore_index=True)
dfML = pd.concat([df1ML, df2ML], ignore_index=True)

df = dfSE.merge(dfML, how='outer')
df
```

Check the output and compare the differences with the previous output.

Merging on index

Sometimes the keys for merging dataframes are located in the dataframes index. In such a situation, we can pass left_index=True or right_index=True to indicate that the index should be accepted as the merge key.

Merging on index is done in the following steps:

1. Consider the following two dataframes:

```
left1 = pd.DataFrame({'key': ['apple','ball','apple', 'apple',
'ball', 'cat'], 'value': range(6)})
right1 = pd.DataFrame({'group_val': [33.4, 5]}, index=['apple',
'ball'])
```

If you print these two dataframes, the output looks like the following screenshot:

	key	value			group_val
0	apple	0	apple		33.4
1	ball	1	ball		5.0
2	apple	2			
3	apple	3			
4	ball	4			
5	cat	5			

Note that the keys in the first dataframe are **apple**, **ball**, and **cat**. In the second dataframe, we have group values for the keys **apple** and **ball**.

2. Now, let's consider two different cases. Firstly, let's try merging using an inner join, which is the default type of merge. In this case, the default merge is the intersection of the keys. Check the following example code:

```
df = pd.merge(left1, right1, left_on='key', right_index=True)
df
```

The output of the preceding code is as follows:

	key	value	group_val
0	apple	0	33.4
2	apple	2	33.4
3	apple	3	33.4
1	ball	1	5.0
4	ball	4	5.0

The output is the intersection of the keys from these dataframes. Since there is no cat key in the second dataframe, it is not included in the final table.

3. Secondly, let's try merging using an outer join, as follows:

```
df = pd.merge(left1, right1, left_on='key', right_index=True,
how='outer')
df
```

The output of the preceding code is as follows:

	key	value	group_val
0	apple	0	33.4
2	apple	2	33.4
3	apple	3	33.4
1	ball	1	5.0
4	ball	4	5.0
5	cat	5	NaN

Note that the last row includes the **cat** key. This is because of the outer join.

Reshaping and pivoting

During EDA, we often need to rearrange data in a dataframe in some consistent manner. This can be done with hierarchical indexing using two actions:

- **Stacking**: Stack rotates from any particular column in the data to the rows.
- **Unstacking**: Unstack rotates from the rows into the column.

We will look at the following example:

1. Let's create a dataframe that records the rainfall, humidity, and wind conditions of five different counties in Norway:

```
data = np.arange(15).reshape((3,5))
indexers = ['Rainfall', 'Humidity', 'Wind']
dframe1 = pd.DataFrame(data, index=indexers, columns=['Bergen',
'Oslo', 'Trondheim', 'Stavanger', 'Kristiansand'])
dframe1
```

The output of the preceding snippet is as follows:

	Bergen	Oslo	Trondheim	Stavanger	Kristiansand
Rainfall	0	1	2	3	4
Humidity	5	6	7	8	9
Wind	10	11	12	13	14

2. Now, using the `stack()` method on the preceding `dframe1`, we can pivot the columns into rows to produce a series:

```
stacked = dframe1.stack()
stacked
```

The output of this stacking is as follows:

```
Rainfall   Bergen         0
           Oslo           1
           Trondheim      2
           Stavanger      3
           Kristiansand   4
Humidity   Bergen         5
           Oslo           6
           Trondheim      7
           Stavanger      8
           Kristiansand   9
Wind       Bergen        10
           Oslo          11
           Trondheim     12
           Stavanger     13
           Kristiansand  14
dtype: int64
```

3. The preceding series stored unstacked in the variable can be rearranged into a dataframe using the `unstack()` method:

```
stacked.unstack()
```

This should revert the series into the original dataframe. Note that there is a chance that unstacking will create missing data if all the values are not present in each of the sub-groups. Confused? Okay, let's look at two series, `series1` and `series2`, and then concatenate them. So far, everything makes sense.

4. Now, let's unstack the concatenated frame:

```
series1 = pd.Series([000, 111, 222, 333], index=['zeros','ones',
'twos', 'threes'])
series2 = pd.Series([444, 555, 666], index=['fours', 'fives',
'sixes'])

frame2 = pd.concat([series1, series2], keys=['Number1', 'Number2'])
frame2.unstack()
```

The output of the preceding unstacking is shown in the following screenshot:

	fives	fours	ones	sixs	threes	twos	zeros
Number1	NaN	NaN	111.0	NaN	333.0	222.0	0.0
Number2	555.0	444.0	NaN	666.0	NaN	NaN	NaN

Since in `series1`, there are no `fours`, `fives`, and `sixes`, their values are stored as **NaN** during the unstacking process. Similarly, there are no `ones`, `twos`, and `zeros` in `series2`, so the corresponding values are stored as **NaN**. Now it makes sense, right? Good.

Transformation techniques

In the *Merging database-style dataframes* section, we saw how we can merge different types of series and dataframes. Now, let's dive more into how we can perform other types of data transformations including cleaning, filtering, deduplication, and others.

Performing data deduplication

It is very likely that your dataframe contains duplicate rows. Removing them is essential to enhance the quality of the dataset. This can be done with the following steps:

1. Let's consider a simple dataframe, as follows:

```
frame3 = pd.DataFrame({'column 1': ['Looping'] * 3 + ['Functions']
* 4, 'column 2': [10, 10, 22, 23, 23, 24, 24]})
frame3
```

The preceding code creates a simple dataframe with two columns. You can clearly see from the following screenshot that in both columns, there are some duplicate entries:

	column 1	column 2
0	Looping	10
1	Looping	10
2	Looping	22
3	Functions	23
4	Functions	23
5	Functions	24
6	Functions	24

2. The `pandas` dataframe comes with a `duplicated()` method that returns a Boolean series stating which of the rows are duplicates:

```
frame3.duplicated()
```

The output of the preceding code is pretty easy to interpret:

```
0    False
1     True
2    False
3    False
4     True
5    False
6     True
dtype: bool
```

The rows that say `True` are the ones that contain duplicated data.

3. Now, we can drop these duplicates using the `drop_duplicates()` method:

```
frame4 = frame3.drop_duplicates()
frame4
```

The output of the preceding code is as follows:

	column 1	column 2
0	Looping	10
2	Looping	22
3	Functions	23
5	Functions	24

Note that rows 1, 4, and 6 are removed. Basically, both the `duplicated()` and `drop_duplicates()` methods consider all of the columns for comparison. Instead of all the columns, we could specify any subset of the columns to detect duplicated items.

4. Let's add a new column and try to find duplicated items based on the second column:

```
frame3['column 3'] = range(7)
frame5 = frame3.drop_duplicates(['column 2'])
frame5
```

The output of the preceding snippet is as follows:

	column 1	column 2	column 3
0	Looping	10	0
2	Looping	22	2
3	Functions	23	3
5	Functions	24	5

Note that both the `duplicated` and `drop_duplicates` methods keep the first observed value during the duplication removal process. If we pass the `take_last=True` argument, the methods return the last one.

Replacing values

Often, it is essential to find and replace some values inside a dataframe. This can be done with the following steps:

1. We can use the `replace` method in such cases:

```
import numpy as np
replaceFrame = pd.DataFrame({'column 1': [200., 3000., -786.,
3000., 234., 444., -786., 332., 3332. ], 'column 2': range(9)})
replaceFrame.replace(to_replace =-786, value= np.nan)
```

The output of the preceding code is as follows:

	column 1	column 2
0	200.0	0
1	3000.0	1
2	NaN	2
3	3000.0	3
4	234.0	4
5	444.0	5
6	NaN	6
7	332.0	7
8	3332.0	8

Note that we just replaced one value with the other values. We can also replace multiple values at once.

2. In order to do so, we display them using a list:

```
replaceFrame = pd.DataFrame({'column 1': [200., 3000., -786.,
3000., 234., 444., -786., 332., 3332. ], 'column 2': range(9)})
replaceFrame.replace(to_replace =[-786, 0], value= [np.nan, 2])
```

In the preceding code, there are two replacements. All -786 values will be replaced by NaN and all 0 values will be replaced by 2. That's pretty straightforward, right?

Handling missing data

Whenever there are missing values, a NaN value is used, which indicates that there is no value specified for that particular index. There could be several reasons why a value could be NaN:

- It can happen when data is retrieved from an external source and there are some incomplete values in the dataset.
- It can also happen when we join two different datasets and some values are not matched.
- Missing values due to data collection errors.
- When the shape of data changes, there are new additional rows or columns that are not determined.
- Reindexing of data can result in incomplete data.

Let's see how we can work with the missing data:

1. Let's assume we have a dataframe as shown here:

```
data = np.arange(15, 30).reshape(5, 3)
dfx = pd.DataFrame(data, index=['apple', 'banana', 'kiwi',
'grapes', 'mango'], columns=['store1', 'store2', 'store3'])
dfx
```

And the output of the preceding code is as follows:

	store1	store2	store3
apple	15	16	17
banana	18	19	20
kiwi	21	22	23
grapes	24	25	26
mango	27	28	29

Assume we have a chain of fruit stores all over town. Currently, the dataframe is showing sales of different fruits from different stores. None of the stores are reporting missing values.

2. Let's add some missing values to our dataframe:

```
dfx['store4'] = np.nan
dfx.loc['watermelon'] = np.arange(15, 19)
dfx.loc['oranges'] = np.nan
dfx['store5'] = np.nan
dfx['store4']['apple'] = 20.
dfx
```

And the output will now look like the following screenshot:

	store1	store2	store3	store4	store5
apple	15.0	16.0	17.0	20.0	NaN
banana	18.0	19.0	20.0	NaN	NaN
kiwi	21.0	22.0	23.0	NaN	NaN
grapes	24.0	25.0	26.0	NaN	NaN
mango	27.0	28.0	29.0	NaN	NaN
watermelon	15.0	16.0	17.0	18.0	NaN
oranges	NaN	NaN	NaN	NaN	NaN

Note that we've added two more stores, `store4` and `store5`, and two more types of fruits, `watermelon` and `oranges`. Assume that we know how many kilos of apples and watermelons were sold from `store4`, but we have not collected any data from `store5`. Moreover, none of the stores reported sales of oranges. We are quite a huge fruit dealer, aren't we?

Note the following characteristics of missing values in the preceding dataframe:

- An entire row can contain `NaN` values.
- An entire column can contain `NaN` values.
- Some (but not necessarily all) values in both a row and a column can be `NaN`.

Based on these characteristics, let's examine `NaN` values in the next section.

NaN values in pandas objects

We can use the isnull() function from the pandas library to identify NaN values:

1. Check the following example:

```
dfx.isnull()
```

The output of the preceding code is as follows:

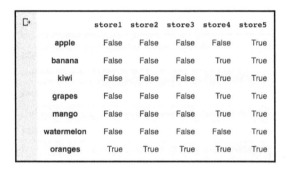

	store1	store2	store3	store4	store5
apple	False	False	False	False	True
banana	False	False	False	True	True
kiwi	False	False	False	True	True
grapes	False	False	False	True	True
mango	False	False	False	True	True
watermelon	False	False	False	False	True
oranges	True	True	True	True	True

Note that the **True** values indicate the values that are NaN. Pretty obvious, right? Alternatively, we can also use the notnull() method to do the same thing. The only difference would be that the function will indicate True for the values which are not null.

2. Check it out in action:

```
dfx.notnull()
```

And the output of this is as follows:

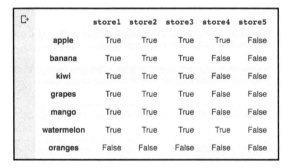

	store1	store2	store3	store4	store5
apple	True	True	True	True	False
banana	True	True	True	False	False
kiwi	True	True	True	False	False
grapes	True	True	True	False	False
mango	True	True	True	False	False
watermelon	True	True	True	True	False
oranges	False	False	False	False	False

Compare these two tables. These two functions, notnull() and isnull(), are the complement to each other.

3. We can use the `sum()` method to count the number of NaN values in each store. How does this work, you ask? Check the following code:

```
dfx.isnull().sum()
```

And the output of the preceding code is as follows:

```
store1  1
store2  1
store3  1
store4  5
store5  7
dtype: int64
```

The fact that *True* is 1 and *False* is 0 is the main logic for summing. The preceding results show that one value was not reported by `store1`, `store2`, and `store3`. Five values were not reported by `store4` and seven values were not reported by `store5`.

4. We can go one level deeper to find the total number of missing values:

```
dfx.isnull().sum().sum()
```

And the output of the preceding code is as follows:

```
15
```

This indicates 15 missing values in our stores. We can use an alternative way to find how many values were actually reported.

5. So, instead of counting the number of missing values, we can count the number of reported values:

```
dfx.count()
```

And the output of the preceding code is as follows:

```
store1  6
store2  6
store3  6
store4  2
store5  0
dtype: int64
```

Pretty elegant, right? We now know two different ways to find the missing values, and also how to count the missing values.

Dropping missing values

One of the ways to handle missing values is to simply remove them from our dataset. We have seen that we can use the `isnull()` and `notnull()` functions from the `pandas` library to determine null values:

```
dfx.store4[dfx.store4.notnull()]
```

The output of the preceding code is as follows:

```
apple 20.0
watermelon 18.0
Name: store4, dtype: float64
```

The output shows that `store4` only reported two items of data. Now, we can use the `dropna()` method to remove the rows:

```
dfx.store4.dropna()
```

The output of the preceding code is as follows:

```
apple 20.0
watermelon 18.0
Name: store4, dtype: float64
```

Note that the `dropna()` method just returns a copy of the dataframe by dropping the rows with NaN. The original dataframe is not changed.

If `dropna()` is applied to the entire dataframe, then it will drop all the rows from the dataframe, because there is at least one NaN value in our dataframe:

```
dfx.dropna()
```

The output of the preceding code is an empty dataframe.

Dropping by rows

We can also drop rows that have NaN values. To do so, we can use the `how=all` argument to drop only those rows entire values are entirely NaN:

```
dfx.dropna(how='all')
```

The output of the preceding code is as follows:

	store1	store2	store3	store4	store5
apple	15.0	16.0	17.0	20.0	NaN
banana	18.0	19.0	20.0	NaN	NaN
kiwi	21.0	22.0	23.0	NaN	NaN
grapes	24.0	25.0	26.0	NaN	NaN
mango	27.0	28.0	29.0	NaN	NaN
watermelon	15.0	16.0	17.0	18.0	NaN

Note that only the orange rows are removed because those entire rows contained NaN values.

Dropping by columns

Furthermore, we can also pass `axis=1` to indicate a check for NaN by columns.

Check the following example:

```
dfx.dropna(how='all', axis=1)
```

And the output of the preceding code is as follows:

	store1	store2	store3	store4
apple	15.0	16.0	17.0	20.0
banana	18.0	19.0	20.0	NaN
kiwi	21.0	22.0	23.0	NaN
grapes	24.0	25.0	26.0	NaN
mango	27.0	28.0	29.0	NaN
watermelon	15.0	16.0	17.0	18.0
oranges	NaN	NaN	NaN	NaN

Note that `store5` is dropped from the dataframe. By passing in `axis=1`, we are instructing pandas to drop columns if all the values in the column are `NaN`. Furthermore, we can also pass another argument, `thresh`, to specify a minimum number of NaNs that must exist before the column should be dropped:

```
dfx.dropna(thresh=5, axis=1)
```

And the output of the preceding code is as follows:

	store1	store2	store3
apple	15.0	16.0	17.0
banana	18.0	19.0	20.0
kiwi	21.0	22.0	23.0
grapes	24.0	25.0	26.0
mango	27.0	28.0	29.0
watermelon	15.0	16.0	17.0
oranges	NaN	NaN	NaN

Compared to the preceding, note that even the `store4` column is now dropped because it has more than five NaN values.

Mathematical operations with NaN

The `pandas` and `numpy` libraries handle NaN values differently for mathematical operations.

Consider the following example:

```
ar1 = np.array([100, 200, np.nan, 300])
ser1 = pd.Series(ar1)

ar1.mean(), ser1.mean()
```

The output of the preceding code is the following:

```
(nan, 200.0)
```

Note the following things:

- When a NumPy function encounters NaN values, it returns NaN.
- Pandas, on the other hand, ignores the NaN values and moves ahead with processing. When performing the sum operation, NaN is treated as 0. If all the values are NaN, the result is also NaN.

Let's compute the total quantity of fruits sold by `store4`:

```
ser2 = dfx.store4
ser2.sum()
```

The output of the preceding code is as follows:

```
38.0
```

Note that `store4` has five NaN values. However, during the summing process, these values are treated as `0` and the result is `38.0`.

Similarly, we can compute averages as shown here:

```
ser2.mean()
```

The output of the code is the following:

```
19.0
```

Note that NaNs are treated as 0s. It is the same for cumulative summing:

```
ser2.cumsum()
```

And the output of the preceding code is as follows:

```
apple 20.0
banana NaN
kiwi NaN
grapes NaN
mango NaN
watermelon 38.0
oranges NaN
Name: store4, dtype: float64
```

Note that only actual values are affected in computing the cumulative sum.

Filling missing values

We can use the `fillna()` method to replace NaN values with any particular values.

Check the following example:

```
filledDf = dfx.fillna(0)
filledDf
```

The output of the preceding code is shown in the following screenshot:

	store1	store2	store3	store4	store5
apple	15.0	16.0	17.0	20.0	0.0
banana	18.0	19.0	20.0	0.0	0.0
kiwi	21.0	22.0	23.0	0.0	0.0
grapes	24.0	25.0	26.0	0.0	0.0
mango	27.0	28.0	29.0	0.0	0.0
watermelon	15.0	16.0	17.0	18.0	0.0
oranges	0.0	0.0	0.0	0.0	0.0

Note that in the preceding dataframe, all the NaN values are replaced by 0. Replacing the values with 0 will affect several statistics including mean, sum, and median.

Check the difference in the following two examples:

```
dfx.mean()
```

And the output of the preceding code is as follows:

```
store1 20.0
store2 21.0
store3 22.0
store4 19.0
store5 NaN
dtype: float64
```

Now, let's compute the mean from the filled dataframe with the following command:

```
filledDf.mean()
```

And the output we get is as follows:

```
store1 17.142857
store2 18.000000
store3 18.857143
store4 5.428571
store5 0.000000
dtype: float64
```

Note that there are slightly different values. Hence, filling with 0 might not be the optimal solution.

Backward and forward filling

NaN values can be filled based on the last known values. To understand this, let's consider taking our store dataframe as an example.

We want to fill `store4` using the forward-filling technique:

```
dfx.store4.fillna(method='ffill')
```

And the output of the preceding code is the following:

```
apple 20.0
banana 20.0
kiwi 20.0
grapes 20.0
mango 20.0
watermelon 18.0
oranges 18.0
Name: store4, dtype: float64
```

Here, from the forward-filling technique, the last known value is `20` and hence the rest of the NaN values are replaced by it.

The direction of the fill can be changed by changing `method='bfill'`. Check the following example:

```
dfx.store4.fillna(method='bfill')
```

And the output of the preceding code is as follows:

```
apple 20.0
banana 18.0
kiwi 18.0
grapes 18.0
mango 18.0
watermelon 18.0
oranges NaN
Name: store4, dtype: float64
```

Note here that the NaN values are replaced by `18.0`.

Interpolating missing values

The pandas library provides the `interpolate()` function both for the series and the dataframe. By default, it performs a linear interpolation of our missing values. Check the following example:

```
ser3 = pd.Series([100, np.nan, np.nan, np.nan, 292])
ser3.interpolate()
```

And the output of the preceding code is the following:

```
0  100.0
1  148.0
2  196.0
3  244.0
4  292.0
dtype: float64
```

Are you wondering how these values are calculated? Well, it is done by taking the first value before and after any sequence of the NaN values. In the preceding series, `ser3`, the first and the last values are `100` and `292` respectively. Hence, it calculates the next value as *(292-100)/(5-1) = 48*. So, the next value after `100` is *100 + 48 = 148*.

> We can perform more complex interpolation techniques, especially with time series data. An example of this interpolation is shown in the notebook provided with this chapter.

Next, we are going to see how we can rename axis indexes.

Renaming axis indexes

Consider the example from the *Reshaping and pivoting* section. Say you want to transform the index terms to capital letters:

```
dframe1.index = dframe1.index.map(str.upper)
dframe1
```

The output of the preceding code is as follows:

	Bergen	Oslo	Trondheim	Stavanger	Kristiansand
RAINFALL	0	1	2	3	4
HUMIDITY	5	6	7	8	9
WIND	10	11	12	13	14

Note that the indexes have been capitalized. If we want to create a transformed version of the dataframe, then we can use the `rename()` method. This method is handy when we do not want to modify the original data. Check the following example:

```
dframe1.rename(index=str.title, columns=str.upper)
```

And the output of the code is as follows:

	BERGEN	OSLO	TRONDHEIM	STAVANGER	KRISTIANSAND
Rainfall	0	1	2	3	4
Humidity	5	6	7	8	9
Wind	10	11	12	13	14

The `rename` method does not make a copy of the dataframe.

Discretization and binning

Often when working with continuous datasets, we need to convert them into discrete or interval forms. Each interval is referred to as a bin, and hence the name *binning* comes into play:

1. Let's say we have data on the heights of a group of students as follows:

    ```
    height = [120, 122, 125, 127, 121, 123, 137, 131, 161, 145, 141,
    132]
    ```

    And we want to convert that dataset into intervals of 118 to 125, 126 to 135, 136 to 160, and finally 160 and higher.

2. To convert the preceding dataset into intervals, we can use the `cut ()` method provided by the `pandas` library:

```
bins = [118, 125, 135, 160, 200]
category = pd.cut(height, bins)
category
```

The output of the preceding code is as follows:

```
[(118, 125], (118, 125], (118, 125], (125, 135], (118, 125], ...,
(125, 135], (160, 200], (135, 160], (135, 160], (125, 135]] Length:
12 Categories (4, interval[int64]): [(118, 125] < (125, 135] <
(135, 160] < (160, 200]]
```

If you look closely at the output, you'll see that there are mathematical notations for intervals. Do you recall what these parentheses mean from your elementary mathematics class? If not, here is a quick recap:

- A parenthesis indicates that the side is open.
- A square bracket means that it is closed or inclusive.

From the preceding code block, `(118, 125]` means the left-hand side is open and the right-hand side is closed. This is mathematically denoted as follows:

$$(a, b] = \{x | a < x \le b\}$$

Hence, `118` is not included, but anything greater than `118` is included, while `125` is included in the interval.

3. We can set a `right=False` argument to change the form of interval:

```
category2 = pd.cut(height, [118, 126, 136, 161, 200], right=False)
category2
```

And the output of the preceding code is as follows:

```
[[118, 126), [118, 126), [118, 126), [126, 136), [118, 126), ...,
[126, 136), [161, 200), [136, 161), [136, 161), [126, 136)] Length:
12 Categories (4, interval[int64]): [[118, 126) < [126, 136) <
[136, 161) < [161, 200)]
```

Note that the output form of closeness has been changed. Now, the results are in the form of *right-closed, left-open*.

4. We can check the number of values in each bin by using the `pd.value_counts()` method:

```
pd.value_counts(category)
```

And the output is as follows:

```
(118, 125]  5
(135, 160]  3
(125, 135]  3
(160, 200]  1
dtype: int64
```

The output shows that there are five values in the interval `[118-125)`.

5. We can also indicate the bin names by passing a list of labels:

```
bin_names = ['Short Height', 'Average height', 'Good Height',
'Taller']
pd.cut(height, bins, labels=bin_names)
```

And the output is as follows:

```
[Short Height, Short Height, Short Height, Average height, Short
Height, ..., Average height, Taller, Good Height, Good Height,
Average height]
Length: 12
Categories (4, object): [Short Height < Average height < Good
Height < Taller]
```

Note that we have passed at least two arguments, the data that needs to be discretized and the required number of bins. Furthermore, we have used a `right=False` argument to change the form of interval.

6. Now, it is essential to note that if we pass just an integer for our bins, it will compute equal-length bins based on the minimum and maximum values in the data. Okay, let's verify what we mentioned here:

```
import numpy as np
pd.cut(np.random.rand(40), 5, precision=2)
```

In the preceding code, we have just passed 5 as the number of required bins, and the output of the preceding code is as follows:

```
[(0.81, 0.99], (0.094, 0.27], (0.81, 0.99], (0.45, 0.63], (0.63,
0.81], ..., (0.81, 0.99], (0.45, 0.63], (0.45, 0.63], (0.81, 0.99],
(0.81, 0.99]] Length: 40
Categories (5, interval[float64]): [(0.094, 0.27] < (0.27, 0.45] <
(0.45, 0.63] < (0.63, 0.81] < (0.81, 0.99]]
```

We can see, based on the number of bins, it created five categories. There isn't anything here that you don't understand, right? Good work so far. Now, let's take this one step further. Another technical term of interest to us from mathematics is *quantiles*. Remember the concept? If not, don't worry, as we are going to learn about quantiles and other measures in Chapter 5, *Descriptive Statistics*. For now, it is sufficient to understand that quantiles divide the range of a probability distribution into continuous intervals with alike probabilities.

Pandas provides a qcut method that forms the bins based on sample quantiles. Let's check this with an example:

```
randomNumbers = np.random.rand(2000)
category3 = pd.qcut(randomNumbers, 4) # cut into quartiles
category3
```

And the output of the preceding code is as follows:

```
[(0.77, 0.999], (0.261, 0.52], (0.261, 0.52], (-0.000565, 0.261],
(-0.000565, 0.261], ..., (0.77, 0.999], (0.77, 0.999], (0.261, 0.52],
(-0.000565, 0.261], (0.261, 0.52]]
Length: 2000
Categories (4, interval[float64]): [(-0.000565, 0.261] < (0.261, 0.52] <
(0.52, 0.77] < (0.77, 0.999]]
```

Note that based on the number of bins, which we set to 4, it converted our data into four different categories. If we count the number of values in each category, we should get equal-sized bins as per our definition. Let's verify that with the following command:

```
pd.value_counts(category3)
```

And the output of the command is as follows:

```
(0.77, 0.999] 500
(0.52, 0.77] 500
(0.261, 0.52] 500
(-0.000565, 0.261] 500
dtype: int64
```

Our claim is hence verified. Each category contains an equal size of 500 values. Note that, similar to `cut`, we can also pass our own bins:

```
pd.qcut(randomNumbers, [0, 0.3, 0.5, 0.7, 1.0])
```

And the output of the preceding code is as follows:

```
[(0.722, 0.999], (-0.000565, 0.309], (0.309, 0.52], (-0.000565, 0.309],
(-0.000565, 0.309], ..., (0.722, 0.999], (0.722, 0.999], (0.309, 0.52],
(-0.000565, 0.309], (0.309, 0.52]] Length: 2000
Categories (4, interval[float64]): [(-0.000565, 0.309] < (0.309, 0.52] <
(0.52, 0.722] < (0.722, 0.999]]
```

Note that it created four different categories based on our code. Congratulations! We successfully learned how to convert continuous datasets into discrete datasets.

Outlier detection and filtering

Outliers are data points that diverge from other observations for several reasons. During the EDA phase, one of our common tasks is to detect and filter these outliers. The main reason for this detection and filtering of outliers is that the presence of such outliers can cause serious issues in statistical analysis. In this section, we are going to perform simple outlier detection and filtering. Let's get started:

1. Load the dataset that is available from the GitHub link as follows:

```
df =
pd.read_csv('https://raw.githubusercontent.com/PacktPublishing/hand
s-on-exploratory-data-analysis-with-
python/master/Chapter%204/sales.csv')
df.head(10)
```

The dataset was synthesized manually by creating a script. If you are interested in looking at how we created the dataset, the script can be found inside the folder named `Chapter 4` in the GitHub repository shared with this book.

The output of the preceding df.head(10) command is shown in the following screenshot:

	Account	Company	Order	SKU	Country	Year	Quantity	UnitPrice	transactionComplete
0	123456779	Kulas Inc	99985	s9-supercomputer	Aruba	1981	5148	545	False
1	123456784	GitHub	99986	s4-supercomputer	Brazil	2001	3262	383	False
2	123456782	Kulas Inc	99990	s10-supercomputer	Montserrat	1973	9119	407	True
3	123456783	My SQ Man	99999	s1-supercomputer	El Salvador	2015	3097	615	False
4	123456787	ABC Dogma	99996	s6-supercomputer	Poland	1970	3356	91	True
5	123456778	Super Sexy Dingo	99996	s9-supercomputer	Costa Rica	2004	2474	136	True
6	123456783	ABC Dogma	99981	s11-supercomputer	Spain	2006	4081	195	False
7	123456785	ABC Dogma	99998	s9-supercomputer	Belarus	2015	6576	603	False
8	123456778	Loolo INC	99997	s8-supercomputer	Mauritius	1999	2460	36	False
9	123456775	Kulas Inc	99997	s7-supercomputer	French Guiana	2004	1831	664	True

2. Now, suppose we want to calculate the total price based on the quantity sold and the unit price. We can simply add a new column, as shown here:

```
df['TotalPrice'] = df['UnitPrice'] * df['Quantity']
df
```

This should add a new column called TotalPrice, as shown in the following screenshot:

	Account	Company	Order	SKU	Country	Year	Quantity	UnitPrice	transactionComplete	TotalPrice
0	123456779	Kulas Inc	99985	s9-supercomputer	Aruba	1981	5148	545	False	2805660
1	123456784	GitHub	99986	s4-supercomputer	Brazil	2001	3262	383	False	1249346
2	123456782	Kulas Inc	99990	s10-supercomputer	Montserrat	1973	9119	407	True	3711433
3	123456783	My SQ Man	99999	s1-supercomputer	El Salvador	2015	3097	615	False	1904655
4	123456787	ABC Dogma	99996	s6-supercomputer	Poland	1970	3356	91	True	305396
5	123456778	Super Sexy Dingo	99996	s9-supercomputer	Costa Rica	2004	2474	136	True	336464
6	123456783	ABC Dogma	99981	s11-supercomputer	Spain	2006	4081	195	False	795795
7	123456785	ABC Dogma	99998	s9-supercomputer	Belarus	2015	6576	603	False	3965328
8	123456778	Loolo INC	99997	s8-supercomputer	Mauritius	1999	2460	36	False	88560
9	123456775	Kulas Inc	99997	s7-supercomputer	French Guiana	2004	1831	664	True	1215784

Now, let's answer some questions based on the preceding table.

Let's find the transaction that exceeded 3,000,000:

```
TotalTransaction = df["TotalPrice"]
TotalTransaction[np.abs(TotalTransaction) > 3000000]
```

The output of the preceding code is as follows:

```
2    3711433
7    3965328
13   4758900
15   5189372
17   3989325
         ...
9977  3475824
9984  5251134
9987  5670420
9991  5735513
9996  3018490
Name: TotalPrice, Length: 2094, dtype: int64
```

Note that, in the preceding example, we have assumed that any price greater than 3,000,000 is an outlier.

Display all the columns and rows from the preceding table if `TotalPrice` is greater than `6741112`, as follows:

```
df[np.abs(TotalTransaction) > 6741112]
```

The output of the preceding code is the following:

	Account	Company	Order	SKU	Country	Year	Quantity	UnitPrice	transactionComplete	TotalPrice
818	123456781	Gen Power	99991	s1-supercomputer	Burkina Faso	1985	9693	696	False	6746328
1402	123456778	Will LLC	99985	s11-supercomputer	Austria	1990	9844	695	True	6841580
2242	123456770	Name IT	99997	s9-supercomputer	Myanmar	1979	9804	692	False	6784368
2876	123456772	Gen Power	99992	s10-supercomputer	Mali	2007	9935	679	False	6745865
3210	123456782	Loolo INC	99991	s8-supercomputer	Kuwait	2006	9886	692	False	6841112
3629	123456779	My SQ Man	99980	s3-supercomputer	Hong Kong	1994	9694	700	False	6785800
7674	123456781	Loolo INC	99989	s6-supercomputer	Sri Lanka	1994	9882	691	False	6828462
8645	123456789	Gen Power	99998	s11-supercomputer	Suriname	2005	9742	699	False	6809658
8684	123456785	Gen Power	99989	s2-supercomputer	Kenya	2013	9805	694	False	6804670

Note that in the output, all the `TotalPrice` values are greater than `6741112`. We can use any sort of conditions, either row-wise or column-wise, to detect and filter outliers.

Permutation and random sampling

Well, now we have some more mathematical terms to learn: *permutation* and *random sampling*. Let's examine how we can perform permutation and random sampling using the `pandas` library:

1. With NumPy's `numpy.random.permutation()` function, we can randomly select or permute a series of rows in a dataframe. Let's understand this with an example:

```
dat = np.arange(80).reshape(10,8)
df = pd.DataFrame(dat)
df
```

And the output of the preceding code is as follows:

	0	1	2	3	4	5	6	7
0	0	1	2	3	4	5	6	7
1	8	9	10	11	12	13	14	15
2	16	17	18	19	20	21	22	23
3	24	25	26	27	28	29	30	31
4	32	33	34	35	36	37	38	39
5	40	41	42	43	44	45	46	47
6	48	49	50	51	52	53	54	55
7	56	57	58	59	60	61	62	63
8	64	65	66	67	68	69	70	71
9	72	73	74	75	76	77	78	79

2. Next, we call the `np.random.permutation()` method. This method takes an argument – the length of the axis we require to be permuted – and gives an array of integers indicating the new ordering:

```
sampler = np.random.permutation(10)
sampler
```

The output of the preceding code is as follows:

```
array([1, 5, 3, 6, 2, 4, 9, 0, 7, 8])
```

3. The preceding output array is used in ix-based indexing for the `take()` function from the `pandas` library. Check the following example for clarification:

```
df.take(sampler)
```

The output of the preceding code is as follows:

	0	1	2	3	4	5	6	7
1	8	9	10	11	12	13	14	15
5	40	41	42	43	44	45	46	47
3	24	25	26	27	28	29	30	31
6	48	49	50	51	52	53	54	55
2	16	17	18	19	20	21	22	23
4	32	33	34	35	36	37	38	39
9	72	73	74	75	76	77	78	79
0	0	1	2	3	4	5	6	7
7	56	57	58	59	60	61	62	63
8	64	65	66	67	68	69	70	71

It is essential that you understand the output. Note that our sampler array contains `array([1, 5, 3, 6, 2, 4, 9, 0, 7, 8])`. Each of these array items represents the rows of the original dataframe. So, from the original dataframe, it pulls the first row, then the fifth row, then the third row, and so on. Compare this with the original dataframe output and it will make more sense.

Random sampling without replacement

To compute random sampling without replacement, follow these steps:

1. To perform random sampling without replacement, we first create a `permutation` array.
2. Next, we slice off the first *n* elements of the array where *n* is the desired size of the subset you want to sample.
3. Then we use the `df.take()` method to obtain actual samples:

```
df.take(np.random.permutation(len(df))[:3])
```

The output of the preceding code is as follows:

	0	1	2	3	4	5	6	7
9	72	73	74	75	76	77	78	79
2	16	17	18	19	20	21	22	23
0	0	1	2	3	4	5	6	7

Note that in the preceding code, we only specified a sample of size 3. Hence, we only get three rows in the random sample.

Random sampling with replacement

To generate random sampling with replacement, follow the given steps:

1. We can generate a random sample with replacement using the `numpy.random.randint()` method and drawing random integers:

```
sack = np.array([4, 8, -2, 7, 5])
sampler = np.random.randint(0, len(sack), size = 10)
sampler
```

We created the sampler using the `np.random.randint()` method. The output of the preceding code is as follows:

```
array([3, 3, 0, 4, 0, 0, 1, 2, 1, 4])
```

2. And now, we can `draw` the required samples:

```
draw = sack.take(sampler)
draw
```

The output of the preceding code is as follows:

```
array([ 7,  7,  4,  5,  4,  4,  8, -2,  8,  5])
```

Compare the index of the sampler and then compare it with the original dataframe. The results are pretty obvious in this case.

Computing indicators/dummy variables

Often, we need to convert a categorical variable into some dummy matrix. Especially for statistical modeling or machine learning model development, it is essential to create dummy variables. Let's get started:

1. Let's say we have a dataframe with data on gender and votes, as shown here:

```
df = pd.DataFrame({'gender': ['female', 'female', 'male',
'unknown', 'male', 'female'], 'votes': range(6, 12, 1)})
df
```

The output of the preceding code is as follows:

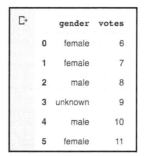

	gender	votes
0	female	6
1	female	7
2	male	8
3	unknown	9
4	male	10
5	female	11

So far, nothing too complicated. Sometimes, however, we need to encode these values in a matrix form with 1 and 0 values.

2. We can do that using the pd.get_dummies() function:

```
pd.get_dummies(df['gender'])
```

And the output of the preceding code is as follows:

	female	male	unknown
0	1	0	0
1	1	0	0
2	0	1	0
3	0	0	1
4	0	1	0
5	1	0	0

Note the pattern. There are five values in the original dataframe with three unique values of male, female, and unknown. Each unique value is transformed into a column and each original value into a row. For example, in the original dataframe, the first value is female, hence it is added as a row with 1 in the female value and the rest of them are 0 values, and so on.

3. Sometimes, we want to add a prefix to the columns. We can do that by adding the prefix argument, as shown here:

```
dummies = pd.get_dummies(df['gender'], prefix='gender')
dummies
```

The output of the preceding code is as follows:

	gender_female	gender_male	gender_unknown
0	1	0	0
1	1	0	0
2	0	1	0
3	0	0	1
4	0	1	0
5	1	0	0

Note the gender prefix added to each of the column names. Not that difficult, right? Great work so far.

Let's look into another type of transformation in the following section.

String manipulation

A lot of data found online is in the form of text, and manipulating these strings is a fundamental part of data transformation. Examining every aspect of string manipulation is beyond the scope of this book. However, we have summarized the major string manipulation operations in the *Appendix*. We highly recommend going through the *Appendix*, in order to comprehend string functions.

Benefits of data transformation

Well, so far we have seen several useful use cases of data transformation.

Let's try to list these benefits:

- Data transformation promotes interoperability between several applications. The main reason for creating a similar format and structure in the dataset is that it becomes compatible with other systems.
- Comprehensibility for both humans and computers is improved when using better-organized data compared to messier data.
- Data transformation ensures a higher degree of data quality and protects applications from several computational challenges such as null values, unexpected duplicates, and incorrect indexings, as well as incompatible structures or formats.
- Data transformation ensures higher performance and scalability for modern analytical databases and dataframes.

In the next section, we will outline some of the challenges encountered in data transformation work.

Challenges

Having discussed the benefits of data transformation, it is worth discussing some of the notable challenges. The process of data transformation can be challenging for several reasons:

- It requires a qualified team of experts and state-of-the-art infrastructure. The cost of attaining such experts and infrastructure can increase the **cost of the operation**.

- Data transformation requires data cleaning before data transformation and data migration. This process of cleansing can be expensively **time-consuming**.
- Generally, the activities of data transformations involve batch processing. This means that sometimes, we might have to wait for a day before the next batch of data is ready for cleansing. This can be very **slow**.

Summary

In this chapter, we discussed several data wrangling techniques, including database-style frame merging, concatenation along an axis, combining different frames, reshaping, removing duplicates, renaming axis indexes, discretization and binning, detecting and filtering outliers, and transformation functions. We have used different datasets to understand different data transformation techniques.

In the next chapter, we are going to discuss in detail different descriptive statistics measures, including the measure of the central tendency and the measure of dispersion. Furthermore, we shall be using Python 3 with different libraries, including SciPy, Pandas, and NumPy, to understand such descriptive measures.

Further reading

- *Pandas Cookbook: Recipes for Scientific Computing, Time Series Analysis and Data Visualization using Python, First Edition,* by *Theodore Petrou, Packt, 2017*
- *Mastering Pandas, Second Edition,* by *Ashish Kumar, Packt,* October 25, 2019
- *Learning Pandas, Second Edition,* by *Michael Heydt, Packt,* June 29, 2017
- *Petr Aubrecht, Zdenek Kouba: Metadata driven data transformation;* retrieved from `http://labe.felk.cvut.cz/~aubrech/bin/Sumatra.pdf`

Section 2: Descriptive Statistics

2

Descriptive statistics help to summarize a provided dataset and identify the most significant features of the data under consideration. The main objective of this section is to familiarize you with descriptive statistics and its main techniques, including the measure of central tendencies and the measure of variability. Moreover, we will be learning different methods of grouping dataset, correlation, and, more importantly, time-series analysis.

This section contains the following chapters:

- Chapter 5, *Descriptive Statistics*
- Chapter 6, *Grouping Datasets*
- Chapter 7, *Correlation*
- Chapter 8, *Time Series Analysis*

Descriptive Statistics

5

In this chapter, we will explore descriptive statistics and their various techniques. Descriptive statistics, as the name suggests, assist in describing and comprehending datasets by providing a short summary pertaining to the dataset provided. The most common types of descriptive statistics include the measure of central tendencies, the measure of deviation, and others. In this chapter, we will become familiar with these techniques and explore those factual measures with visualization. We will use tools such as box plot to get bits of knowledge from statistics.

In this chapter, we'll cover the following topics:

- Understanding statistics
- Measures of central tendency
- Measures of dispersion

Technical requirements

The code for this chapter can be found in this book's GitHub repository, `https://github.com/PacktPublishing/hands-on-exploratory-data-analysis-with-python`, inside the `Chapter 5` folder:

- The dataset used in this chapter is available under open access in Kaggle. It can be downloaded from here: `https://www.kaggle.com/toramky/automobile-dataset`.

Understanding statistics

In data science, both qualitative and quantitative analyses are important aspects. In particular, the quantitative analysis of any dataset requires an understanding of statistical concepts. Statistics is a branch of mathematics that deals with collecting, organizing, and interpreting data. Hence, by using statistical concepts, we can understand the nature of the data, a summary of the dataset, and the type of distribution that the data has.

Distribution function

In order to understand the concept of the distribution function, it is essential to understand the concept of a continuous function. So, what do we mean when we refer to a **continuous function**? Basically, a continuous function is any function that does not have any unexpected changes in value. These abrupt or unexpected changes are referred to as **discontinuities**. For example, consider the following cubic function:

$$y(x) = x^3 + x^2 - 5x + 3$$

If you plot the graph of this function, you will see that there are no jumps or holes in the series of values. Hence, this function is continuous:

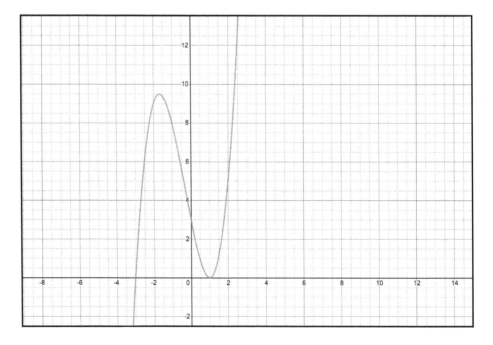

Having understood the continuous function, let's now try to understand what the **probability density function** (**PDF**) is. The PDF can be defined in terms of a continuous function, in other words, for any continuous function, the PDF is the probability that the variate has the value of x.

Now, if you have been paying attention, an obvious question should pop up in your mind. What if the function is associated with discrete random variables rather than continuous random variables? Well, then the function is referred to as a **probability mass function** (**PMF**). For a more formal definition, refer to reference [6] in the *Further reading* section.

The **probability distribution** or **probability function** of a discrete random variable is a list of probabilities linked to each of its attainable values. Let's assume that a random variable, A, takes all values over an interval of real numbers. Then, the probability that A is in the list of outcomes Z, P(Z), is the area above Z and under a curve that describes a function p(a) satisfying the following conditions:

1. The curve cannot have negative values (p(a) > 0 for all a).
2. The total area under the curve is always equal to 1.

Such curves are referred to as density curves. Continuous probability distributions include normal distribution, exponential distribution, uniform distribution, gamma distribution, Poisson distribution, and binomial distribution.

Uniform distribution

The uniform probability distribution function of any continuous uniform distribution is given by the following equation:

$$f(x) = \begin{cases} \frac{1}{b-1} \text{ for a} <= \text{x} <= \text{b}, \\ 0 \text{ for x} < \text{a or x} > \text{b} \end{cases}$$

Let's plot the graph for uniform distribution using the Python libraries, seaborn and matplotlib. First of all, let's import the important libraries needed to generate the graph:

```
import matplotlib.pyplot as plt
from IPython.display import Math, Latex
from IPython.core.display import Image
import seaborn as sns

sns.set(color_codes=True)
sns.set(rc={'figure.figsize':(10,6)})
```

Now, let's generate a uniform distribution:

```
from scipy.stats import uniform
number = 10000
start = 20
width = 25

uniform_data = uniform.rvs(size=number, loc=start, scale=width)
axis = sns.distplot(uniform_data, bins=100, kde=True, color='skyblue',
hist_kws={"linewidth": 15})
axis.set(xlabel='Uniform Distribution ', ylabel='Frequency')
```

The code is pretty obvious, right? We simply import the uniform function from the stats library and generate the data. Once we generate the dataset, we plot the graph. The output graph of the preceding code is as follows:

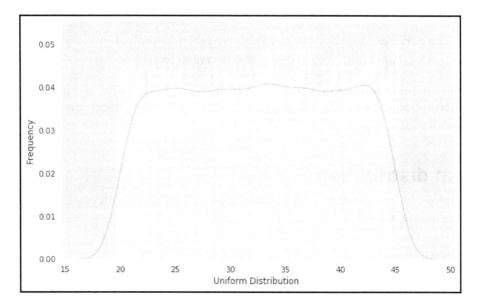

The `uniform` function is used to generate a uniform continuous variable between the given start location (`loc`) and the width of the arguments (`scale`). The `size` arguments specify the number of random variates taken under consideration. The graph illustrates the fact that the dataset is uniformly distributed.

Normal distribution

Normal distribution, or **Gaussian distribution**, is a function that distributes the list of random variables in a graph that is shaped like a symmetrical bell. I am pretty sure that you will have encountered this term numerous times in your data science career. But have you understood its concept? Well, a normal distribution has a density curve that is symmetrical about its mean, with its spread typically defined by its standard deviation. It has two parameters – the mean and the standard deviation. The fact that the normal distribution is principally based on the central limit theorem makes it relevant. If the size of all possible samples in a population is n, and the mean is μ and the variance $\sigma2$, then the distribution approaches a normal distribution. Mathematically, it is given as follows:

$$f(x) = \frac{1}{\sigma\sqrt{2\Pi}} e^{-\frac{(x-\mu)^2}{2\sigma^2}} \qquad X \sim N(\mu, \sigma^2)$$

Now, let's see how we can draw an illustration for normal distribution using the Python `stats` library:

```
from scipy.stats import norm

normal_data = norm.rvs(size=90000,loc=20,scale=30)
axis = sns.distplot(normal_data, bins=100, kde=True, color='skyblue',
hist_kws={"linewidth": 15,'alpha':0.568})
axis.set(xlabel='Normal Distribution', ylabel='Frequency')
```

The output of the preceding code is as follows:

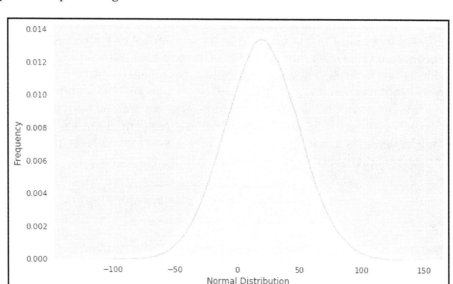

We can get a normal distribution graph using the `scipy.stats` modules by the `norm.rvs()` method. It allows the `loc` argument to set the mean of the distribution, the `scale` argument to set the standard deviation, and finally the `size` argument to indicate the number of random variables.

Exponential distribution

A process in which some events occur continuously and independently at a constant average rate is referred to as a **Poisson point process**. The exponential distribution describes the time between events in such a Poisson point process, and the probability density function of the exponential distribution is given as follows:

$$f(x; \lambda) = \begin{cases} \lambda e^{-\lambda x} & x \geq 0, \\ 0 & x < 0 \end{cases}$$

We can visualize an exponentially distributed random variable using the `scipy.stats` module by applying the `expon.rvs()` function. Check the following code:

```
# Exponential distribution
from scipy.stats import expon

expon_data = expon.rvs(scale=1,loc=0,size=1000)
axis = sns.distplot(expon_data, kde=True, bins=100, color='skyblue',
hist_kws={"linewidth": 15})
axis.set(xlabel='Exponential Distribution', ylabel='Frequency')
```

The output of the preceding code is as follows:

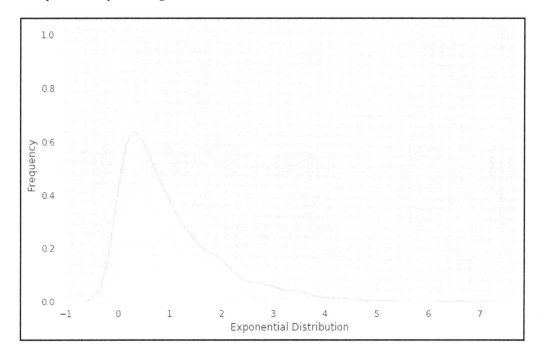

The graph shown in the preceding diagram illustrates the decreasing exponential function. The curve is decreasing over the *x* axis.

Binomlal distribution

Binomial distribution, as the name suggests, has only two possible outcomes, success or failure. The outcomes do not need to be equally likely and each trial is independent of the other.

Let's generate a binomial distribution graph using the `scipy.stats` module by the `binom` method:

```
from scipy.stats import binom

binomial_data = binom.rvs(n=10, p=0.8,size=10000)

axis = sns.distplot(binomial_data, kde=False, color='red',
hist_kws={"linewidth": 15})
axis.set(xlabel='Binomial Distribution', ylabel='Frequency')
```

The output of the preceding code is given in the following diagram:

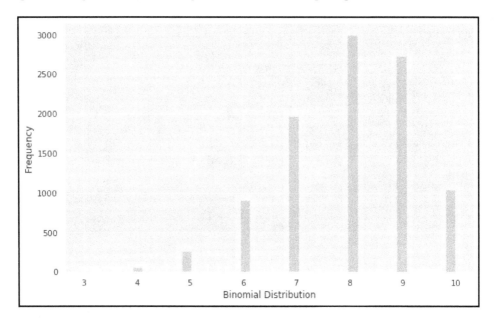

The `binom.rvs()` method from the `scipy.stats` module takes n as the number of trial arguments, and p as the probability of success as shape parameters to generate the graph.

Cumulative distribution function

Now, the **cumulative distribution function** (CDF) is the probability that the variable takes a value that is less than or equal to x. Mathematically, it is written as follows:

$$f(x) = P[X \leq x] = \alpha$$

When a distribution is a scalar continuous, it provides the area under the PDF, ranging from minus infinity to x. The CDF specifies the distribution of multivariate random variables.

Descriptive statistics

Descriptive statistics deals with the formulation of simple summaries of data so that they can be clearly understood. The summaries of data may be either numerical representations or visualizations with simple graphs for further understanding. Typically, such summaries help in the initial phase of statistical analysis. There are two types of descriptive statistics:

1. Measures of central tendency
2. Measures of variability (spread)

Measures of central tendency include `mean`, `median`, and `mode`, while measures of variability include `standard deviation` (or variance), the minimum and maximum values of the variables, `kurtosis`, and `skewness`. We are going to discuss these two categories in the next section.

Measures of central tendency

The measure of central tendency tends to describe the average or mean value of datasets that is supposed to provide an optimal summarization of the entire set of measurements. This value is a number that is in some way central to the set. The most common measures for analyzing the distribution frequency of data are the mean, median, and mode.

Mean/average

The mean, or average, is a number around which the observed continuous variables are distributed. This number estimates the value of the entire dataset. Mathematically, it is the result of the division of the sum of numbers by the number of integers in the dataset.

Let x be a set of integers:

x = (12,2,3,5,8,9,6,4,2)

Hence, the mean value of *x* can be calculated as follows:

$$Mean(x) = \frac{12 + 2 + 3 + 5 + 8 + 9 + 6 + 4 + 2}{9} = 5.66$$

Next, let's look at the median.

Median

Given a dataset that is sorted either in ascending or descending order, the median divides the data into two parts. The general formula for calculating the median is as follows:

$$\text{median position} = \frac{(n + 1)}{2} \text{th observation}$$

Here, n is the number of items in the data. The steps involved in calculating the median are as follows:

1. Sort the numbers in either ascending or descending order.
2. If n is odd, find the $(n+1)/2^{th}$ term. The value corresponding to this term is the median.
3. If n is even, find the $(n+1)/2^{th}$ term. The median value is the average of numbers on either side of the median position.

For a set of integers such as x, we must arrange them in ascending order and then select the middle integer.

x in ascending order = (2,2,3,4,5,6,8,9,12).

Here, the median is 5.

Mode

The mode is the integer that appears the maximum number of times in the dataset. It happens to be the value with the highest frequency in the dataset. In the x dataset in the median example, the mode is 2 because it occurs twice in the set.

Python provides different libraries for operating descriptive statistics in the dataset. Commonly used libraries are `pandas`, `numpy`, and `scipy`. These measures of central tendency can simply be calculated by the `numpy` and `pandas` functionalities.

To practice descriptive statistics, we would require a dataset that has multiple numerical records in it. Here is a dataset of automobiles that enlists different features and attributes of cars, such as symboling, normalized losses, aspiration, and many others, an analysis of which will provide some valuable insight and findings in relation to automobiles in this dataset.

Let's begin by importing the datasets and the Python libraries required:

```
import pandas as pd
import numpy as np
```

Now, let's load the automobile database:

```
df = pd.read_csv("data.csv")
df.head()
```

In the preceding code, we assume that you have the database stored in your current drive. Alternatively, you can change the path to the correct location. By now, you should be familiar with data loading techniques. The output of the code is given here:

	symboling	normalized-losses	make	aspiration	num-of-doors	body-style	drive-wheels	engine-location	wheel-base	length	width	height	curb-weight	engine-type	num-of-cylinders	engine-size
0	3	122	alfa-romero	std	two	convertible	rwd	front	88.6	0.811148	0.890278	48.8	2548	dohc	four	130
1	3	122	alfa-romero	std	two	convertible	rwd	front	88.6	0.811148	0.890278	48.8	2548	dohc	four	130
2	1	122	alfa-romero	std	two	hatchback	rwd	front	94.5	0.822681	0.909722	52.4	2823	ohcv	six	152
3	2	164	audi	std	four	sedan	fwd	front	99.8	0.848630	0.919444	54.3	2337	ohc	four	109
4	2	164	audi	std	four	sedan	4wd	front	99.4	0.848630	0.922222	54.3	2824	ohc	five	136

Data cleaning: In the previous chapter, we discussed several ways in which we can clean our dataset. We need to clean numeric columns. Since we have already discussed several ways in which we can clean the dataset, I have skipped the codes for doing so. However, you can find a section entitled *Data cleaning* in the Python notebook attached to this chapter in the GitHub repository.

Now, let's start by computing measures of central tendencies. Before establishing these for all the rows, let's see how we can get central tendencies for a single column. For example, we want to obtain the mean, median, and mode for the column that represents the height. In pandas, we can get an individual column easily by specifying the column name as `dataframe["column_name"]`. In our case, our DataFrame is stored in the `df` variable. Hence, we can get all the data items for height as `df["height"]`. Now, pandas provides easy built-in functions to measure central tendencies. Let's compute this as follows:

```
height =df["height"]
mean = height.mean()
median =height.median()
mode = height.mode()
print(mean , median, mode)
```

The output of the preceding code is as follows:

```
53.766666666666715 54.1 0 50.8
dtype: float64
```

Now, the important thing here is to interpret the results. Just with these simple statistics, we can understand that the average height of the cars is around `53.766` and that there are a lot of cars whose mode value is `50.8`. Similarly, we can get measures of the central tendencies for any columns whose data types are numeric. A list of similar functions that are helpful is shown in the following screenshot:

Serial Number	Function Name	Description
1	count()	Number of non-null observations
2	sum()	Sum of values
3	mean()	Mean of Values
4	median()	Median of Values
5	mode()	Mode of values
6	std()	Standard Deviation of the Values
7	min()	Minimum Value
8	max()	Maximum Value
9	abs()	Absolute Value
10	prod()	Product of Values
11	cumsum()	Cumulative Sum
12	cumprod()	Cumulative Product

In addition to finding statistics for a single column, it is possible to find descriptive statistics for the entire dataset at once. Pandas provides a very useful function, df.describe, for doing so:

```
df.describe()
```

The output of the preceding code is shown in the following screenshot:

	symboling	wheel-base	length	width	height	curb-weight	engine-size	compression-ratio	city-mpg	highway-mpg
count	205.000000	205.000000	205.000000	205.000000	205.000000	205.000000	205.000000	205.000000	205.000000	205.000000
mean	0.834146	98.756585	174.049268	65.907805	53.724878	2555.565854	126.907317	10.142537	25.219512	30.751220
std	1.245307	6.021776	12.337289	2.145204	2.443522	520.680204	41.642693	3.972040	6.542142	6.886443
min	-2.000000	86.600000	141.100000	60.300000	47.800000	1488.000000	61.000000	7.000000	13.000000	16.000000
25%	0.000000	94.500000	166.300000	64.100000	52.000000	2145.000000	97.000000	8.600000	19.000000	25.000000
50%	1.000000	97.000000	173.200000	65.500000	54.100000	2414.000000	120.000000	9.000000	24.000000	30.000000
75%	2.000000	102.400000	183.100000	66.900000	55.500000	2935.000000	141.000000	9.400000	30.000000	34.000000
max	3.000000	120.900000	208.100000	72.300000	59.800000	4066.000000	326.000000	23.000000	49.000000	54.000000

If you have used pandas before, I am pretty sure you have heard about or probably used this function several times. But have you really understood the output you obtained? In the preceding table, you can see that we have statistics for all the columns, excluding NaN values. The function takes both numeric and objects series under consideration during the calculation. In the rows, we get the count, mean, standard deviation, minimum value, percentiles, and maximum values of that column. We can easily understand our dataset in a better way. In fact, if you check the preceding table, you can answer the following questions:

- What is the total number of rows we have in our dataset?
- What is the average length, width, height, price, and compression ratio of the cars?
- What is the minimum height of the car? What is the maximum height of the car?
- What is the maximum standard deviation of the curb weight of the cars?.

We can now, in fact, answer a lot of questions, just based on one table. Pretty good, right? Now, whenever you start any data science work, it is always considered good practice to perform a number of sanity checks. By sanity checks, I mean understanding your data before actually fitting machine learning models. Getting a description of the dataset is one such sanity check.

In the case of categorical variables that have discrete values, we can summarize the categorical data by using the `value_counts()` function. Well, an example is better than a precept. In our dataset, we have a categorical data column, `make`. Let's first count the total number of entries according to such categories, and then take the first 30 largest values and draw a bar chart:

```
df.make.value_counts().nlargest(30).plot(kind='bar', figsize=(14,8))
plt.title("Number of cars by make")
plt.ylabel('Number of cars')
plt.xlabel('Make of the cars')
```

By now, the preceding code should be pretty familiar. We are using the `value_counts()` function from the pandas library. Once we have the list, we are getting the first 30 largest values by using the `nlargest()` function. Finally, we exploit the plot function provided by the pandas library. The output of the preceding code snippet is shown here:

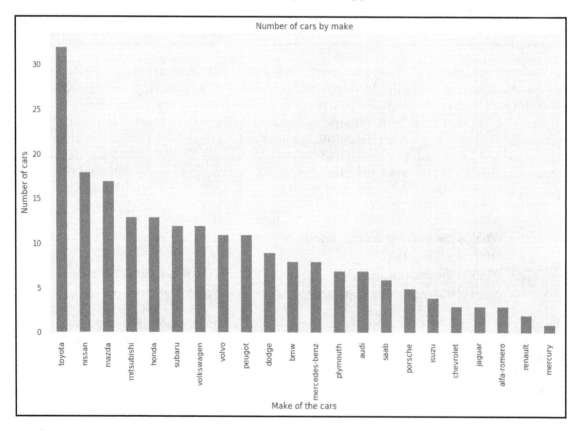

The table, as shown, is helpful. To add a degree of comprehension, we can use visualization techniques as shown in the preceding diagram. It is pretty clear from the diagram that Toyota's brand is the most popular brand. Similarly, we can easily visualize successive brands on the list.

Measures of dispersion

The second type of descriptive statistics is the measure of **dispersion**, also known as a **measure of variability**. It is used to describe the variability in a dataset, which can be a sample or population. It is usually used in conjunction with a measure of central tendency, to provide an overall description of a set of data. A measure of dispersion/variability/spread gives us an idea of how well the central tendency represents the data. If we are analyzing the dataset closely, sometimes, the mean/average might not be the best representation of the data because it will vary when there are large variations between the data. In such a case, a measure of dispersion will represent the variability in a dataset much more accurately.

Multiple techniques provide the measures of dispersion in our dataset. Some commonly used methods are standard deviation (or variance), the minimum and maximum values of the variables, range, kurtosis, and skewness.

Standard deviation

In simple language, the standard deviation is the average/mean of the difference between each value in the dataset with its average/mean; that is, how data is spread out from the mean. If the standard deviation of the dataset is low, then the data points tend to be close to the mean of the dataset, otherwise, the data points are spread out over a wider range of values.

Different Python libraries have functions to get the standard deviation of the dataset. The NumPy library has the `numpy.std(dataset)` function. The statistics library has the `statistics.stdev(dataset).` function. Using the pandas library, we calculate the standard deviation in our `df` data frame using the `df.std()` function:

```
#standard variance of dataset using std() function
std_dev =df.std()
print(std_dev)
# standard variance of the specific column
sv_height=df.loc[:,"height"].std()
print(sv_height)
```

The output of the preceding code is as follows:

```
symboling                     1.254802
normalized-losses            31.996250
wheel-base                    6.066366
length                        0.059213
width                         0.029187
height                        2.447822
curb-weight                 517.296727
engine-size                  41.546834
bore                          0.268072
stroke                        0.319256
compression-ratio             4.004965
horsepower                   37.365700
peak-rpm                    478.113805
city-mpg                      6.423220
highway-mpg                   6.815150
price                      7947.066342
city-L/100km                  2.534599
diesel                        0.300083
gas                           0.300083
dtype: float64
2.44782216129631
```

Next, let's look at variance.

Variance

Variance is the square of the average/mean of the difference between each value in the dataset with its average/mean; that is, it is the square of standard deviation.

Different Python libraries have functions to obtain the variance of the dataset. The NumPy library has the `numpy.var(dataset)` function. The statistics library has the `statistics.variance(dataset)` function. Using the pandas library, we calculate the variance in our `df` data frame using the `df.var()` function:

```
# variance of dataset using var() function
variance=df.var()
print(variance)

# variance of the specific column
var_height=df.loc[:,"height"].var()
print(var_height)
```

The output of the preceding code is as follows:

```
symboling            1.574527e+00
normalized-losses    1.023760e+03
wheel-base           3.680079e+01
length               3.506151e-03
width                8.518865e-04
height               5.991833e+00
curb-weight          2.675959e+05
engine-size          1.726139e+03
bore                 7.186252e-02
stroke               1.019245e-01
compression-ratio    1.603975e+01
horsepower           1.396195e+03
peak-rpm             2.285928e+05
city-mpg             4.125776e+01
highway-mpg          4.644627e+01
price                6.315586e+07
city-L/100km         6.424193e+00
diesel               9.004975e-02
gas                  9.004975e-02
dtype: float64
5.991833333333338
```

It is essential to note the following observations from the code snippet provided here:

- It is important to note that `df.var()` will calculate the variance in the given data frame across the column by default. In addition, we can specify `axis=0` to indicate that we need to calculate variance by column or by row.
- Specifying `df.var(axis=1)` will calculate the row-wise variance in the given data frame.
- Finally, it is also possible to calculate the variance in any particular column by specifying the location. For example, `df.loc[:, "height"].var()` calculates the variance in the column height in the preceding dataset.

Skewness

In probability theory and statistics, skewness is a measure of the asymmetry of the variable in the dataset about its mean. The skewness value can be positive or negative, or undefined. The skewness value tells us whether the data is skewed or symmetric. Here's an illustration of a positively skewed dataset, symmetrical data, and some negatively skewed data:

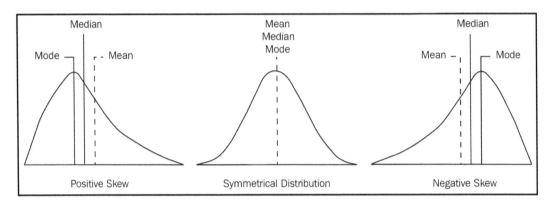

Note the following observations from the preceding diagram:

- The graph on the right-hand side has a tail that is longer than the tail on the right-hand side. This indicates that the distribution of the data is skewed to the left. If you select any point in the left-hand longer tail, the mean is less than the mode. This condition is referred to as **negative skewness**.
- The graph on the left-hand side has a tail that is longer on the right-hand side. If you select any point on the right-hand tail, the mean value is greater than the mode. This condition is referred to as **positive skewness**.
- The graph in the middle has a right-hand tail that is the same as the left-hand tail. This condition is referred to as a **symmetrical condition**.

Different Python libraries have functions to get the skewness of the dataset. The SciPy library has a `scipy.stats.skew(dataset)` function. Using the pandas library, we can calculate the skewness in our `df` data frame using the `df.skew()` function.

Here, in our data frame of automobiles, let's get the skewness using the `df.skew()` function:

```
df.skew()
```

The output of the preceding code is as follows:

```
symboling              0.204275
normalized-losses      0.209007
wheel-base             1.041170
length                 0.154086
width                  0.900685
height                 0.064134
curb-weight            0.668942
engine-size            1.934993
bore                   0.013419
stroke                -0.669515
compression-ratio      2.682640
horsepower             9.985047
peak-rpm               0.073094
city-mpg               0.673533
highway-mpg            0.549104
price                  1.812335
dtype: float64
```

In addition, we can also compute skew at a column level. For example, the skew of the column height can be computed using the `df.loc[:, "height"].skew()`. function.

Kurtosis

We have already discussed normal distribution. Do you remember the bell-shaped graph? If not, just check out the first section of this chapter again. You may well ask yourself, why should you remember that? It is necessary in order to understand the concept of kurtosis. Basically, kurtosis is a statistical measure that illustrates how heavily the tails of distribution differ from those of a normal distribution. This technique can identify whether a given distribution contains extreme values.

 But hold on, isn't that similar to what we do with skewness? Not really. Skewness typically measures the symmetry of the given distribution. On the other hand, kurtosis measures the heaviness of the distribution tails.

Kurtosis, unlike skewness, is not about the peakedness or flatness. It is the measure of outlier presence in a given distribution. Both high and low kurtosis are an indicator that data needs further investigation. The higher the kurtosis, the higher the outliers.

Types of kurtosis

There are three types of kurtosis—mesokurtic, leptokurtic, and platykurtic. Let's look at these one by one:

- **Mesokurtic**: If any dataset follows a normal distribution, it follows a mesokurtic distribution. It has kurtosis around 0.
- **Leptokurtic**: In this case, the distribution has kurtosis greater than 3 and the fat tails indicate that the distribution produces more outliers.
- **Platykurtic**: In this case, the distribution has negative kurtosis and the tails are very thin compared to the normal distribution.

All three types of kurtosis are shown in the following diagram:

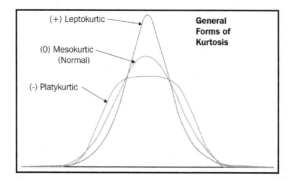

Different Python libraries have functions to get the kurtosis of the dataset. The SciPy library has the `scipy.stats.kurtosis(dataset)` function. Using the pandas library, we calculate the kurtosis of our `df` data frame using the `df.kurt()` function:

```
# Kurtosis of data in data using skew() function
kurtosis =df.kurt()
print(kurtosis)

# Kurtosis of the specific column
sk_height=df.loc[:,"height"].kurt()
print(sk_height)
```

The output of the preceding code is given here:

```
symboling           -0.676271
wheel-base           1.017039
length              -0.082895
width                0.702764
height              -0.443812
curb-weight         -0.042854
engine-size          5.305682
compression-ratio    5.233054
city-mpg             0.578648
highway-mpg          0.440070
price                3.354218
dtype: float64
-0.4438123650575503
```

Similarly, we can compute the kurtosis of any particular data column. For example, we can compute the kurtosis of the column height as `df.loc[:, "height"].kurt()`.

Calculating percentiles

Percentiles measure the percentage of values in any dataset that lie below a certain value. In order to calculate percentiles, we need to make sure our list is sorted. An example would be if you were to say that the 80th percentile of data is 130: then what does that mean? Well, it simply means that 80% of the values lie below 130. Pretty easy, right? We will use the following formula for this:

$$\text{The formula for calculating percentile of X} = \frac{\text{Number of values less than X}}{\text{Total number of observations}} * 100$$

Suppose we have the given data: 1, 2, 2, 3, 4, 5, 6, 7, 7, 8, 9, 10. Then the percentile value of 4 = (4/12) * 100 = 33.33%.

This simply means that 33.33% of the data is less than 4.

Now, let's compute the percentile of the `height` column from the same data frame we have been using so far:

```
height = df["height"]
percentile = np.percentile(height, 50,)
print(percentile)
```

The output of the preceding code is as follows:

```
54.1
```

> The preceding formula is very simple. But do you see any pattern with the measures of central tendencies? What would be the 50th percentile? This corresponds to the median. Were you able to deduce that?

Quartiles

Given a dataset sorted in ascending order, quartiles are the values that split the given dataset into quarters. Quartiles refer to the three data points that divide the given dataset into four equal parts, such that each split makes 25% of the dataset. In terms of percentiles, the 25th percentile is referred to as the first quartile (Q1), the 50th percentile is referred to as the second quartile (Q2), and the 75th percentile is referred to as the third quartile (Q3).

Based on the quartile, there is another measure called inter-quartile range that also measures the variability in the dataset. It is defined as follows:

$$IQR = Q3 - Q1$$

IQR is not affected by the presence of outliers. Let's get the IQR for the `price` column from the same dataframe we have been using so far:

```
price = df.price.sort_values()
Q1 = np.percentile(price, 25)
Q2 = np.percentile(price, 50)
Q3 = np.percentile(price, 75)

IQR = Q3 - Q1
IQR
```

The output of the preceding snippet is as follows:

```
8718.5
```

Next, let's visualize the quartiles using the box plot.

Visualizing quartiles

First of all, let's generate some data. Let's assume that the following are the scores obtained by students in three different subjects:

```
scorePhysics =
[34,35,35,35,35,35,36,36,37,37,37,37,37,38,38,38,39,39,40,40,40,40,40,41,42
,42,42,42,42,42,42,42,43,43,43,43,44,44,44,44,44,44,45,45,45,45,45,46,46,46
,46,46,46,47,47,47,47,47,47,48,48,48,48,48,49,49,49,49,49,49,49,49,52,52,52
,53,53,53,53,53,53,53,53,54,54,54,54,54,54,54,55,55,55,55,55,56,56,56,56,56
,56,57,57,57,58,58,59,59,59,59,59,59,59,60,60,60,60,60,60,60,61,61,61,61,61
,62,62,63,63,63,63,63,64,64,64,64,64,64,64,65,65,65,66,66,67,67,68,68,68,68
,68,68,68,69,70,71,71,71,72,72,72,72,73,73,74,75,76,76,76,76,77,77,78,79,79
,80,80,81,84,84,85,85,87,87,88]
scoreLiterature =
[49,49,50,51,51,52,52,52,52,53,54,54,55,55,55,55,56,56,56,56,56,57,57,57,58
,58,58,59,59,59,60,60,60,60,60,60,60,61,61,61,62,62,62,62,63,63,67,67,68,68
,68,68,68,68,69,69,69,69,69,69,70,71,71,71,71,72,72,72,72,73,73,73,73,74,74
,74,74,74,75,75,75,76,76,76,77,77,78,78,78,79,79,79,80,80,82,83,85,88]
scoreComputer =
[56,57,58,58,58,60,60,61,61,61,61,61,61,62,62,62,62,63,63,63,63,63,64,64,64
,64,65,65,66,66,67,67,67,67,67,67,67,68,68,68,69,69,70,70,70,71,71,71,73,73
,74,75,75,76,76,77,77,77,78,78,81,82,84,89,90]
```

Now, if we want to plot the box plot for a single subject, we can do that using the plt.boxplot() function:

```
plt.boxplot(scoreComputer, showmeans=True, whis = 99)
```

Let's print the box plot for scores from the computer subject:

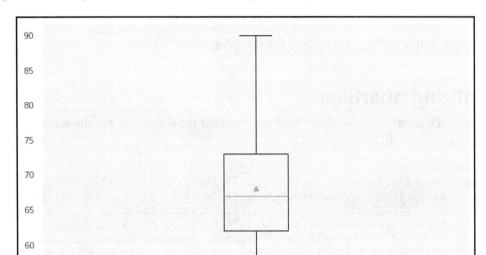

The preceding diagram illustrates the fact that the box goes from the upper to the lower quartile (around 62 and 73), while the whiskers (the bars extending from the box) go to a minimum of 56 and a maximum of 90. The red line is the median (around 67), whereas the little triangle (green color) is the mean.

Now, let's add box plots to other subjects as well. We can do this easily by combining all the scores into a single variable:

```
scores=[scorePhysics, scoreLiterature, scoreComputer]
```

Next, we plot the box plot:

```
box = plt.boxplot(scores, showmeans=True, whis=99)

plt.setp(box['boxes'][0], color='blue')
plt.setp(box['caps'][0], color='blue')
plt.setp(box['caps'][1], color='blue')
plt.setp(box['whiskers'][0], color='blue')
plt.setp(box['whiskers'][1], color='blue')

plt.setp(box['boxes'][1], color='red')
plt.setp(box['caps'][2], color='red')
plt.setp(box['caps'][3], color='red')
plt.setp(box['whiskers'][2], color='red')
```

```
plt.setp(box['whiskers'][3], color='red')

plt.ylim([20, 95])
plt.grid(True, axis='y')
plt.title('Distribution of the scores in three subjects', fontsize=18)
plt.ylabel('Total score in that subject')
plt.xticks([1,2,3], ['Physics','Literature','Computer'])

plt.show()
```

The output of the preceding code is given here:

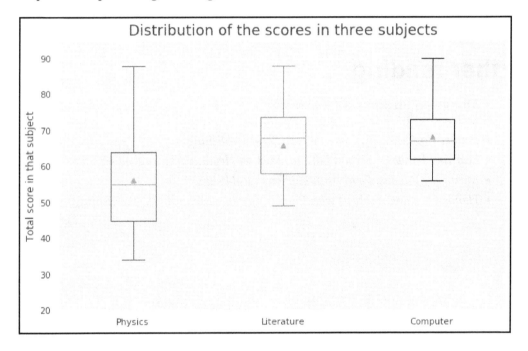

From the graph, it is clear that the minimum score obtained by the students was around 32, while the maximum score obtained was 90, which was in the computer science subject.

Summary

In this chapter, we discussed several aspects of descriptive statistics. A descriptive statistic is commonly referred to as a summary statistic that quantitatively describes a given dataset. We discussed the most common summary measures used in this field, including measures of central tendency (mean, median, and mode) and measures of variability (standard deviation, minimum, maximum, kurtosis, and skewness).

In the next chapter, we will continue more advanced descriptive statistics by using grouping techniques. These grouping techniques are provided by the pandas library.

Further reading

- *Measures of Skewness and Kurtosis*: `https://www.itl.nist.gov/div898/handbook/eda/section3/eda35b.htm`
- *Pandas Cookbook, Theodore Petrou, Packt Publishing*
- *Learning Pandas – Second Edition, Michael Heydt, Packt Publishing*
- *Mastering Pandas, Femi Anthony, Packt Publishing*
- *Hands-On Data Analysis with Pandas, Stefanie Molin, Packt Publishing*

6
Grouping Datasets

During data analysis, it is often essential to cluster or group data together based on certain criteria. For example, an e-commerce store might want to group all the sales that were done during the Christmas period or the orders that were received on Black Friday. These grouping concepts occur in several parts of data analysis. In this chapter, we will cover the fundamentals of grouping techniques and how doing this can improve data analysis. We will discuss different `groupby()` mechanics that will accumulate our dataset into various classes that we can perform aggregation on. We will also figure out how to dissect this categorical data with visualization by utilizing pivot tables and cross-tabulations.

In this chapter, we will cover the following topics:

- Understanding groupby()
- Groupby mechanics
- Data aggregation
- Pivot tables and cross-tabulations

Technical requirements

The code for this chapter can be found in this book's GitHub repository, `https://github.com/PacktPublishing/hands-on-exploratory-data-analysis-with-python`, inside the `Chapter 6` folder.

The dataset we'll be using in this chapter is available under open access through Kaggle. It can be downloaded from `https://www.kaggle.com/toramky/automobile-dataset`.

In this chapter, we are going to use the `pandas` library, so make sure you have it installed.

Understanding groupby()

During the data analysis phase, categorizing a dataset into multiple categories or groups is often essential. We can do such categorization using the `pandas` library. The pandas `groupby` function is one of the most efficient and time-saving features for doing this. `Groupby` provides functionalities that allow us to split-apply-combine throughout the dataframe; that is, this function can be used for splitting, applying, and combining dataframes.

Similar to the **Structured Query Language** (**SQL**), we can use pandas and Python to execute more complex group operations by using any built-in functions that accept the `pandas` object or the `numpy` array.

In the next section, we are going to look into the groupby mechanics using the `pandas` library.

Groupby mechanics

While working with the `pandas` dataframes, our analysis may require us to split our data by certain criteria. Groupby mechanics amass our dataset into various classes in which we can perform exercises and make changes, such as the following:

- Grouping by features, hierarchically
- Aggregating a dataset by groups
- Applying custom aggregation functions to groups
- Transforming a dataset groupwise

The pandas `groupby` method performs two essential functions:

- It splits the data into groups based on some criteria.
- It applies a function to each group independently.

To work with `groupby` functionalities, we need a dataset that has multiple numerical as well as categorical records in it so that we can group by different categories and ranges.

Let's take a look at a dataset of automobiles that enlists the different features and attributes of cars, such as `symbolling`, `normalized-losses`, `make`, `aspiration`, `body-style`, `drive-wheels`, `engine-location`, and many others. Let's get started:

1. Let's start by importing the required Python libraries and datasets:

```
import pandas as pd
df = pd.read_csv("/content/automobileEDA.csv")
df.head()
```

Here, we're assuming that you have the database stored in your current drive. If you don't, you can change the path to the correct location. By now, you should be familiar with the appropriate data loading techniques for doing this, so we won't cover this again here.

The output of the preceding code is as follows:

	symboling	normalized-losses	make	aspiration	num-of-doors	body-style	drive-wheels	engine-location	wheel-base	length	width	height	curb-weight	engine-type	num-of-cylinders	engine-size
0	3	122	alfa-romero	std	two	convertible	rwd	front	88.6	0.811148	0.890278	48.8	2548	dohc	four	130
1	3	122	alfa-romero	std	two	convertible	rwd	front	88.6	0.811148	0.890278	48.8	2548	dohc	four	130
2	1	122	alfa-romero	std	two	hatchback	rwd	front	94.5	0.822681	0.909722	52.4	2823	ohcv	six	152
3	2	164	audi	std	four	sedan	fwd	front	99.8	0.848630	0.919444	54.3	2337	ohc	four	109
4	2	164	audi	std	four	sedan	4wd	front	99.4	0.848630	0.922222	54.3	2824	ohc	five	136

As you can see, there are multiple columns with categorical variables.

2. Using the `groupby()` function lets us group this dataset on the basis of the `body-style` column:

```
df.groupby('body-style').groups.keys()
```

The output of the preceding code is as follows:

```
dict_keys(['convertible', 'hardtop', 'hatchback', 'sedan',
'wagon'])
```

From the preceding output, we know that the `body-style` column has five unique values, including `convertible`, `hardtop`, `hatchback`, `sedan`, and `wagon`.

3. Now, we can group the data based on the `body-style` column. Next, let's print the values contained in that group that have the `body-style` value of `convertible`. This can be done using the following code:

```
# Group the dataset by the column body-style
style = df.groupby('body-style')

# Get values items from group with value convertible
style.get_group("convertible")
```

The output of the preceding code is as follows:

	symboling	normalized-losses	make	aspiration	num-of-doors	body-style	drive-wheels	engine-location	wheel-base	length	width	height	curb-weight	engine-type	num-of-cylinders	engine-size
0	3	122	alfa-romero	std	two	convertible	rwd	front	88.6	0.811148	0.890278	48.8	2548	dohc	four	130
1	3	122	alfa-romero	std	two	convertible	rwd	front	88.6	0.811148	0.890278	48.8	2548	dohc	four	130
69	3	142	mercedes-benz	std	two	convertible	rwd	front	96.6	0.866410	0.979167	50.8	3685	ohcv	eight	234
125	3	122	porsche	std	two	convertible	rwd	rear	89.5	0.811629	0.902778	51.6	2800	ohcf	six	194
168	2	134	toyota	std	two	convertible	rwd	front	98.4	0.846708	0.911111	53.0	2975	ohc	four	146
185	3	122	volkswagen	std	two	convertible	fwd	front	94.5	0.765497	0.891667	55.6	2254	ohc	four	109

In the preceding example, we have grouped by using a single `body-style` column. We can also select a subset of columns. We'll learn how to do this in the next section.

Selecting a subset of columns

To form groups based on multiple categories, we can simply specify the column names in the `groupby()` function. Grouping will be done simultaneously with the first category, the second category, and so on.

Let's `groupby` using two categories, `body-style` and `drive wheels`, as follows:

```
double_grouping = df.groupby(["body-style","drive-wheels"])
double_grouping.first()
```

The output of the preceding code is as follows:

		symboling	normalized-losses	make	aspiration	num-of-doors	engine-location	wheel-base	length	width	height	curb-weight	engine-type	num-of-cylinders	engine-size	fue syst
body-style	drive-wheels															
convertible	fwd	3	122	volkswagen	std	two	front	94.5	0.765497	0.891667	55.6	2254	ohc	four	109	m
	rwd	3	122	alfa-romero	std	two	front	88.6	0.811148	0.890278	48.8	2548	dohc	four	130	m
hardtop	fwd	2	168	nissan	std	two	front	95.1	0.780394	0.886111	53.3	2008	ohc	four	97	2t
	rwd	0	93	mercedes-benz	turbo	two	front	106.7	0.901009	0.976389	54.9	3495	ohc	five	183	
hatchback	4wd	2	83	subaru	std	two	front	93.3	0.755887	0.886111	55.7	2240	ohcf	four	108	2t
	fwd	2	121	chevrolet	std	two	front	88.4	0.678039	0.837500	53.2	1488	l	three	61	2t
	rwd	1	122	alfa-romero	std	two	front	94.5	0.822681	0.909722	52.4	2823	ohcv	six	152	m
sedan	4wd	2	164	audi	std	four	front	99.4	0.848630	0.922222	54.3	2824	ohc	five	136	m
	fwd	2	164	audi	std	four	front	99.8	0.848630	0.919444	54.3	2337	ohc	four	109	m
	rwd	2	192	bmw	std	two	front	101.2	0.849592	0.900000	54.3	2395	ohc	four	108	m
wagon	4wd	0	85	subaru	std	four	front	96.9	0.834214	0.908333	54.9	2420	ohcf	four	108	2t
	fwd	1	122	audi	std	four	front	105.8	0.925997	0.991667	55.7	2954	ohc	five	136	m
	rwd	-1	93	mercedes-benz	turbo	four	front	110.0	0.917347	0.976389	58.7	3750	ohc	five	183	

Not only can we group the dataset with specific criteria, but we can also perform arithmetic operations directly on the whole group at the same time and print the output as a series or dataframe. There are functions such as max(), min(), mean(), first(), and last() that can be directly applied to the GroupBy object in order to obtain summary statistics for each group.

In the next section, we are going to discuss these functions one by one.

Max and min

Let's compute the maximum and minimum entry for each group. Here, we will find the maximum and minimum for the normalized-losses column:

```
# max() will print the maximum entry of each group
style['normalized-losses'].max()

# min() will print the minimum entry of each group
style['normalized-losses'].min()
```

The output of the preceding code is as follows:

```
body-style
convertible 122
hardtop 93
hatchback 65
sedan 65
wagon 74
Name: normalized-losses, dtype: int64
```

As illustrated in the preceding output, the minimum value for each category is presented.

Mean

We can find the mean values for the numerical column in each group. This can be done using the df.mean() method.

The code for finding the mean is as follows:

```
# mean() will print mean of numerical column in each group
style.mean()
```

The output of the preceding code is as follows:

	symboling	normalized-losses	wheel-base	length	width	height	curb-weight	engine-size	bore	stroke	compression-ratio	horsepower
body-style												
convertible	2.833333	127.333333	92.700000	0.818757	0.910880	51.433333	2801.666667	157.166667	3.491667	3.043333	8.933333	131.666667
hardtop	1.875000	128.625000	98.500000	0.850252	0.925174	52.850000	2810.625000	176.250000	3.608750	3.322500	10.725000	142.250000
hatchback	1.617647	130.897059	95.435294	0.799078	0.904228	52.133824	2322.852941	112.852941	3.236015	3.280312	9.042941	97.768473
sedan	0.329787	120.893617	100.750000	0.855583	0.921070	54.387234	2625.893617	131.691489	3.345106	3.270638	10.965957	103.808511
wagon	-0.160000	98.560000	102.156000	0.871235	0.920222	56.728000	2784.240000	123.840000	3.406400	3.175600	10.316000	98.010246

Note that we can get the average of each column by specifying a column, as follows:

```
# get mean of each column of specific group
style.get_group("convertible").mean()
```

The output of the preceding code is as follows:

```
symboling                    2.833333
normalized-losses          127.333333
wheel-base                  92.700000
length                       0.818757
width                        0.910880
height                      51.433333
curb-weight               2801.666667
engine-size                157.166667
bore                         3.491667
stroke                       3.043333
compression-ratio            8.933333
horsepower                 131.666667
peak-rpm                  5158.333333
city-mpg                    20.500000
highway-mpg                 26.000000
price                    21890.500000
city-L/100km                11.745886
diesel                       0.000000
gas                          1.000000
dtype: float64
```

Next, we can also count the number of `symboling/records` in each group. To do so, use the following code:

```
# get the number of symboling/records in each group
style['symboling'].count()
```

The output of the preceding code is as follows:

```
body-style
convertible 6
hardtop 8
hatchback 68
sedan 94
wagon 25
Name: symboling, dtype: int64
```

Having understood the counting part, in the next section, we are going to discuss different types of data aggregation techniques.

Data aggregation

Aggregation is the process of implementing any mathematical operation on a dataset or a subset of it. Aggregation is one of the many techniques in pandas that's used to manipulate the data in the dataframe for data analysis.

The `Dataframe.aggregate()` function is used to apply aggregation across one or more columns. Some of the most frequently used aggregations are as follows:

- `sum`: Returns the sum of the values for the requested axis
- `min`: Returns the minimum of the values for the requested axis
- `max`: Returns the maximum of the values for the requested axis

We can apply aggregation in a `DataFrame, df,` as `df.aggregate()` or `df.agg()`.

Since aggregation only works with numeric type columns, let's take some of the numeric columns from the dataset and apply some aggregation functions to them:

```
# new dataframe that consist length,width,height,curb-weight and price
new_dataset = df.filter(["length","width","height","curb-
weight","price"],axis=1)
new_dataset
```

The output of the preceding code snippet is as follows:

	length	width	height	curb-weight	price
0	0.811148	0.890278	48.8	2548	13495.0
1	0.811148	0.890278	48.8	2548	16500.0
2	0.822681	0.909722	52.4	2823	16500.0
3	0.848630	0.919444	54.3	2337	13950.0
4	0.848630	0.922222	54.3	2824	17450.0
...	...	...	...	...	...
196	0.907256	0.956944	55.5	2952	16845.0
197	0.907256	0.955556	55.5	3049	19045.0
198	0.907256	0.956944	55.5	3012	21485.0
199	0.907256	0.956944	55.5	3217	22470.0
200	0.907256	0.956944	55.5	3062	22625.0

201 rows × 5 columns

Next, let's apply a single aggregation to get the mean of the columns. To do this, we can use the agg() method, as shown in the following code:

```
# applying single aggregation for mean over the columns
new_dataset.agg("mean", axis="rows")
```

The output of the preceding code is as follows:

```
length 0.837102
width 0.915126
height 53.766667
curb-weight 2555.666667
price 13207.129353
dtype: float64
```

We can aggregate more than one function together. For example, we can find the sum and the minimum of all the columns at once by using the following code:

```
# applying aggregation sum and minimum across all the columns
new_dataset.agg(['sum', 'min'])
```

The output of the preceding code is as follows:

	length	width	height	curb-weight	price
sum	168.257568	183.940278	10807.1	513689	2654633.0
min	0.678039	0.837500	47.8	1488	5118.0

The output is a dataframe with rows containing the result of the respective aggregation that was applied to the columns. To apply aggregation functions across different columns, you can pass a dictionary with a key containing the column names and values containing the list of aggregation functions for any specific column:

```
# find aggregation for these columns
new_dataset.aggregate({"length":['sum', 'min'],
            "width":['max', 'min'],
            "height":['min', 'sum'],
            "curb-weight":['sum']})
# if any specific aggregation is not applied on a column
# thon it has NaN value corresponding to it
```

The output of the preceding code is as follows:

	length	width	height	curb-weight
max	NaN	1.0000	NaN	NaN
min	0.678039	0.8375	47.8	NaN
sum	168.257568	NaN	10807.1	513689.0

Check the preceding output. The maximum, minimum, and the sum of rows present the values for each column. Note that some values are NaN based on their column values.

Group-wise operations

The most important operations groupBy implements are aggregate, filter, transform, and apply. An efficient way of implementing aggregation functions in the dataset is by doing so after grouping the required columns. The aggregated function will return a single aggregated value for each group. Once these groups have been created, we can apply several aggregation operations to that grouped data.

Let's group the DataFrame, df, by body-style and drive-wheels and extract stats from each group by passing a dictionary of aggregation functions:

```
# Group the data frame df by body-style and drive-wheels and extract stats
from each group
df.groupby(
    ["body-style","drive-wheels"]
).agg(
    {
        'height':min, # minimum height of car in each group
        'length': max, # maximum length of car in each group
        'price': 'mean', # average price of car in each group
    }
)
```

The output of the preceding code is as follows:

		height	length	price
body-style	drive-wheels			
convertible	fwd	55.6	0.765497	11595.000000
	rwd	48.8	0.866410	23949.600000
hardtop	fwd	53.3	0.780394	8249.000000
	rwd	51.6	0.957232	24202.714286
hatchback	4wd	55.7	0.755887	7603.000000
	fwd	49.4	0.896684	8396.387755
	rwd	49.6	0.881788	14337.777778
sedan	4wd	54.3	0.848630	12647.333333
	fwd	50.6	0.925997	9811.800000
	rwd	47.8	1.000000	21711.833333
wagon	4wd	54.9	0.834214	9095.750000
	fwd	53.0	0.925997	9997.333333
	rwd	54.1	0.955790	16994.222222

The preceding code groups the dataframe according to `body-style` and then `driver-wheels`. Then, the aggregate functions are applied to the `height`, `length`, and `price` columns, which return the minimum height, maximum length, and average price in the respective groups.

We can make an aggregation dictionary of functions we want to perform in groups, and then use it later:

```
# create dictionary of aggregations
aggregations=(
    {
        'height':min, # minimum height of car in each group
        'length': max, # maximum length of car in each group
        'price': 'mean', # average price of car in each group
    }
)
# implementing aggregations in groups
df.groupby(
    ["body-style","drive-wheels"]
).agg(aggregations)
```

The output of the preceding code is as follows:

body-style	drive-wheels	height	length	price
convertible	fwd	55.6	0.765497	11595.000000
	rwd	48.8	0.866410	23949.600000
hardtop	fwd	53.3	0.780394	8249.000000
	rwd	51.6	0.957232	24202.714286
hatchback	4wd	55.7	0.755887	7603.000000
	fwd	49.4	0.896684	8396.387755
	rwd	49.6	0.881788	14337.777778
sedan	4wd	54.3	0.848630	12647.333333
	fwd	50.6	0.925997	9811.800000
	rwd	47.8	1.000000	21711.833333
wagon	4wd	54.9	0.834214	9095.750000
	fwd	53.0	0.925997	9997.333333
	rwd	54.1	0.955790	16994.222222

We can use numpy functions in aggregation as well:

```
# import the numpy library as np
import numpy as np
# using numpy libraries for operations
df.groupby(
    ["body-style","drive-wheels"])["price"].agg([np.sum, np.mean, np.std])
```

The output of the preceding code is as follows:

		sum	mean	std
body-style	drive-wheels			
convertible	fwd	11595.0	11595.000000	NaN
	rwd	119748.0	23949.600000	11165.099700
hardtop	fwd	8249.0	8249.000000	NaN
	rwd	169419.0	24202.714286	14493.311190
hatchback	4wd	7603.0	7603.000000	NaN
	fwd	411423.0	8396.387755	3004.675695
	rwd	258080.0	14337.777778	3831.795195
sedan	4wd	37942.0	12647.333333	4280.814681
	fwd	539649.0	9811.800000	3519.517598
	rwd	781626.0	21711.833333	9194.820239
wagon	4wd	36383.0	9095.750000	1775.652063
	fwd	119968.0	9997.333333	3584.185551
	rwd	152948.0	16994.222222	4686.703313

As shown in the preceding screenshot, we selected two categories, `body-style` and `drive-wheels`. The sum, mean, and standard deviation for each row can be seen here. Pretty straightforward, right? Now, let's learn how to rename grouped aggregated columns.

Renaming grouped aggregation columns

Don't you think the output dataframe would be more informative if we could rename the column name with the operation we performed in that column or group?

We can perform aggregation in each group and rename the columns according to the operation performed. This is useful for understanding the output dataset:

```
df.groupby(
    ["body-style","drive-wheels"]).agg(
    # Get max of the price column for each group
    max_price=('price', max),
    # Get min of the price column for each group
    min_price=('price', min),
    # Get sum of the price column for each group
    total_price=('price', 'mean')
)
```

The output of the preceding code is as follows:

body-style	drive-wheels	max_price	min_price	total_price
convertible	fwd	11595.0	11595.0	11595.000000
	rwd	37028.0	13495.0	23949.600000
hardtop	fwd	8249.0	8249.0	8249.000000
	rwd	45400.0	8449.0	24202.714286
hatchback	4wd	7603.0	7603.0	7603.000000
	fwd	18150.0	5118.0	8396.387755
	rwd	22018.0	8238.0	14337.777778
sedan	4wd	17450.0	9233.0	12647.333333
	fwd	23875.0	5499.0	9811.800000
	rwd	41315.0	6785.0	21711.833333
wagon	4wd	11694.0	7898.0	9095.750000
	fwd	18920.0	6918.0	9997.333333
	rwd	28248.0	12440.0	16994.222222

As shown in the preceding screenshot, we only selected two categories: body-style and drive-wheels. For each row in these categories, the maximum price, the minimum price, and the total price is computed in the successive columns.

Group-wise transformations

Working with groupby() and aggregation, you must have thought, *why can't we group data, apply aggregation, and append the result into the dataframe directly? Is it possible to do all this in a single step?* Yes, it is.

Performing a transformation on a group or a column returns an object that is indexed by the same axis length as itself. It is an operation that's used in conjunction with groupby(). The aggregation operation has to return a reduced version of the data, whereas the transformation operation can return a transformed version of the full data. Let's take a look:

1. Let's begin by using a simple transformation function to increase the price of each car by 10% using the lambda function:

```
df["price"]=df["price"].transform(lambda x:x + x/10)
df.loc[:,'price']
```

The output of the preceding code is as follows:

```
0 14844.5
1 18150.0
2 18150.0
3 15345.0
4 19195.0
       ...
196 18529.5
197 20949.5
198 23633.5
199 24717.0
200 24887.5
Name: price, Length: 201, dtype: float64
```

2. Let's observe the average price of cars for each grouping by `body-style` and `drive-wheels`:

    ```
    df.groupby(["body-style","drive-
    wheels"])["price"].transform('mean')
    ```

    The output of the preceding code is as follows:

    ```
    0 26344.560000
    1 26344.560000
    2 15771.555556
    3 10792.980000
    4 13912.066667
           ...
    196 23883.016667
    197 23883.016667
    198 23883.016667
    199 23883.016667
    200 23883.016667
    Name: price, Length: 201, dtype: float64
    ```

    If you look at the preceding output, you will notice how this returns a different sized dataset from our normal `groupby()` functions.

3. Now, create a new column for an average price in the original dataframe:

    ```
    df["average-price"]=df.groupby(["body-style","drive-
    wheels"])["price"].transform('mean')

    # selecting columns body-style,drive-wheels,price and average-price
    df.loc[:,["body-style","drive-wheels","price","average-price"]]
    ```

The output of the preceding code is as follows:

	body-style	drive-wheels	price	average-price
0	convertible	rwd	14844.5	26344.560000
1	convertible	rwd	18150.0	26344.560000
2	hatchback	rwd	18150.0	15771.555556
3	sedan	fwd	15345.0	10792.980000
4	sedan	4wd	19195.0	13912.066667
...	...	...	...	...
196	sedan	rwd	18529.5	23883.016667
197	sedan	rwd	20949.5	23883.016667
198	sedan	rwd	23633.5	23883.016667
199	sedan	rwd	24717.0	23883.016667
200	sedan	rwd	24887.5	23883.016667

201 rows × 4 columns

The output shown in the preceding screenshot is pretty obvious. We computed the price and the average price for two categories: `body-style` and `drive-wheels`. Next, we are going to discuss how to use pivot tables and cross-tabulation techniques.

Pivot tables and cross-tabulations

Pandas offers several options for grouping and summarizing data. We've already discussed `groupby`, aggregation, and transformation, but there are other options available, such as `pivot_table` and `crosstab`. First, let's understand pivot tables.

Pivot tables

The `pandas.pivot_table()` function creates a spreadsheet-style pivot table as a dataframe. The levels in the pivot table will be stored in MultiIndex objects (hierarchical indexes) on the index and columns of the resulting dataframe.

The simplest pivot tables must have a dataframe and an index/list of the index. Let's take a look at how to do this:

1. Let's make a pivot table of a new dataframe that consists of the `body-style`, `drive-wheels`, `length`, `width`, `height`, `curb-weight`, and `price` columns:

```
new_dataset1 = df.filter(["body-style","drive-wheels",
                          "length","width","height","curb-
weight","price"],axis=1)
#simplest pivot table with dataframe df and index body-style
table = pd.pivot_table(new_dataset1, index =["body-style"])
table
```

The output of the preceding code is as follows:

	curb-weight	height	length	price	width
body-style					
convertible	2801.666667	51.433333	0.818757	24079.550000	0.910880
hardtop	2810.625000	52.850000	0.850252	24429.350000	0.925174
hatchback	2322.852941	52.133824	0.799078	10953.185294	0.904228
sedan	2625.893617	54.387234	0.855583	15905.730851	0.921070
wagon	2784.240000	56.728000	0.871235	13609.156000	0.920222

The output table is similar to how we group a dataframe with respect to `body-style`. The values in the preceding table are the mean of the values in the corresponding category. Let's make a more precise pivot table.

2. Now, design a pivot table with the `new_dataset1` dataframe and make `body-style` and `drive-wheels` as an index. Note that providing multiple indexes will make a grouping of the dataframe first and then summarize the data:

```
#pivot table with dataframe df and index body-style and drive-
wheels
table = pd.pivot_table(new_dataset1, index =["body-style","drive-
wheels"])
table
```

The output of the preceding code is as follows:

body-style	drive-wheels	curb-weight	height	length	price	width
convertible	fwd	2254.000000	55.600000	0.765497	12754.500000	0.891667
	rwd	2911.200000	50.600000	0.829409	26344.560000	0.914722
hardtop	fwd	2008.000000	53.300000	0.780394	9073.900000	0.886111
	rwd	2925.285714	52.785714	0.860232	26622.985714	0.930754
hatchback	4wd	2240.000000	55.700000	0.755887	8363.300000	0.886111
	fwd	2181.551020	52.442857	0.787818	9236.026531	0.898214
	rwd	2712.111111	51.094444	0.832132	15771.555556	0.921605
sedan	4wd	2573.000000	54.300000	0.833894	13912.066667	0.912963
	fwd	2313.018182	53.956364	0.828404	10792.980000	0.908182
	rwd	3108.305556	55.052778	0.898913	23883.016667	0.941435
wagon	4wd	2617.500000	57.000000	0.824844	10005.325000	0.895833
	fwd	2464.333333	56.008333	0.843064	10997.066667	0.910185
	rwd	3284.888889	57.566667	0.929414	18693.644444	0.944444

The output is a pivot table grouped by `body-style` and `drive-wheels`. It contains the average of the numerical values of the corresponding columns.

The syntax for the pivot table takes some arguments, such as c, values, index, column, and aggregation function. We can apply the aggregation function to a pivot table at the same time. We can pass the aggregation function, values, and columns that aggregation will be applied to, in order to create a pivot table of a summarized subset of a dataframe:

```
# import numpy for aggregation function
import numpy as np

# new data set with few columns
new_dataset3 = df.filter(["body-style","drive-
wheels","price"],axis=1)

table = pd.pivot_table(new_dataset3, values='price', index=["body-
style"],
                       columns=["drive-
wheels"],aggfunc=np.mean,fill_value=0)
table
```

In terms of syntax, the preceding code represents the following:

- A pivot table with a dataset called `new_dataset3`.
- The values are the columns that the aggregation function is to be applied to.
- The index is a column for grouping data.
- Columns for specifying the category of data.
- `aggfunc` is the aggregation function to be applied.
- `fill_value` is used to fill in missing values.

The output of the preceding code is as follows:

drive-wheels	4wd	fwd	rwd
body-style			
convertible	0.000000	12754.500000	26344.560000
hardtop	0.000000	9073.900000	26622.985714
hatchback	8363.300000	9236.026531	15771.555556
sedan	13912.066667	10792.980000	23883.016667
wagon	10005.325000	10997.066667	18693.644444

The preceding pivot table represents the average price of cars with different `body-style` and available `drive-wheels` in those `body-style`.

3. We can also apply a different aggregation function to different columns:

```
table = pd.pivot_table(new_dataset1,
values=['price','height','width'],
                        index =["body-style","drive-wheels"],
                        aggfunc={'price': np.mean,'height': [min,
max],'width': [min, max]},
                        fill_value=0)
table
```

The output of the preceding code is as follows:

body-style	drive-wheels	height max	min	price mean	width max	min
convertible	fwd	55.6	55.6	12754.500000	0.891667	0.891667
	rwd	53.0	48.8	26344.560000	0.979167	0.890278
hardtop	fwd	53.3	53.3	9073.900000	0.886111	0.886111
	rwd	55.4	51.6	26622.985714	1.000000	0.902778
hatchback	4wd	55.7	55.7	8363.300000	0.886111	0.886111
	fwd	56.1	49.4	9236.026531	0.925000	0.837500
	rwd	54.8	49.6	15771.555556	0.948611	0.888889
sedan	4wd	54.3	54.3	13912.066667	0.922222	0.908333
	fwd	56.1	50.6	10792.980000	0.991667	0.868056
	rwd	56.7	47.8	23883.016667	0.995833	0.858333
wagon	4wd	59.1	54.9	10005.325000	0.908333	0.883333
	fwd	59.8	53.0	10997.066667	0.991667	0.883333
	rwd	58.7	54.1	18693.644444	0.976389	0.923611

This pivot table represents the maximum and minimum of the height and width and the average price of cars in the respective categories mentioned in the index.

Cross-tabulations

We can customize the `pandas` dataframe with another technique called cross-tabulation. This allows us to cope with `groupby` and aggregation for better data analysis. pandas has the `crosstab` function, which helps when it comes to building a cross-tabulation table. The cross-tabulation table shows the frequency with which certain groups of data appear. Let's take a look:

1. Let's use `pd.crosstab()` to look at how many different body styles cars are made by different makers:

```
pd.crosstab(df["make"], df["body-style"])
```

The output of the preceding code is as follows:

body-style	convertible	hardtop	hatchback	sedan	wagon
make					
alfa-romero	2	0	1	0	0
audi	0	0	0	5	1
bmw	0	0	0	8	0
chevrolet	0	0	2	1	0
dodge	0	0	5	3	1
honda	0	0	7	5	1
isuzu	0	0	1	1	0
jaguar	0	0	0	3	0
mazda	0	0	10	7	0
mercedes-benz	1	2	0	4	1
mercury	0	0	1	0	0

Let's apply margins and the `margins_name` attribute to display the row-wise and column-wise sum of the cross tables, as shown in the following code:

```
# apply margins and margins_name attribute to displays the row wise
# and column wise sum of the cross table
pd.crosstab(df["make"], df["body-
style"],margins=True,margins_name="Total Made")
```

The output of the preceding code is as follows:

body-style	convertible	hardtop	hatchback	sedan	wagon	Total Made
make						
alfa-romero	2	0	1	0	0	3
audi	0	0	0	5	1	6
bmw	0	0	0	8	0	8
chevrolet	0	0	2	1	0	3
dodge	0	0	5	3	1	9
honda	0	0	7	5	1	13
isuzu	0	0	1	1	0	2
jaguar	0	0	0	3	0	3
mazda	0	0	10	7	0	17
mercedes-benz	1	2	0	4	1	8
mercury	0	0	1	0	0	1
mitsubishi	0	0	9	4	0	13
nissan	0	1	5	9	3	18
peugot	0	0	0	7	4	11

Applying multiple columns in the `crosstab` function for the row index or column index or both will print the output with grouping automatically.

2. Let's see how the data is distributed by the `body-type` and `drive_wheels` columns within the maker of car and their door type in a `crosstab`:

```
pd.crosstab([df["make"],df["num-of-doors"]], [df["body-
style"],df["drive-wheels"]],
        margins=True,margins_name="Total Made")
```

The output of the preceding code is as follows:

make	body-style	convertible		hardtop		hatchback			sedan			wagon			Total Made
	drive-wheels	fwd	rwd	fwd	rwd	4wd	fwd	rwd	4wd	fwd	rwd	4wd	fwd	rwd	
	num-of-doors														
alfa-romero	two	0	2	0	0	0	0	1	0	0	0	0	0	0	3
audi	four	0	0	0	0	0	0	0	1	3	0	0	1	0	5
	two	0	0	0	0	0	0	0	0	1	0	0	0	0	1
bmw	four	0	0	0	0	0	0	0	0	0	5	0	0	0	5
	two	0	0	0	0	0	0	0	0	0	3	0	0	0	3
chevrolet	four	0	0	0	0	0	0	0	0	1	0	0	0	0	1
	two	0	0	0	0	0	2	0	0	0	0	0	0	0	2
dodge	four	0	0	0	0	0	1	0	0	3	0	0	1	0	5
	two	0	0	0	0	0	4	0	0	0	0	0	0	0	4
honda	four	0	0	0	0	0	0	0	0	4	0	0	1	0	5
	two	0	0	0	0	0	7	0	0	1	0	0	0	0	8
isuzu	four	0	0	0	0	0	0	0	0	0	1	0	0	0	1

Now, let's rename the column and row index. Renaming gives us a better understanding of cross-tabulation, as shown in the following code:

```
# rename the columns and row index for better understanding of
crosstab
pd.crosstab([df["make"],df["num-of-doors"]], [df["body-
style"],df["drive-wheels"]],
            rownames=['Auto Manufacturer', "Doors"],
            colnames=['Body Style', "Drive Type"],
            margins=True,margins_name="Total Made").head()
```

The output of the preceding code is as follows:

Auto Manufacturer	Body Style	convertible		hardtop		hatchback			sedan			wagon			Total Made
	Drive Type	fwd	rwd	fwd	rwd	4wd	fwd	rwd	4wd	fwd	rwd	4wd	fwd	rwd	
	Doors														
alfa-romero	two	0	2	0	0	0	0	1	0	0	0	0	0	0	3
audi	four	0	0	0	0	0	0	0	1	3	0	0	1	0	5
	two	0	0	0	0	0	0	0	0	1	0	0	0	0	1
bmw	four	0	0	0	0	0	0	0	0	0	5	0	0	0	5
	two	0	0	0	0	0	0	0	0	0	3	0	0	0	3

These were some cross-tabulation examples that gave us the frequency distributions of data in the respective categories.

The pivot table syntax of `pd.crosstab` also takes some arguments, such as dataframe columns, values, normalize, and the aggregation function. We can apply the aggregation function to a cross table at the same time. Passing the aggregation function and values, which are the columns that aggregation will be applied to, gives us a cross table of a summarized subset of the dataframe.

3. First, let's look at the average `curb-weight` of cars made by different makers with respect to their `body-style` by applying the `mean()` aggregation function to the `crosstable`:

```
# values are the column in which aggregation function is to be
applied
# aggfunc is the aggregation function to be applied
# round() to round the output

pd.crosstab(df["make"], df["body-style"],values=df["curb-weight"],
            aggfunc='mean').round(0)
```

The output of the preceding code is as follows:

body-style	convertible	hardtop	hatchback	sedan	wagon
make					
alfa-romero	2548.0	NaN	2823.0	NaN	NaN
audi	NaN	NaN	NaN	2720.0	2954.0
bmw	NaN	NaN	NaN	2929.0	NaN
chevrolet	NaN	NaN	1681.0	1909.0	NaN
dodge	NaN	NaN	2132.0	2056.0	2535.0
honda	NaN	NaN	1970.0	2289.0	2024.0
isuzu	NaN	NaN	2734.0	2337.0	NaN
jaguar	NaN	NaN	NaN	4027.0	NaN
mazda	NaN	NaN	2254.0	2361.0	NaN
mercedes-benz	3685.0	3605.0	NaN	3731.0	3750.0
mercury	NaN	NaN	2910.0	NaN	NaN
mitsubishi	NaN	NaN	2377.0	2394.0	NaN
nissan	NaN	2008.0	2740.0	2238.0	2452.0
peugot	NaN	NaN	NaN	3143.0	3358.0

A normalized `crosstab` will show the percentage of time each combination occurs. This can be accomplished using the `normalize` parameter, as follows:

```
pd.crosstab(df["make"], df["body-style"],normalize=True).head(10)
```

The output of the preceding code is as follows:

body-style	convertible	hardtop	hatchback	sedan	wagon
make					
alfa-romero	0.009950	0.00000	0.004975	0.000000	0.000000
audi	0.000000	0.00000	0.000000	0.024876	0.004975
bmw	0.000000	0.00000	0.000000	0.039801	0.000000
chevrolet	0.000000	0.00000	0.009950	0.004975	0.000000
dodge	0.000000	0.00000	0.024876	0.014925	0.004975
honda	0.000000	0.00000	0.034826	0.024876	0.004975
isuzu	0.000000	0.00000	0.004975	0.004975	0.000000
jaguar	0.000000	0.00000	0.000000	0.014925	0.000000
mazda	0.000000	0.00000	0.049751	0.034826	0.000000
mercedes-benz	0.004975	0.00995	0.000000	0.019900	0.004975

Cross-tabulation techniques can be handy when we're trying to analyze two or more variables. This helps us inspect the relationships between them.

Summary

Grouping data into similar categories is an essential operation in any data analysis task. In this chapter, we discussed different grouping techniques, including groupby mechanics, rearranging, reshaping data structures, data aggregation methods, and cross-tabulation methods. In addition to this, we also checked various examples for each case.

In the next chapter, we are going to learn about correlation, which describes how two or more variables can be related. In addition to this, we will look at different types of correlation techniques and their applications with suitable examples.

Further reading

- *Pandas Cookbook: Recipes for Scientific Computing, Time Series Analysis and Data Visualization using Python 1st Edition,* by *Theodore Petrou, PACKT Publication,* 2017
- *Mastering pandas - Second Edition,* by *Ashish Kumar, PACKT Publication,* October 25, 2019
- *Learning pandas - Second Edition,* by *Michael Heydt, PACKT Publication,* June 29, 2017

7
Correlation

In this chapter, we will explore the correlation between different factors and estimate to what degree these different factors are reliable. Additionally, we will learn about the different types of examinations we can carry out in order to discover the relationship between data including univariate analysis, bivariate analysis, and multivariate analysis. We will perform these analyses using the Titanic dataset. We'll also introduce Simpson's paradox. Likewise, we will take an insightful look at the well-known fact that correlation does *not* imply causation.

In this chapter, we will cover the following topics:

- Introducing correlation
- Understanding univariate analysis
- Understanding bivariate analysis
- Understanding multivariate analysis
- Discussing multivariate analysis using the Titanic dataset
- Outlining Simpson's paradox
- Correlation does not imply causation

Technical requirements

The code for this chapter can be found in the GitHub repository (`https://github.com/PacktPublishing/hands-on-exploratory-data-analysis-with-python`) inside the `chapter 7` folder:

- **Dataset A**: The automobile dataset used in this chapter is inside the `chapter 7/automobile.csv` folder.
- **Dataset B**: The Titanic dataset used in this chapter is available with Open ML. You can download it at `https://www.openml.org/d/40945`. The dataset has been downloaded for you inside the folder.
- **GitHub**: `https://github.com/PacktPublishing/hands-on-exploratory-data-analysis-with-python/tree/master/Chapter%207`.

Introducing correlation

Any dataset that we want to analyze will have different fields (that is, columns) of multiple observations (that is, variables) representing different facts. The columns of a dataset are, most probably, related to one another because they are collected from the same event. One field of record may or may not affect the value of another field. To examine the type of relationships these columns have and to analyze the causes and effects between them, we have to work to find the dependencies that exist among variables. The strength of such a relationship between two fields of a dataset is called **correlation**, which is represented by a numerical value between -1 and 1.

In other words, the statistical technique that examines the relationship and explains whether, and how strongly, pairs of variables are related to one another is known as correlation. Correlation answers questions such as how one variable changes with respect to another. If it does change, then to what degree or strength? Additionally, if the relation between those variables is strong enough, then we can make predictions for future behavior.

For example, height and weight are both related; that is, taller people tend to be heavier than shorter people. If we have a new person who is taller than the average height that we observed before, then they are more likely to weigh more than the average weight we observed.

Correlation tells us how variables change together, both in the same or opposite directions and in the magnitude (that is, strength) of the relationship. To find the correlation, we calculate the Pearson correlation coefficient, symbolized by ρ (the Greek letter *rho*). This is obtained by dividing the covariance by the product of the standard deviations of the variables:

$$\rho xy = \frac{\sigma xy}{\sigma x \sigma y}$$

In terms of the strength of the relationship, the value of the correlation between two variables, *A* and *B*, varies between +1 and -1. If the correlation is +1, then it is said to be a perfect positive/linear correlation (that is, variable A is directly proportional to variable B), while a correlation of -1 is a perfect negative correlation (that is, variable A is inversely proportional to variable B). Note that values closer to 0 are not supposed to be correlated at all. If correlation coefficients are near to 1 in absolute value, then the variables are said to be strongly correlated; in comparison, those that are closer to 0.5 are said to be weakly correlated.

Let's take a look at some examples using scatter plots. Scatter plots show how much one variable is affected by another:

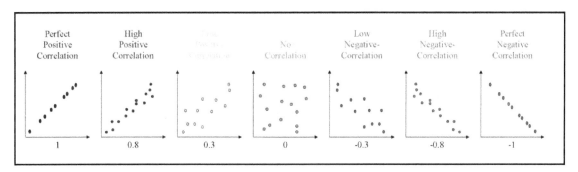

As depicted in the first and last charts, the closer the distance between the data points when plotted to make a straight line, the higher the correlation between the associated variables. The higher the correlation between them, the stronger the relationship between the variables. The more scattered the data points get when plotted (thus making no patterns), the lower the correlation between the two variables. Here, you should observe the following four important points:

- When the data points plot has a straight line going through the origin to the x and y values, then the variables are said to have a **positive correlation**.
- When the data points plot to generate a line that goes from a high value on the y axis to a high value on the x axis, the variables are said to have a **negative correlation**.
- A perfect correlation has a value of 1.
- A perfect negative correlation has a value of -1.

A highly positive correlation is given a value closer to 1. A highly negative correlation is given a value closer to -1. In the preceding diagram, +0.8 gives a high positive correlation and -0.8 gives a high negative correlation. The closer the number is to 0 (in the diagram, this is +0.3 and -0.3), the weaker the correlation.

Before analyzing the correlation in our dataset, let's learn about the various types of analysis.

Types of analysis

In this section, we are going to explore different types of analysis. We will start with univariate analysis, then move on to bivariate analysis, and, finally, we will discuss multivariate analysis.

Understanding univariate analysis

Remember the variables we worked with in `Chapter 5`, *Descriptive Statistics*, for measures of descriptive statistics? There we had a set of integers ranging from 2 to 12. We calculated the mean, median, and mode of that set and analyzed the distribution patterns of integers. Then, we calculated the mean, mode, median, and standard deviation of the values available in the height column of each type of automobile dataset. Such an analysis on a single type of dataset is called **univariate analysis**.

Univariate analysis is the simplest form of analyzing data. It means that our data has only one type of variable and that we perform analysis over it. The main purpose of univariate analysis is to take data, summarize that data, and find patterns among the values. It doesn't deal with causes or relationships between the values. Several techniques that describe the patterns found in univariate data include central tendency (that is the mean, mode, and median) and dispersion (that is, the range, variance, maximum and minimum quartiles (including the interquartile range), and standard deviation).

Why don't you try doing an analysis over the same set of data again? This time, remember that this is univariate analysis:

1. Start by importing the required libraries and loading the dataset:

```
#import libraries
import matplotlib.pyplot as plt
import seaborn as sns
import pandas as pd
```

2. Now, load the data:

```
# loading dataset as Pandas dataframe
df = pd.read_csv("data.csv")
df.head()
```

The output of this code is given as follows:

	symboling	normalized-losses	make	aspiration	num-of-doors	body-style	drive-wheels	engine-location	wheel-base	length	width	height	curb-weight	engine-type	num-of-cylinders	engine-size	fuel-system	bore	stroke	com
0	3	122	alfa-romero	std	two	convertible	rwd	front	88.6	0.811148	0.890278	48.8	2548	dohc	four	130	mpfi	3.47	2.68	
1	3	122	alfa-romero	std	two	convertible	rwd	front	88.6	0.811148	0.890278	48.8	2548	dohc	four	130	mpfi	3.47	2.68	
2	1	122	alfa-romero	std	two	hatchback	rwd	front	94.5	0.822681	0.909722	52.4	2823	ohcv	six	152	mpfi	2.68	3.47	
3	2	164	audi	std	four	sedan	fwd	front	99.8	0.848630	0.919444	54.3	2337	ohc	four	109	mpfi	3.19	3.40	
4	2	164	audi	std	four	sedan	4wd	front	99.4	0.848630	0.922222	54.3	2824	ohc	five	136	mpfi	3.19	3.40	

3. First, check the data types of each column. By now, you must be familiar with the following:

```
df.dtypes
```

The output is as follows:

```
symboling int64
normalized-losses int64
make object
aspiration object
num-of-doors object
body-style object
drive-wheels object
engine-location object
wheel-base float64
length float64
width float64
height float64
curb-weight int64
engine-type object
num-of-cylinders object
engine-size int64
fuel-system object
bore float64
stroke float64
compression-ratio float64
horsepower float64
peak-rpm float64
city-mpg int64
highway-mpg int64
price float64
city-L/100km float64
horsepower-binned object
diesel int64
gas int64
dtype: object
```

4. Now compute the measure of central tendency of the height column. Recall that we discussed several descriptive statistics in `Chapter 5`, *Descriptive Statistics:*

```
#calculate mean, median and mode of dat set height
mean = df["height"].mean()
median =df["height"].median()
mode = df["height"].mode()
print(mean , median, mode)
```

The output of those descriptive functions is as follows:

```
53.766666666666715 54.1 0 50.8
dtype: float64
```

5. Now, let's visualize this analysis in the graph:

```
#distribution plot
sns.FacetGrid(df,size=5).map(sns.distplot,"height").add_legend()
```

The code will generate a distribution plot of values in the height column:

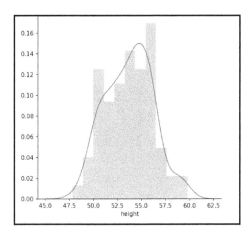

From the graph, we can observe that the maximum height of maximum cars ranges from 53 to 57. Now, let's do the same with the price column:

```
#distribution plot
sns.FacetGrid(df,size=5).map(sns.distplot,"price").add_legend()
```

The output of this code is given as follows:

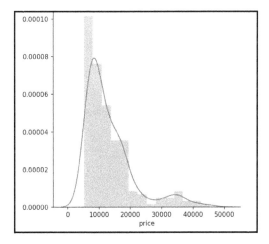

Looking at this diagram, we can say that the price ranges from 5,000 to 45,000, but the maximum car price ranges between 5,000 and 10,000.

A box plot is also an effective method for the visual representation of statistical measures such as the median and quartiles in univariate analysis:

```
#boxplot for price of cars
sns.boxplot(x="price",data=df)
plt.show()
```

The box plot generated from the preceding code is given as follows:

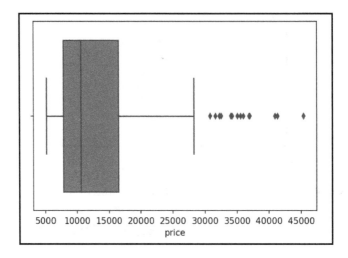

The right border of the box is Q3, that is, the third quartile, and the left border of the box is Q1, that is, the first quartile. Lines extend from both sides of the box boundaries toward the minimum and maximum. Based on the convention that our plotting tool uses, though, they may only extend to a certain statistic; any values beyond these statistics are marked as outliers (using points).

This analysis was for a dataset with a single type of variable only. Now, let's take a look at the next form of analysis for a dataset with two types of variables, known as bivariate analysis.

Understanding bivariate analysis

As its name suggests, this is the analysis of more than one (that is, exactly two) type of variable. Bivariate analysis is used to find out whether there is a relationship between two different variables. When we create a scatter plot by plotting one variable against another on a Cartesian plane (think of the *x* and *y* axes), it gives us a picture of what the data is trying to tell us. If the data points seem to fit the line or curve, then there is a relationship or correlation between the two variables. Generally, bivariate analysis helps us to predict a value for one variable (that is, a dependent variable) if we are aware of the value of the independent variable.

Here's a diagram showing a scatter plot of advertising dollars and sales rates over a period of time:

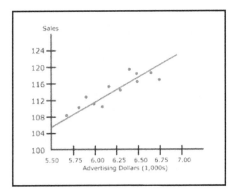

This diagram is the scatter plot for bivariate analysis, where **Sales** and **Advertising Dollars** are two variables. While plotting a scatter plot, we can see that the sales values are dependent on the advertising dollars; that is, as the advertising dollars increase, the sales values also increase. This understanding of the relationship between two variables will guide us in our future predictions:

1. It's now time to perform bivariate analysis on our automobiles dataset. Let's look at whether horsepower is a dependent factor for the pricing of cars or not:

```
# plot the relationship between "horsepower" and "price"
plt.scatter(df["price"], df["horsepower"])
plt.title("Scatter Plot for horsepower vs price")
plt.xlabel("horsepower")
plt.ylabel("price")
```

This code will generate a scatter plot with a `price` range on the *y* axis and `horsepower` values on the *x* axis, as follows:

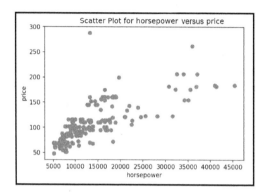

As you can see in the preceding diagram, the horsepower of cars is a dependent factor for the price. As the horsepower of a car increases, the price of the car also increases.

A box plot is also a nice way in which to view some statistical measures along with the relationship between two values.

2. Now, let's draw a box plot between the engine location of cars and their price:

```
#boxplot
sns.boxplot(x="engine-location",y="price",data=df)
plt.show()
```

This code will generate a box plot with the price range on the *y* axis and the types of engine locations on the *x* axis:

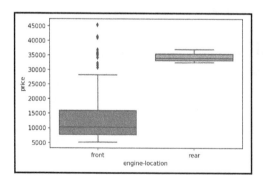

This diagram shows that the price of cars having a **front engine-location** is much lower than that of cars having a **rear engine-location**. Additionally, there are some outliers that have a front engine location but the price is much higher.

3. Next, plot another box plot with the price range and the driver wheel type:

```
#boxplot to visualize the distribution of "price" with types of
"drive-wheels"
sns.boxplot(x="drive-wheels", y="price",data=df)
```

The output of this code is given as follows:

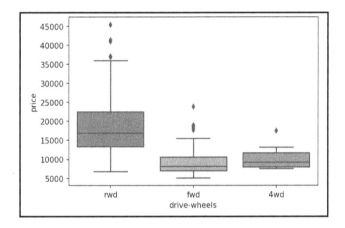

This diagram shows the range of prices of cars with different wheel types. Here, the box plot shows the average and median price in respective wheel types and some outliers too.

This was a brief introduction, along with a few practice examples of bivariate analysis. Now, let's learn about a more efficient type of practice for data analysis, multivariate analysis.

Understanding multivariate analysis

Multivariate analysis is the analysis of three or more variables. This allows us to look at correlations (that is, how one variable changes with respect to another) and attempt to make predictions for future behavior more accurately than with bivariate analysis.

Initially, we explored the visualization of univariate analysis and bivariate analysis; likewise, let's visualize the concept of multivariate analysis.

One common way of plotting multivariate data is to make a matrix scatter plot, known as a pair plot. A matrix plot or pair plot shows each pair of variables plotted against each other. The pair plot allows us to see both the distribution of single variables and the relationships between two variables:

1. We can use the `scatter_matrix()` function from the `pandas.tools.plotting` package or the `seaborn.pairplot()` function from the `seaborn` package to do this:

```
# pair plot with plot type regression
sns.pairplot(df,vars = ['normalized-losses', 'price','horsepower'],
kind="reg")
plt.show()
```

This code will plot a 3 x 3 matrix of different plots for data in the normalized losses, price, and horsepower columns:

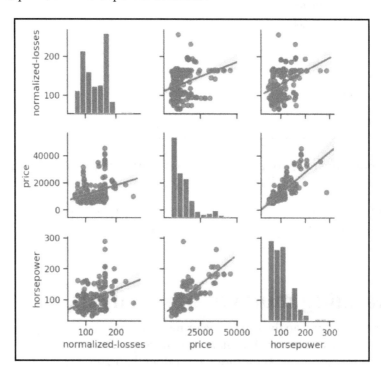

As shown in the preceding diagram, the histogram on the diagonal allows us to illustrate the distribution of a single variable. The regression plots on the upper and the lower triangles demonstrate the relationship between two variables. The middle plot in the first row shows the regression plot; this represents that there is no correlation between normalized losses and the price of cars. In comparison, the middle regression plot in the bottom row illustrates that there is a huge correlation between price and horsepower.

2. Similarly, we can carry out multivariate analysis using a pair plot by specifying the colors, labels, plot type, diagonal plot type, and variables. So, let's make another pair plot:

```
#pair plot (matrix scatterplot) of few columns
sns.set(style="ticks", color_codes=True)
sns.pairplot(df,vars = ['symboling', 'normalized-losses','wheel-
base'], hue="drive-wheels")
plt.show()
```

The output of this code is given as follows:

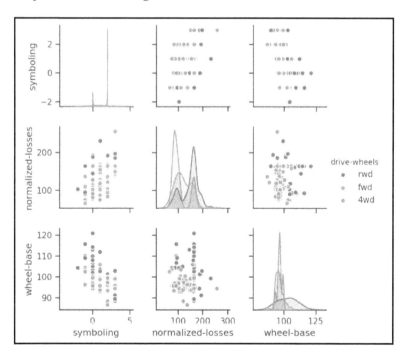

This is a pair plot of records of the symboling, normalized-losses, wheel-base, and drive-wheels columns.

The density plots on the diagonal allow us to see the distribution of a single variable, while the scatter plots on the upper and lower triangles show the relationship (or correlation) between two variables. The hue parameter is the column name used for the labels of the data points; in this diagram, the drive-wheels type is labeled by color. The left-most plot in the second row shows the scatter plot of normalized-losses versus wheel-base.

As discussed earlier, correlation analysis is an efficient technique for finding out whether any of the variables in a multivariate dataset are correlated. To calculate the linear (Pearson) correlation coefficient for a pair of variables, we can use the `dataframe.corr(method ='pearson')` function from the `pandas` package and the `pearsonr()` function from the `scipy.stats` package:

3. For example, to calculate the correlation coefficient for the price and horsepower, use the following:

```
from scipy import stats
corr = stats.pearsonr(df["price"], df["horsepower"])
print("p-value:\t", corr[1])
print("cor:\t\t", corr[0])
```

The output is as follows:

```
p-value: 6.369057428260101e-48
cor: 0.8095745670036559
```

Here, the correlation between these two variables is 0.80957, which is close to +1. Therefore, we can make sure that both price and horsepower are highly positively correlated.

4. Using the pandas `corr(` function, the correlation between the entire numerical record can be calculated as follows:

```
correlation = df.corr(method='pearson')
correlation
```

The output of this code is given as follows:

	symboling	normalized-losses	wheel-base	length	width	height	curb-weight	engine-size	bore	stroke	compression-ratio	horsepower	peak-rpm	city-mpg	highway-mpg	p
symboling	1.000000	0.466264	-0.535987	-0.365404	-0.242423	-0.550160	-0.233118	-0.110581	-0.140019	-0.008245	-0.182196	0.075819	0.279740	-0.036527	0.036233	-0.08
normalized-losses	0.466264	1.000000	-0.056661	0.019424	0.086802	-0.373737	0.099404	0.112360	-0.029862	0.055563	-0.114713	0.217299	0.239543	-0.225016	-0.181877	0.13
wheel-base	-0.535987	-0.056661	1.000000	0.876024	0.814507	0.590742	0.782097	0.572027	0.493244	0.158502	0.250313	0.371147	-0.360305	-0.470606	-0.543304	0.58
length	-0.365404	0.019424	0.876024	1.000000	0.857170	0.492063	0.880665	0.685025	0.608971	0.124139	0.159733	0.579821	-0.285970	-0.665192	-0.698142	0.69
width	-0.242423	0.086802	0.814507	0.857170	1.000000	0.306002	0.866201	0.729436	0.544885	0.188829	0.189867	0.615077	-0.245800	-0.633531	-0.680635	0.75
height	-0.550160	-0.373737	0.590742	0.492063	0.306002	1.000000	0.307581	0.074694	0.180449	-0.062704	0.259737	-0.087027	-0.309974	-0.049800	-0.104812	0.13
curb-weight	-0.233118	0.099404	0.782097	0.880665	0.866201	0.307581	1.000000	0.849072	0.644060	0.167562	0.156433	0.757976	-0.279361	-0.749543	-0.794889	0.83
engine-size	-0.110581	0.112360	0.572027	0.685025	0.729436	0.074694	0.849072	1.000000	0.572609	0.209523	0.028889	0.822676	-0.256733	-0.650546	-0.679571	0.87
bore	-0.140019	-0.029862	0.493244	0.608971	0.544885	0.180449	0.644060	0.572609	1.000000	-0.055390	0.001263	0.566936	-0.267392	-0.582027	-0.591309	0.54
stroke	-0.008245	0.055563	0.158502	0.124139	0.188829	-0.062704	0.167562	0.209523	-0.055390	1.000000	0.187923	0.098462	-0.065713	-0.034696	-0.035201	0.08
compression-ratio	-0.182196	-0.114713	0.250313	0.159733	0.189867	0.259737	0.156433	0.028889	0.001263	0.187923	1.000000	-0.214514	-0.435780	0.331425	0.268465	0.07
horsepower	0.075819	0.217299	0.371147	0.579821	0.615077	-0.087027	0.757976	0.822676	0.566936	0.098462	-0.214514	1.000000	0.107885	-0.822214	-0.804575	0.80
peak-rpm	0.279740	0.239543	-0.360305	-0.285970	-0.245800	-0.309974	-0.279361	-0.256733	-0.267392	-0.065713	-0.435780	0.107885	1.000000	-0.115413	-0.058598	-0.10
city-mpg	-0.036527	-0.225016	-0.470606	-0.665192	-0.633531	-0.049800	-0.749543	-0.650546	-0.582027	-0.034696	0.331425	-0.822214	-0.115413	1.000000	0.972044	-0.68
highway-mpg	0.036233	-0.181877	-0.543304	-0.698142	-0.680635	-0.104812	-0.794889	-0.679571	-0.591309	-0.035201	0.268465	-0.804575	-0.058598	0.972044	1.000000	-0.70
price	-0.082391	0.133999	0.584642	0.690628	0.751265	0.135486	0.834415	0.872335	0.543155	0.082310	0.071107	0.809575	-0.101616	-0.686571	-0.704692	1.00

5. Now, let's visualize this correlation analysis using a heatmap. A heatmap is the best technique to make this look beautiful and easier to interpret:

```
sns.heatmap(correlation,xticklabels=correlation.columns,
            yticklabels=correlation.columns)
```

The output of this code is given as follows:

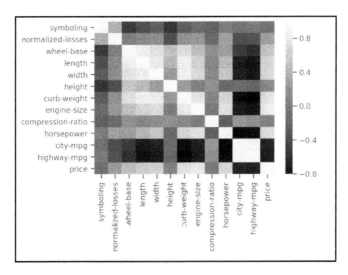

A coefficient close to 1 means that there's a very strong positive correlation between the two variables. The diagonal line is the correlation of the variables to themselves – so they'll, of course, be 1.

This was a brief introduction to, along with a few practice examples of multivariate analysis. Now, let's practice them with the popular dataset, Titanic, which is frequently used for practicing data analysis and machine learning algorithms all around the world. The data source is mentioned in the *Technical requirements* section of this chapter.

Discussing multivariate analysis using the Titanic dataset

On April 15, 1912, the largest passenger liner ever made at the time collided with an iceberg during her maiden voyage. When the Titanic sank, it killed 1,502 out of 2,224 passengers and crew. The `titanic.csv` (https://web.stanford.edu/class/archive/cs/cs109/cs109.1166/stuff/titanic.csv) file contains data for 887 real Titanic passengers. Each row represents one person. The columns describe different attributes about the person in the ship where the `PassengerId` column is a unique ID of the passenger, `Survived` is the number that survived (1) or died (0), `Pclass` is the passenger's class (that is, first, second, or third), `Name` is the passenger's name, `Sex` is the passenger's sex, `Age` is the passenger's age, `Siblings/Spouses Aboard` is the number of siblings/spouses aboard the Titanic, `Parents/Children Aboard` is the number of parents/children aboard the Titanic, `Ticket` is the ticket number, `Fare` is the fare for each ticket, `Cabin` is the cabin number, and `Embarked` is where the passenger got on the ship (for instance: C refers to Cherbourg, S refers to Southampton, and Q refers to Queenstown).

Let's analyze the Titanic dataset and identify those attributes that have maximum dependencies on the survival of the passengers:

1. First load the dataset and the required libraries:

```
# load python libraries
import numpy as np
import pandas as pd
import seaborn as sns
import matplotlib.pyplot as plt
#load dataset
titanic=pd.read_csv("/content/titanic.csv")
titanic.head()
```

The output of this code is given as follows:

	PassengerId	Survived	Pclass	Name	Sex	Age	SibSp	Parch	Ticket	Fare	Cabin	Embarked
0	1	0	3	Braund, Mr. Owen Harris	male	22.0	1	0	A/5 21171	7.2500	NaN	S
1	2	1	1	Cumings, Mrs. John Bradley (Florence Briggs Th...	female	38.0	1	0	PC 17599	71.2833	C85	C
2	3	1	3	Heikkinen, Miss. Laina	female	26.0	0	0	STON/O2 3101282	7.9250	NaN	S
3	4	1	1	Futrelle, Mrs. Jacques Heath (Lily May Peel)	female	35.0	1	0	113803	53.1000	C123	S
4	5	0	3	Allen, Mr. William Henry	male	35.0	0	0	373450	8.0500	NaN	S

Let's take a look at the shape of the DataFrame in the code:

```
titanic.shape
```

The output is as follows:

```
(891, 12)
```

3. Let's take a look at the number of records missing in the dataset:

```
total = titanic.isnull().sum().sort_values(ascending=False)
total
```

The output is as follows:

```
Cabin 687
Age 177
Embarked 2
Fare 0
Ticket 0
Parch 0
SibSp 0
Sex 0
Name 0
Pclass 0
Survived 0
PassengerId 0
dtype: int64
```

All the records appear to be fine except for `Embarked`, `Age`, and `Cabin`. The `Cabin` feature requires further investigation to fill up so many, but let's not use it in our analysis because 77% of it is missing. Additionally, it will be quite tricky to deal with the `Age` feature, which has 177 missing values. We cannot ignore the age factor because it might correlate with the survival rate. The `Embarked` feature has only two missing values, which can easily be filled.

Since the `PassengerId`, `Ticket`, and `Name` columns have unique values, they do not correlate with a high survival rate.

4. First, let's find out the percentages of women and men who survived the disaster:

```
#percentage of women survived
women = titanic.loc[titanic.Sex == 'female']["Survived"]
rate_women = sum(women)/len(women)

#percentage of men survived
men = titanic.loc[titanic.Sex == 'male']["Survived"]
rate_men = sum(men)/len(men)

print(str(rate_women) +" % of women who survived." )
print(str(rate_men) + " % of men who survived." )
```

The output is as follows:

```
0.7420382165605095 % of women who survived.
0.18890814558058924 % of men who survived.
```

5. Here, you can see the number of women who survived was high, so gender could be an attribute that contributes to analyzing the survival of any variable (person). Let's visualize this information using the survival numbers of males and females:

```
titanic['Survived'] = titanic['Survived'].map({0:"not_survived",
1:"survived"})

fig, ax = plt.subplots(1, 2, figsize = (10, 8))
titanic["Sex"].value_counts().plot.bar(color = "skyblue", ax =
ax[0])
ax[0].set_title("Number Of Passengers By Sex")
ax[0].set_ylabel("Population")
sns.countplot("Sex", hue = "Survived", data = titanic, ax = ax[1])
ax[1].set_title("Sex: Survived vs Dead")
plt.show()
```

The output of this code is given as follows:

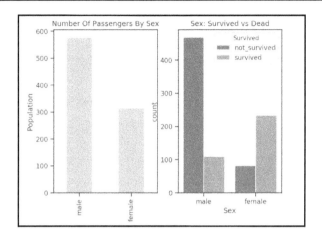

6. Let's visualize the number of survivors and deaths from different Pclasses:

```
fig, ax = plt.subplots(1, 2, figsize = (10, 8))
titanic["Pclass"].value_counts().plot.bar(color = "skyblue", ax =
ax[0])
ax[0].set_title("Number Of Passengers By Pclass")
ax[0].set_ylabel("Population")
sns.countplot("Pclass", hue = "Survived", data = titanic, ax =
ax[1])
ax[1].set_title("Pclass: Survived vs Dead")
plt.show()
```

The output of this code is given as follows:

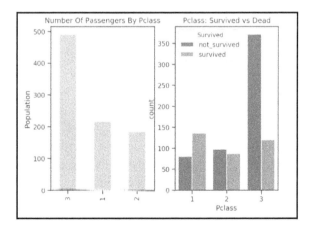

7. Well, it looks like the number of passengers in `Pclass` **3** was high, and the majority of them could not survive. In `Pclass` **2**, the number of deaths is high. And, `Pclass` **1** shows the maximum number of passengers who survived:

```
fig, ax = plt.subplots(1, 2, figsize = (10, 8))
titanic["Embarked"].value_counts().plot.bar(color = "skyblue", ax =
ax[0])
ax[0].set_title("Number Of Passengers By Embarked")
ax[0].set_ylabel("Number")
sns.countplot("Embarked", hue = "Survived", data = titanic, ax =
ax[1])
ax[1].set_title("Embarked: Survived vs Unsurvived")
plt.show()
```

The output of the code is given as follows:

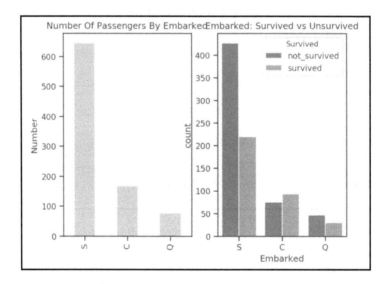

Most passengers seemed to arrive on to the ship from S (Southampton) and nearly 450 of them did not survive.

8. To visualize the `Age` records, we will plot the distribution of data using the `distplot()` method. As we previously analyzed, there are 177 null values in the `Age` records, so we will drop them before plotting the data:

```
sns.distplot(titanic['Age'].dropna())
```

The output of this code is given as follows:

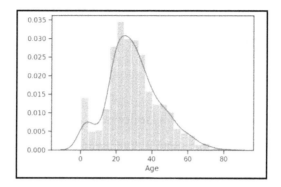

9. Now, let's first carry out a multivariate analysis on the Titanic dataset using the Survived, Pclass, Fear, and Age variables:

```
sns.set(style="ticks", color_codes=True)
sns.pairplot(titanic,vars = [ 'Fare','Age','Pclass'],
hue="Survived")
plt.show()
```

The output of this code is given as follows:

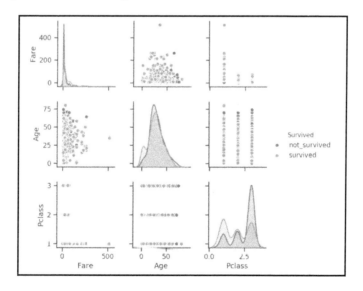

10. Now, let's view the correlation table with a heatmap. Note that the first `Embarked` map records with integer values so that we can include `Embarked` in our correlation analysis too:

```
titanic['Embarked'] = titanic['Embarked'].map({"S":1,
"C":2,"Q":2,"NaN":0})
Tcorrelation = titanic.corr(method='pearson')
Tcorrelation
```

The output of this code is given as follows:

	PassengerId	Survived	Pclass	Age	SibSp	Parch	Fare	Embarked
PassengerId	1.000000	-0.005007	-0.035144	0.036847	-0.057527	-0.001652	0.012658	-0.022269
Survived	-0.005007	1.000000	-0.338481	-0.077221	-0.035322	0.081629	0.257307	0.151777
Pclass	-0.035144	-0.338481	1.000000	-0.369226	0.083081	0.018443	-0.549500	-0.076466
Age	0.036847	-0.077221	-0.369226	1.000000	-0.308247	-0.189119	0.096067	0.025431
SibSp	-0.057527	-0.035322	0.083081	-0.308247	1.000000	0.414838	0.159651	-0.069438
Parch	-0.001652	0.081629	0.018443	-0.189119	0.414838	1.000000	0.216225	-0.061512
Fare	0.012658	0.257307	-0.549500	0.096067	0.159651	0.216225	1.000000	0.163758
Embarked	-0.022269	0.151777	-0.076466	0.025431	-0.069438	-0.061512	0.163758	1.000000

11. The result is pretty straightforward. It shows the correlation between the individual columns. As you can see, in this table, `PassengerId` shows a weak positive relationship with the `Fare` and `Age` columns:

```
sns.heatmap(Tcorrelation,xticklabels=Tcorrelation.columns,
            yticklabels=Tcorrelation.columns)
```

The output of this code is given as follows:

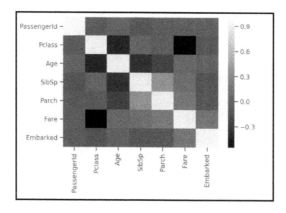

You can get the same dataset in Kaggle if you want to practice more analysis and prediction algorithms.

So far, you have learned about correlation and types of data analysis. You have made different analyses over the dataset too. Now we need to closely consider the facts before making any conclusions on the analysis based on the output we get.

Outlining Simpson's paradox

Usually, the decisions we make from our dataset are influenced by the output of statistical measures we apply to them. Those outputs tell us about the type of correlation and the basic visualizations of the dataset. However, sometimes, the decisions differ when we segregate the data into groups and apply statistical measures, or when we aggregate it together and then apply statistical measures. This kind of anomalous behavior in the results of the same dataset is generally called **Simpson's paradox**. Put simply, Simpson's paradox is the difference that appears in a trend of analysis when a dataset is analyzed in two different situations: first, when data is separated into groups and, second, when data is aggregated.

Here's a table that represents the recommendation rate for two different game consoles by males and females individually and also combined:

	Recommendation PS4	Recommendation Xbox One
Male	50/150=30%	180/360=50%
Female	200/250=80%	36/40=90%
Combined	250/400=62.5%	216/400=54%

The preceding table presents the recommendation rate of two different game consoles: PS4 and Xbox One by males and females, both individually and combined.

Suppose you are going to buy a game console that has a maximum recommendation. As shown in the preceding table, Xbox One is recommended by a higher percentage of both men and women than the PS4. However, using the same data when combined, the PS4 has a higher recommended percentage (62.5%) according to all users. So, how would you decide which one to go with? The calculations look fine but, logically, the decision making does not seem okay. This is Simpson's paradox. The same dataset here proves two opposing arguments.

Well, the main issue, in this case, is that when we only see the percentages of the separate data, it does not consider the sample size. Since each fraction shows the number of users who would recommend the game console by the number asked, it is relevant to consider the entire sample size. The sample size in the separate data of males and females differs by a large amount. For example, the recommendations of males for the PS4 is 50, while the recommendation for Xbox One is 180. There is a huge difference in these numbers. Xbox One has far more responses from men than from women, while the case is the opposite for the PS4. Because fewer men recommend the PlayStation, which results in a lower average rating for the PS4 when the data is combined, it leads to the paradox.

In order to come to a single decision regarding which console we should go with, we need to decide whether the data can be combined or whether we should look at it separately. In this case, we have to find out which console is most likely to satisfy both males and females. There might be other factors influencing these reviews, but we don't have this data, so we look for the maximum number of good reviews irrespective of the gender bias. Here, aggregating the data makes the most sense. We will combine the review and go with the overall average. Since our aim is to combine the reviews and see the total average, the aggregation of the data makes more sense.

It looks like Simpson's paradox is a far-fetched problem that is theoretically possible but never occurs in practice because our statistical analysis of the overall available data is accurate. However, there are many well-known studies of Simpson's paradox in the real world.

One real-world example is with mental health treatments such as depression. The following is a table about the effectiveness of two types of therapies given to patients:

	Therapy A	Therapy B
Mild depression	81/87=93%	234/270=87%
Severe depression	192/263=73%	55/80=69%
Both	273/350=78%	289/350=83%

As you can see, in the preceding table, there are two types of therapies: **Therapy A** and **Therapy B**. Therapy A seems to work better for both mild and severe depression, but aggregating the data reveals that treatment B works better for both cases. How is this possible? Well, we cannot conclude that the results after the data aggregation are correct, because the sample size differs in each type of therapy. In order to come to a single decision regarding which therapies we should go with, we need to think practically: how was the data generated? And what factors influence the results that are not seen at all?

In reality, mild depression is considered to be a less serious case by doctors and therapy A is cheaper than therapy B. Therefore, doctors recommend the simpler therapy, A, for mild depression.

The details and facts of the two therapy types are not mentioned in our dataset. The kind of depression and seriousness of the case leads to confounding variables (confounding variables are something we don't see in the data table but they can be determined by background analysis of the data) because it affects the decision regarding what treatment and recovery method to select. So, the factor that decides which treatment works better for the patient is dependent on the confounding variable, which is the seriousness of the case here. To determine which therapy works better, we require a report of the seriousness of the cases and then need to compare the recovery rates with both therapies rather than aggregated data across groups.

Answering the questions we want from a set of data sometimes requires more analysis than just looking at the available data. The lesson to take from Simpson's paradox is that data alone is insufficient. Data is never purely objective and neither is the final plot. Therefore, we must consider whether we are getting the whole story when dealing with a set of data.

Another fact that must be considered before concluding the analysis based on the output we get is that **correlation does not imply causation**. This is so important in the field of statistics that Wikipedia has a separate article on this statement.

Correlation does not imply causation

Correlation does not imply causation is an interesting phrase that you will hear mostly in statistics and when learning about data science in detail. But what does it mean? Well, it merely indicates that just because two things correlate does not always mean that one causes the other. For example, the Norwegian winter is cold, and people tend to spend more money on buying hot foods such as soup than they do in summer. However, this does not mean that cold weather causes people to spend more money on soup. Therefore, although the expenditure of people in Norway is related to cold weather, the spending is not the cause of the cold weather. Hence, correlation is not causation.

Note that there are two essential terms in this phrase: correlation and causation. **Correlation** reveals how strongly a pair of variables are related to each other and change together. **Causation** explains that any change in the value of one variable will cause a difference in the amount of another variable. In this case, one variable makes the other variable happen. This phenomenon is known as **cause and effect**. For example, when you exercise (X), the amount of calories (Y) you burn is higher every minute. Hence, X causes Y. According to the theory of logic, we can say the following:

$$X \rightarrow Y$$

The most common example found in any data analysis book is about the sales of ice cream and the rise and fall of homicide. According to this example, as there is an increase in ice cream sales, there is an increase in the number of homicides. Based on the correlation, these two events are highly co-related. However, the consumption of ice cream is not causing the death of people. These two things are not based on the cause and effect theory. Therefore, correlation does not mean causation.

So, what is the takeaway from this critical phrase? Well, first of all, we should not form our conclusions too quickly based on correlation. It is essential to invest some time in finding the underlying factors of the data in order to understand any critical, hidden factors.

Summary

In this chapter, we discussed correlation. Correlation is a statistical measure that can be used to inspect how a pair of variables are related. Understanding these relationships can help you to decide the most important features from a set of variables. Once we understand the correlation, we can use it to make better predictions. The higher the relationship between the variables, the higher the accuracy of the prediction. Since correlation is of higher importance, in this chapter, we have covered several methods of correlation and the different types of analysis, including univariate analysis, bivariate analysis, and multivariate analysis.

In the next chapter, we will take a closer look at time series analysis. We will use several real-life databases, including time series analysis, in order to perform exploratory data analysis.

Further reading

- *Associations and Correlations*, by *Lee Baker, Packt Publishing,* June 28, 2019
- *Data Science with Python,* by *Rohan Chopra, Aaron England,* and *Mohamed Noordeen Alaudeen, Packt Publishing,* July 2019
- *Hands-On Data Analysis with NumPy and Pandas,* by *Curtis Miller, Packt Publishing,* June 2018

8
Time Series Analysis

Time series data includes timestamps and is often generated while monitoring the industrial process or tracking any business metrics. An ordered sequence of timestamp values at equally spaced intervals is referred to as a *time series*. Analysis of such a time series is used in many applications such as sales forecasting, utility studies, budget analysis, economic forecasting, inventory studies, and so on. There are a plethora of methods that can be used to model and forecast time series.

In this chapter, we are going to explore **Time Series Analysis** (**TSA**) using Python libraries. Time series data is in the form of a sequence of quantitative observations about a system or process and is made at successive points in time.

In this chapter, we are going to cover the following topics:

- Understanding time series datasets
- TSA with Open Power System Data

Technical requirements

All the code and datasets used in this chapter can be found inside the GitHub repository (`https://github.com/PacktPublishing/hands-on-exploratory-data-analysis-with-python`):

- **Code**: The code you'll need for this chapter can be found inside the folder marked `Chapter 8/`.
- **Datasets**: We are going to use Open Power System Data for TSA. It can be downloaded from `https://open-power-system-data.org/`. You can also find the dataset inside the GitHub repository inside `Chapter 9/datasets`.

Understanding the time series dataset

The most essential question would be, *what do we mean by time series data?* Of course, we have heard about it on several occasions. Perhaps we can define it? Sure we can. Essentially, a time series is a collection of observations made sequentially in time. Note that there are two important key phrases here—**a collection of observations** and **sequentially in time**. Since it is a series, it has to be a collection of observations, and since it deals with time, it has to deal with it in a sequential fashion.

Let's take an example of time series data:

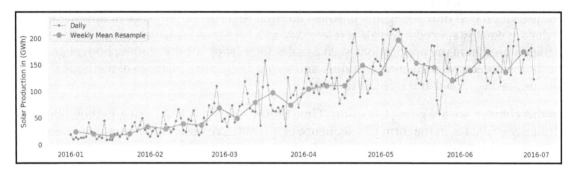

The preceding screenshot illustrates solar energy production (measured in **Gigawatt Hours (GWh)**) for the first six months of 2016. It also shows the consumption of electricity on both a daily and weekly basis.

Fundamentals of TSA

In order to understand the time series dataset, let's randomly generate a normalized dataset:

1. We can generate the dataset using the numpy library:

```
import os
import numpy as np
%matplotlib inline
from matplotlib import pyplot as plt
import seaborn as sns

zero_mean_series = np.random.normal(loc=0.0, scale=1., size=50)
zero_mean_series
```

We have used the NumPy library to generate random datasets. So, the output given here will be different for you. The output of the preceding code is given here:

```
array([-0.73140395, -2.4944216 , -1.44929237, -0.40077112,
0.23713083, 0.89632516, -0.90228469, -0.96464949, 1.48135275,
0.64530002, -1.70897785,  0.54863901, -1.14941457, -1.49177657,
-2.04298133, 1.40936481,  0.65621356, -0.37571958, -0.04877503,
-0.84619236, -1.46231312,  2.42031845, -0.91949491,  0.80903063,
0.67885337, -0.1082256 , -0.16953567,  0.93628661,  2.57639376,
-0.01489153, 0.9011697 , -0.29900988,  0.04519547,  0.71230853,
-0.00626227, 1.27565662, -0.42432848,  1.44748288,  0.29585819,
0.70547011, -0.6838063 ,  1.61502839, -0.04388889,  1.06261716,
0.17708138, 0.3723592 , -0.77185183, -3.3487284 ,  0.59464475,
-0.89005505])
```

2. Next, we are going to use the `seaborn` library to plot the time series data. Check the code snippet given here:

```
plt.figure(figsize=(16, 8))
g = sns.lineplot(data=zero_mean_series)
g.set_title('Zero mean model')
g.set_xlabel('Time index')
plt.show()
```

We plotted the time series graph using the `seaborn.lineplot()` function which is a built-in method provided by the `seaborn` library. The output of the preceding code is given here:

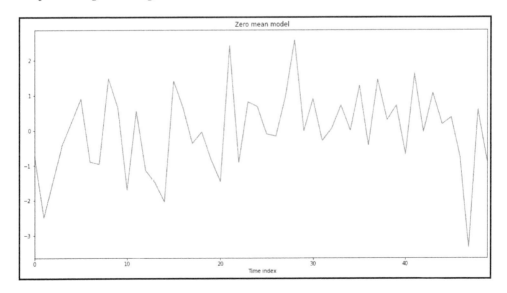

3. We can perform a cumulative sum over the list and then plot the data using a time series plot. The plot gives more interesting results. Check the following code snippet:

```
random_walk = np.cumsum(zero_mean_series)
random_walk
```

It generates an array of the cumulative sum as shown here:

```
array([ -0.73140395,   -3.22582556,   -4.67511792,
-5.07588904,-4.83875821,   -3.94243305,   -4.84471774,
-5.80936723,-4.32801448,   -3.68271446,   -5.39169231,   -4.8430533
,-5.99246787,   -7.48424444,   -9.52722576,   -8.11786095,-7.46164739,
-7.83736697,   -7.886142  ,   -8.73233436, -10.19464748,
-7.77432903,   -8.69382394,   -7.88479331,-7.20593994,   -7.31416554,
-7.4837012 ,   -6.5474146 ,-3.97102084,   -3.98591237,   -3.08474267,
-3.38375255,-3.33855708,   -2.62624855,   -2.63251082,
-1.35685419,-1.78118268,   -0.3336998 ,   -0.03784161,
0.66762849,-0.01617781,    1.59885058,    1.55496169,    2.61757885,
2.79466023,    3.16701943,    2.3951676 ,   -0.9535608 ,-0.35891606,
-1.2489711 ])
```

Note that for any particular value, the next value is the sum of previous values.

4. Now, if we plot the list using the time series plot as shown here, we get an interesting graph that shows the change in values over time:

```
plt.figure(figsize=(16, 8))
g = sns.lineplot(data=random_walk)
g.set_title('Random Walk')
g.set_xlabel('Time index')
plt.show()
```

The output of the preceding code is given here:

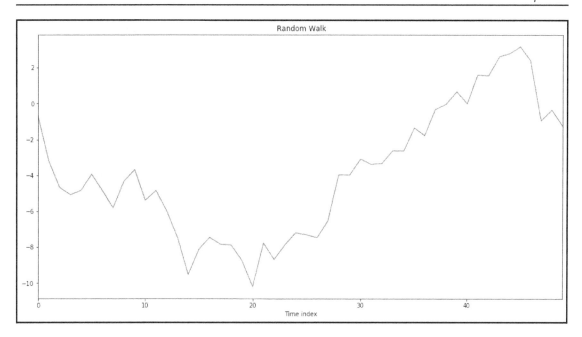

Note the graph shown in the preceding diagram. It shows the change of values over time. Great – so far, we have generated different time series data and plotted it using the built-in `seaborn.tsplot()` method.

Univariate time series

When we capture a sequence of observations for the same variable over a particular duration of time, the series is referred to as **univariate time series.** In general, in a univariate time series, the observations are taken over regular time periods, such as the change in temperature over time throughout a day.

Characteristics of time series data

When working with time series data, there are several unique characteristics that can be observed. In general, time series tend to exhibit the following characteristics:

- When looking at time series data, it is essential to see if there is any **trend**. Observing a trend means that the average measurement values seem either to decrease or increase over time.
- Time series data may contain a notable amount of **outliers**. These outliers can be noted when plotted on a graph.

- Some data in time series tends to repeat over a certain interval in some patterns. We refer to such repeating patterns as **seasonality**.
- Sometimes, there is an uneven change in time series data. We refer to such uneven changes as **abrupt changes**. Observing abrupt changes in time series is essential as it reveals essential underlying phenomena.
- Some series tend to follow **constant variance** over time. Hence, it is essential to look at the time series data and see whether or not the data exhibits constant variance over time.

The characteristics listed previously help us to make better analyses when it comes to TSA. Now that we know what to see and expect in time series data, it would be useful to see some real examples in action. Next, let's import a real database and perform various TSA methods on it.

TSA with Open Power System Data

In this section, we are going to use Open Power System Data to understand TSA. We'll look at the time series data structures, time-based indexing, and several ways to visualize time series data.

We will start by importing the dataset. Look at the code snippet given here:

```
# load time series dataset
df_power =
pd.read_csv("https://raw.githubusercontent.com/jenfly/opsd/master/opsd_germ
any_daily.csv")
df_power.columns
```

The output of the preceding code is given here:

```
Index(['Consumption', 'Wind', 'Solar', 'Wind+Solar'], dtype='object')
```

The columns of the dataframe are described here:

- **Date**: The date is in the format `yyyy-mm-dd`.
- **Consumption**: This indicates electricity consumption in GWh.
- **Solar**: This indicates solar power production in GWh.
- **Wind+Solar**: This represents the sum of solar and wind power production in GWh.

Note the date column, which contains the time series dataset. We can use this dataset to discover how electricity consumption and production varies over time in Germany.

Data cleaning

Let's now clean our dataset for outliers:

1. We can start by checking the shape of the dataset:

```
df_power.shape
```

The output of the preceding code is given here:

```
(4383, 5)
```

The dataframe contains 4,283 rows and 5 columns.

2. We can also check few entries inside the dataframe. Let's examine the last 10 entries:

```
df_power.tail(10)
```

The output of the preceding code is given here:

	Date	Consumption	Wind	Solar	Wind+Solar
4373	2017-12-22	1423.23782	228.773	10.065	238.838
4374	2017-12-23	1272.17085	748.074	8.450	756.524
4375	2017-12-24	1141.75730	812.422	9.949	822.371
4376	2017-12-25	1111.28338	587.810	15.765	603.575
4377	2017-12-26	1130.11683	717.453	30.923	748.376
4378	2017-12-27	1263.94091	394.507	16.530	411.037
4379	2017-12-28	1299.86398	506.424	14.162	520.586
4380	2017-12-29	1295.08753	584.277	29.854	614.131
4381	2017-12-30	1215.44897	721.247	7.467	728.714
4382	2017-12-31	1107.11488	721.176	19.980	741.156

3. Next, let's review the data types of each column in our `df_power` dataframe:

```
df_power.dtypes
```

The output of the preceding code is given here:

```
Date object
Consumption float64
Wind float64
Solar float64
Wind+Solar float64
dtype: object
```

4. Note that the `Date` column has a data type of `object`. This is not correct. So, the next step is to correct the `Date` column, as shown here:

```
#convert object to datetime format
df_power['Date'] = pd.to_datetime(df_power['Date'])
```

5. It should convert the `Date` column to `Datetime` format. We can verify this again:

```
df_power.dtypes
```

The output of the preceding code is given here:

```
Date datetime64[ns]
Consumption float64
Wind float64
Solar float64
Wind+Solar float64
dtype: object
```

Note that the `Date` column has been changed into the correct data type.

6. Let's next change the index of our dataframe to the `Date` column:

```
df_power = df_power.set_index('Date')
df_power.tail(3)
```

The output of the preceding code is given here:

Date	Consumption	Wind	Solar	Wind+Solar
2017-12-29	1295.08753	584.277	29.854	614.131
2017-12-30	1215.44897	721.247	7.467	728.714
2017-12-31	1107.11488	721.176	19.980	741.156

Note from the preceding screenshot that the `Date` column has been set as `DatetimeIndex`.

7. We can simply verify this by using the code snippet given here:

```
df_power.index
```

The output of the preceding code is given here:

```
DatetimeIndex(['2006-01-01', '2006-01-02', '2006-01-03',
'2006-01-04', '2006-01-05', '2006-01-06', '2006-01-07',
'2006-01-08', '2006-01-09', '2006-01-10', ... '2017-12-22',
'2017-12-23', '2017-12-24', '2017-12-25', '2017-12-26',
'2017-12-27', '2017-12-28', '2017-12-29', '2017-12-30',
'2017-12-31'],dtype='datetime64[ns]', name='Date', length=4383,
freq=None)
```

8. Since our index is the `DatetimeIndex` object, now we can use it to analyze the dataframe. Let's add more columns to our dataframe to make our lives easier. Let's add `Year`, `Month`, and `Weekday Name`:

```
# Add columns with year, month, and weekday name
df_power['Year'] = df_power.index.year
df_power['Month'] = df_power.index.month
df_power['Weekday Name'] = df_power.index.weekday_name
```

9. Let's display five random rows from the dataframe:

```
# Display a random sampling of 5 rows
df_power.sample(5, random_state=0)
```

The output of this code is given here:

	Consumption	Wind	Solar	Wind+Solar	Year	Month	Weekday Name
Date							
2008-08-23	1152.011	NaN	NaN	NaN	2008	8	Saturday
2013-08-08	1291.984	79.666	93.371	173.037	2013	8	Thursday
2009-08-27	1281.057	NaN	NaN	NaN	2009	8	Thursday
2015-10-02	1391.050	81.229	160.641	241.870	2015	10	Friday
2009-06-02	1201.522	NaN	NaN	NaN	2009	6	Tuesday

Note that we added three more columns—`Year`, `Month`, and `Weekday Name`. Adding these columns helps to make the analysis of data easier.

Time-based indexing

Time-based indexing is a very powerful method of the `pandas` library when it comes to time series data. Having time-based indexing allows using a formatted string to select data. See the following code, for example:

```
df_power.loc['2015-10-02']
```

The output of the preceding code is given here:

```
Consumption 1391.05
Wind 81.229
Solar 160.641
Wind+Solar 241.87
Year 2015
Month 10
Weekday Name Friday
Name: 2015-10-02 00:00:00, dtype: object
```

Note that we used the pandas dataframe `loc` accessor. In the preceding example, we used a date as a string to select a row. We can use all sorts of techniques to access rows just as we can do with a normal dataframe index.

Visualizing time series

Let's visualize the time series dataset. We will continue using the same `df_power` dataframe:

1. The first step is to import the `seaborn` and `matplotlib` libraries:

```
import matplotlib.pyplot as plt
import seaborn as sns
sns.set(rc={'figure.figsize':(11, 4)})
plt.rcParams['figure.figsize'] = (8,5)
plt.rcParams['figure.dpi'] = 150
```

2. Next, let's generate a line plot of the full time series of Germany's daily electricity consumption:

```
df_power['Consumption'].plot(linewidth=0.5)
```

The output of the preceding code is given here:

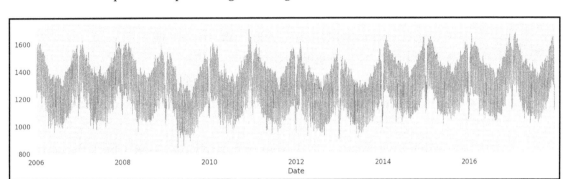

As depicted in the preceding screenshot, the y-axis shows the electricity consumption and the x-axis shows the year. However, there are too many datasets to cover all the years.

3. Let's use the dots to plot the data for all the other columns:

```
cols_to_plot = ['Consumption', 'Solar', 'Wind']
axes = df_power[cols_to_plot].plot(marker='.', alpha=0.5,
linestyle='None',figsize=(14, 6), subplots=True)
for ax in axes:
    ax.set_ylabel('Daily Totals (GWh)')
```

The output of the preceding code is given here:

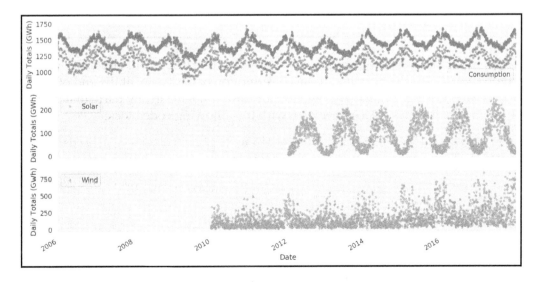

The output shows that electricity consumption can be broken down into two distinct patterns:

- One cluster roughly from 1,400 GWh and above
- Another cluster roughly below 1,400 GWh

Moreover, solar production is higher in summer and lower in winter. Over the years, there seems to have been a strong increasing trend in the output of wind power.

4. We can further investigate a single year to have a closer look. Check the code given here:

```
ax = df_power.loc['2016', 'Consumption'].plot()
ax.set_ylabel('Daily Consumption (GWh)');
```

The output of the preceding code is given here:

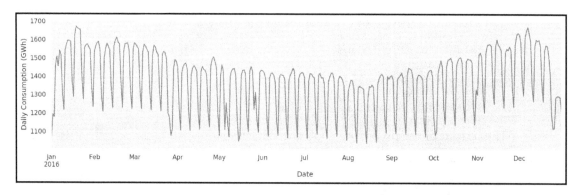

From the preceding screenshot, we can see clearly the consumption of electricity for 2016. The graph shows a drastic decrease in the consumption of electricity at the end of the year (December) and during August. We can look for further details in any particular month. Let's examine the month of December 2016 with the following code block:

```
ax = df_power.loc['2016-12', 'Consumption'].plot(marker='o', linestyle='-')
ax.set_ylabel('Daily Consumption (GWh)');
```

The output of the preceding code is given here:

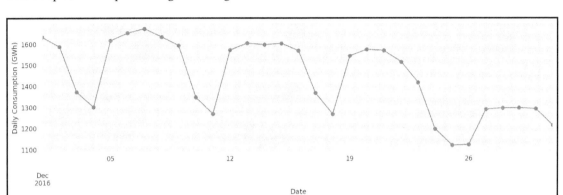

As shown in the preceding graph, electricity consumption is higher on weekdays and lowest at the weekends. We can see the consumption for each day of the month. We can zoom in further to see how consumption plays out in the last week of December.

In order to indicate a particular week of December, we can supply a specific date range as shown here:

```
ax = df_power.loc['2016-12-23':'2016-12-30',
'Consumption'].plot(marker='o', linestyle='-')
ax.set_ylabel('Daily Consumption (GWh)');
```

As illustrated in the preceding code, we want to see the electricity consumption between 2016-12-23 and 2016-12-30. The output of the preceding code is given here:

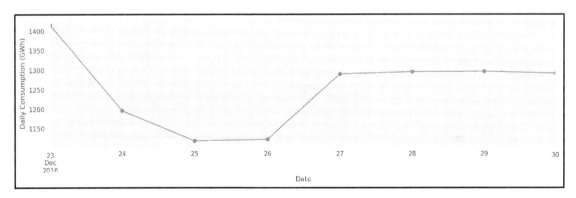

As illustrated in the preceding screenshot, electricity consumption was lowest on the day of Christmas, probably because people were busy partying. After Christmas, the consumption increased.

Grouping time series data

We can group the data by different time periods and present them in box plots:

1. We can first group the data by months and then use the box plots to visualize the data:

```
fig, axes = plt.subplots(3, 1, figsize=(8, 7), sharex=True)
for name, ax in zip(['Consumption', 'Solar', 'Wind'], axes):
    sns.boxplot(data=df_power, x='Month', y=name, ax=ax)
    ax.set_ylabel('GWh')
    ax.set_title(name)
    if ax != axes[-1]:
        ax.set_xlabel('')
```

The output of the preceding code is given here:

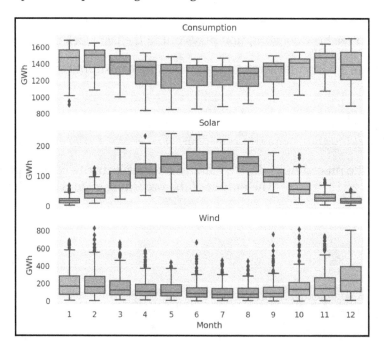

The preceding plot illustrates that electricity consumption is generally higher in the winter and lower in the summer. Wind production is higher during the summer. Moreover, there are many outliers associated with electricity consumption, wind production, and solar production.

2. Next, we can group the consumption of electricity by the day of the week, and present it in a box plot:

```
sns.boxplot(data=df_power, x='Weekday Name', y='Consumption');
```

The output of the preceding code is given here:

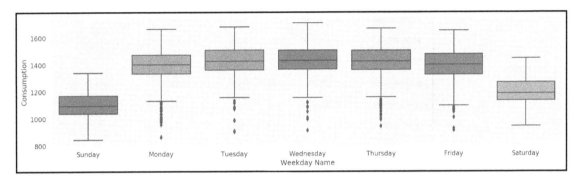

The preceding screenshot shows that electricity consumption is higher on weekdays than on weekends. Interestingly, there are more outliers on the weekdays.

Resampling time series data

It is often required to resample the dataset at lower or higher frequencies. This resampling is done based on aggregation or grouping operations. For example, we can resample the data based on the weekly mean time series as follows:

1. We can use the code given here to resample our data:

```
columns = ['Consumption', 'Wind', 'Solar', 'Wind+Solar']

power_weekly_mean = df_power[columns].resample('W').mean()
power_weekly_mean
```

The output of the preceding code is given here:

	Consumption	Wind	Solar	Wind+Solar
Date				
2006-01-01	1069.184000	NaN	NaN	NaN
2006-01-08	1381.300143	NaN	NaN	NaN
2006-01-15	1486.730286	NaN	NaN	NaN
2006-01-22	1490.031143	NaN	NaN	NaN
2006-01-29	1514.176857	NaN	NaN	NaN
2006-02-05	1501.403286	NaN	NaN	NaN
2006-02-12	1498.217143	NaN	NaN	NaN
2006-02-19	1446.507429	NaN	NaN	NaN
2006-02-26	1447.651429	NaN	NaN	NaN
2006-03-05	1439.727857	NaN	NaN	NaN

As shown in the preceding screenshot, the first row, labeled `2006-01-01`, includes the average of all the data. We can plot the daily and weekly time series to compare the dataset over the six-month period.

2. Let's see the last six months of 2016. Let's start by initializing the variable:

```
start, end = '2016-01', '2016-06'
```

3. Next, let's plot the graph using the code given here:

```
fig, ax = plt.subplots()

ax.plot(df_power.loc[start:end, 'Solar'],
marker='.', linestyle='-', linewidth=0.5, label='Daily')
ax.plot(power_weekly_mean.loc[start:end, 'Solar'],
marker='o', markersize=8, linestyle='-', label='Weekly Mean
Resample')
ax.set_ylabel('Solar Production in (GWh)')
ax.legend();
```

The output of the preceding code is given here:

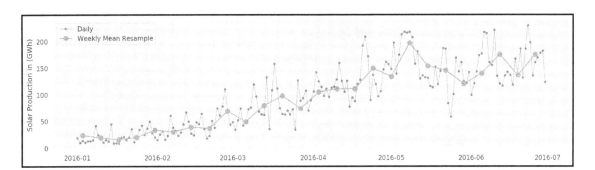

The preceding screenshot shows that the weekly mean time series is increasing over time and is much smoother than the daily time series.

Summary

In this chapter, we have discussed how to import, clean, analyze, and visualize time series datasets using the pandas library. Moreover, we visualized a time series dataset using the `matplotlib` and `seaborn` libraries. Finally, we used Python to load and examine the Open Power System Data dataset and performed several techniques associated with TSA.

In the next chapter, we are going to learn about different methods for model development using classical machine learning techniques and three different types of machine learning, namely, supervised learning, unsupervised machine learning, and reinforcement learning.

Further reading

- *Practical Time Series Analysis*, by *Dr. Avishek Pal* and *Dr. PKS Prakash*, *Packt Publishing*
- *Python Machine Learning - Third Edition*, by *Sebastian Raschka* and *Vahid Mirjalili*, *Packt Publishing*
- *Data Analysis with Python*, by *David Taieb*, *Packt Publishing*
- *Regression Analysis with Python*, by *Luca Massaron* and *Alberto Boschetti*, *Packt Publishing*
- *Statistics for Machine Learning*, by *Pratap Dangeti*, *Packt Publishing*

- *Statistics for Data Science,* by *James D. Miller, Packt Publishing*
- *Data Science Algorithms in a Week - Second Edition,* by *Dávid Natingga, Packt Publishing*
- *Machine Learning with scikit-learn Quick Start Guide,* by *Kevin Jolly, Packt Publishing*

Section 3: Model Development and Evaluation

3

One of the main aims of EDA is to prepare your dataset to develop a useful model capable of characterizing sensed data. To create such models, we first need to understand the dataset. If our data set is labeled, we will be performing supervised learning tasks, and if our data is unlabeled, then we will be performing unsupervised learning tasks. Moreover, once we create these models, we need to quantify how effective our model is. We can do this by performing several evaluations on these models. In this section, We are going to discuss in-depth how to use EDA for model development and evaluation. The main objective of this section is to allow you to use EDA techniques on real datasets, prepare different types of models, and evaluate them.

This section contains the following chapters:

- Chapter 9, *Hypothesis Testing and Regression*
- Chapter 10, *Model Development and Evaluation*
- Chapter 11, *EDA on Wine Quality Data*

Hypothesis Testing and Regression

9

In this chapter, we will dive into two important concepts, hypothesis testing and regression. First, we will discuss several aspects of hypothesis testing, the basic principles of hypothesis testing and types of hypothesis testing and run through some working examples. Next, we will discuss types of regression and develop models using the scikit-learn library.

In this chapter, we will cover the following topics:

- Hypothesis testing
- p-hacking
- Understanding regression
- Types of regression
- Model development and evaluation

Technical requirements

The code for this chapter can be found in the GitHub repository (`https://github.com/PacktPublishing/hands-on-exploratory-data-analysis-with-python`) inside the folder for `Chapter 9`, *Hypothesis Testing and Regression*.

Hypothesis testing

Hypothesis testing is often used to facilitate statistical decisions using experimental datasets. The testing is used to validate assumptions about a population parameter. For example, consider the following statements:

- The average score of students taking the Machine Learning course at the University of Nepal is 78.
- The average height of boys is higher than that of girls among the students taking the Machine Learning course.

In all these examples, we assume some statistical facts to prove those statements. A situation like this is where hypothesis testing helps. A hypothesis test assesses two mutually exclusive statements about any particular **population** and determines which statement is best established by the **sample** data. Here, we used two essential keywords: population and sample. A population includes all the elements from a set of data, whereas a sample consists of one or more observations taken from any particular population.

In the next section, we are going to discuss hypothesis testing and discuss how we can use Python libraries to perform hypothesis testing.

Hypothesis testing principle

Hypothesis testing is based on two fundamental principles of statistics, namely, normalization and standard normalization:

- **Normalization**: The concept of normalization differs with respect to the context. To understand the concept of normalization easily, it is the process of adjusting values measured on different scales to common scales before performing descriptive statistics, and it is denoted by the following equation:

$$X_{changed} = \frac{X - X_{min}}{X_{max} - X_{min}}$$

- **Standard normalization**: Standard normalization is similar to normalization except it has a mean of 0 and a standard deviation of 1. Standard normalization is denoted by the following equation:

$$X_{changed} = \frac{X - \mu}{\sigma}$$

Besides these concepts, we need to know about some important parameters of hypothesis testing:

- The **null hypothesis** is the most basic assumption made based on the knowledge about the domain. For example, the average typing speed of a person is 38-40 words per minute.
- An **alternative hypothesis** is a different hypothesis that opposes the null hypothesis. The main task here is whether we accept or reject the alternative hypothesis based on the experimentation results. For example, the average typing speed of a person is always less than 38-40 words per minute. We can either accept or reject this hypothesis based on certain facts. For example, we can find a person who can type at a speed of 38 words per minute and it will disprove this hypothesis. Hence, we can reject this statement.
- **Type I error** and **Type II error**: When we either accept or reject a hypothesis, there are two types of errors that we could make. They are referred to as Type I and Type II errors:
    - **False-positive**: A Type I error is when we reject the null hypothesis (H0) when H0 is true.
    - **False-negative**: A Type II error is when we do not reject the null hypothesis (H0) when H0 is false.
- **P-values**: This is also referred to as the probability value or asymptotic significance. It is the probability for a particular statistical model given that the null hypothesis is true. Generally, if the P-value is lower than a predetermined threshold, we reject the null hypothesis.
- **Level of significance**: This is one of the most important concepts that you should be familiar with before using the hypothesis. The level of significance is the degree of importance with which we are either accepting or rejecting the null hypothesis. We must note that 100% accuracy is not possible for accepting or rejecting. We generally select a level of significance based on our subject and domain. Generally, it is 0.05 or 5%. It means that our output should be 95% confident that it supports our null hypothesis.

To summarize, see the condition before either selecting or rejecting the null hypothesis:

```
# Reject H0
p <= α
# Accept the null hypothesis
p > α
```

Generally, we set the significance level before we start calculating new values. Next, we will see how we can use the stats library to perform hypothesis testing.

statsmodels library

Let's perform hypothesis testing using the stats library. Let's consider the following scenario.

In a study about mental health in youth, 48% of parents believed that social media was the cause of their teenagers' stress:

- **Population**: Parent with a teenager (age >= 18)
- **Parameter of interest**: p
- **Null hypothesis**: p = 0.48
- **Alternative hypothesis**: p > 0.48

Data: 4,500 people were surveyed, and 65% of those who were surveyed believed that their teenagers' stress is due to social media.

Let's start the hypothesis testing:

1. First, import the required libraries:

   ```
   import statsmodels.api as sm
   import numpy as np
   import matplotlib.pyplot as plt
   import pandas as pd
   ```

2. Next, let's declare the variables:

   ```
   n = 4500
   pnull= 0.48
   phat = 0.65
   ```

3. Now, we can use the `proportions_ztest` method to calculate the new P-value. Check out the following snippet:

   ```
   sm.stats.proportions_ztest(phat * n, n, pnull,
   alternative='larger')
   ```

   The output of the preceding code is as follows:

   ```
   (23.90916877786327, 1.2294951052777303e-126)
   ```

Our calculated P-value of `1.2294951052777303e-126` is pretty small, and we can reject the null hypothesis, which is that social media is the cause of teenagers' stress.

Average reading time

Let's say a reading competition was conducted with some adults. The data looks like the following:

```
[236, 239, 209, 246, 246, 245, 215, 212, 242, 241, 219, 242, 236, 211, 216,
214, 203, 223, 200, 238, 215, 227, 222, 204, 200, 208, 204, 230, 216, 204,
201, 202, 240, 209, 246, 224, 243, 247, 215,249, 239, 211, 227, 211, 247,
235, 200, 240, 213, 213, 209, 219,209, 222, 244, 226, 205, 230, 238, 218,
242, 238, 243, 248, 228,243, 211, 217, 200, 237, 234, 207, 217, 211, 224,
217, 205, 233, 222, 218, 202, 205, 216, 233, 220, 218, 249, 237, 223]
```

Now, our hypothesis question is this: **Is the average reading speed of random students (adults) more than 212 words per minute?**

We can break down the preceding concept into the following parameters:

- **Population**: All adults
- **Parameter of interest**: μ, the population of a classroom
- **Null hypothesis**: $\mu = 212$
- **Alternative hypothesis**: $\mu > 212$
- **Confidence level**: $\alpha = 0.05$

We know all the required parameters. Now, we can use a Z-test from the `statsmodels` package with `alternate="larger"`:

```
import numpy as np

sdata = np.random.randint(200, 250, 89)
sm.stats.ztest(sdata, value = 80, alternative = "larger")
```

The output of the preceding code is as follows:

```
(91.63511530225408, 0.0)
```

Since the computed P-value (0.0) is lower than the standard confidence level ($\alpha = 0.05$), we can **reject the null hypothesis**. That means the statement *the average reading speed of adults is 212 words per minute* is rejected.

Types of hypothesis testing

There are different types of hypothesis testing. The most commonly used ones are as follows:

- Z-test
- T-test
- ANOVA test
- Chi-squared test

Going through each type of test is beyond the scope of this book. We recommend checking out Wikipedia or the links in the *Further reading* section to get detailed information about them. However, we are going to look at the Z-test and the T-test in this book. In the preceding examples, we only used the Z-test.

T-test

The T-test is a type of test most commonly used in inferential statistics. This test is most commonly used in scenarios where we need to understand if there is a significant difference between the means of two groups. For example, say we have a dataset of students from certain classes. The dataset contains the height of each student. We are checking whether the average height is 175 cm or not:

- **Population**: All students in that class
- **Parameter of interest**: μ, the population of a classroom
- **Null hypothesis**: The average height is $\mu = 175$
- **Alternative hypothesis**: $\mu > 175$
- **Confidence level**: $\alpha = 0.05$

We have listed all the parameters. Now, we can use hypothesis testing:

1. Let's first set up the dataset:

```
import numpy as np
height = np.array([172, 184, 174, 168, 174, 183, 173, 173, 184,
179, 171, 173, 181, 183, 172, 178, 170, 182, 181, 172, 175, 170,
168, 178, 170, 181, 180, 173, 183, 180, 177, 181, 171, 173, 171,
182, 180, 170, 172, 175, 178, 174, 184, 177, 181, 180, 178, 179,
175, 170, 182, 176, 183, 179, 177])
```

2. Next, we are going to use the stats module from the SciPy library. Note that in the previous examples, we used the statsmodels API library. We could also continue using that, but our intention here is to introduce you to the new modules of the SciPy library. Let's import the library:

```
from scipy.stats import ttest_1samp
import numpy as np
```

3. Now, let's use the NumPy library to compute the average height:

```
height_average = np.mean(height)
print("Average height is = {0:.3f}".format(height_average))
```

The output of the preceding code is as follows:

```
Average height is = 175.618
```

4. Now, let's use the T-test to compute the new P-value:

```
tset,pval = ttest_1samp(height, 175)

print("P-value = {}".format(pval))

if pval < 0.05:
 print("We are rejecting the null Hypothesis.")
else:
   print("We are accepting the null hypothesis.")
```

The output of the preceding code is as follows:

```
Average height is = 175.618
P-value = 0.35408130524750125
We are accepting the null hypothesis
```

Note that our significance level (alpha = 0.05) and the computed P-value is 0.354. Since it is greater than alpha, we are accepting the null hypothesis. This means that the average height of students is 175 cm with a 95% confidence value.

p-hacking

p-hacking is a serious methodological issue. It is also referred to as data fishing, data butchery, or data dredging. It is the misuse of data analysis to detect patterns in data that can be statistically meaningful. This is done by conducting one or more tests and only publishing those that come back with higher-significance results.

We have seen in the previous section, *Hypothesis testing*, that we rely on the P-value to draw a conclusion. In simple words, this means we compute the P-value, which is the probability of the results. If the P-value is small, the result is declared to be statistically significant. This means if you create a hypothesis and test it with some criteria and report a P-value less than 0.05, the readers are likely to believe that you have found a real correlation or effect. However, this could be totally false in real life. There could be no effect or correlation at all. So, whatever is reported is a **false positive**. This is seen a lot in the field of publications. Many journals will only publish studies that can report at least one statistically significant effect. As a result of this, the researchers try to wrangle the dataset, or experiment to get a significantly lower P-value. This is called p-hacking.

Having covered the concept of data dredging, it's now time we start learning how to build models. We will start with one of the most common and basic models—regression.

Understanding regression

We use correlation in statistical terms to denote the association between two quantitative variables. Note that we have used the term quantitative variables. This should be meaningful to you. If not, we suggest you pause here and go through Chapter 1, *Exploratory Data Analysis Fundamentals*.

When it comes to quantitative variables and correlation, we also assume that the relationship is linear, that is, one variable increases or decreases by a fixed amount when there is an increase or decrease in another variable. To determine a similar relationship, there is the other method that's often used in these situations, **regression**, which includes determining the best straight line for the relationship. A simple equation, called the **regression equation**, can represent the relation:

$$Y = a + bX + u$$

Let's examine this formula:

- Y = The dependent variable (the variable that you are trying to predict). It is often referred to as the **outcome variable**.
- X = The independent variable (the variable that you are using to predict Y). It is often referred to as the **predictor**, or the **covariate** or **feature**.
- a = The intercept.
- b = The slope.
- u = The regression residual.

If y represents the dependent variable and x represents the independent variable, this relationship is described as the regression of y on x. The relationship between x and y is generally represented by an equation. The equation shows how much y changes with respect to x.

There are several reasons why people use regression analysis. The most obvious reasons are as follows:

- We can use regression analysis to predict future economic conditions, trends, or values.
- We can use regression analysis to determine the relationship between two or more variables.
- We can use regression analysis to understand how one variable changes when another also change.

In a later section, we will use the regression function for model development to predict the dependent variable while implementing a new explanatory variable in our function. Basically, we will build a prediction model. So, let's dive further into the regression.

Types of regression

The two main regression types are linear regression and multiple linear regression. Most simple data can be represented by linear regression. Some complex data follows multiple linear regression. We will examine the types of regression with Python in this chapter. Finally, we will end the discussion with different aspects of a nonlinear example.

Simple linear regression

Linear regression, which is also called **simple linear regression**, defines the relationship between two variables using a straight line. During linear regression, our aim is to draw a line closest to the data by finding the slope and intercept that define the line. The equation for simple linear regression is generally given as follows:

$$Y = a + bX + u$$

X is a single feature, Y is a target, and a and b are the intercept and slope respectively. The question is, how do we choose a and b? The answer is to choose the line that minimizes the error function, u. This error function is also known as loss or **cost function**, which is the sum of the square (to ignore the positive and negative cancelation) of the difference of the vertical distance between the line and the data point.

This calculation is called the **Ordinary Least Squares (OLS)**. Note that explaining every aspect of regression is beyond the scope of this book, and we suggest you explore the *Further reading* section to broaden your knowledge about the subject.

Multiple linear regression

In the case of **multiple linear regression**, two more independent variables or explanatory variables show a linear relationship with the target or dependent variables. Most of the linearly describable phenomena in nature are captured by multiple linear regression. For example, the price of any item depends on the quantity being purchased, the time of the year, and the number of items available in the inventory. For instance, the price of a bottle of wine depends primarily on how many bottles you bought. Also, the price is a bit higher during festivals such as Christmas. Moreover, if there are a limited number of bottles in the inventory, the price is likely to go even higher. In this case, the price of wine is dependent on three variables: quantity, time of year, and stock quantity. This type of relationship can be captured using multiple linear regression.

The equation for multiple linear regression is generally given as follows:

$$Y = a + b1X1 + b2X2 + b3X3 + \ldots + btXt + u$$

Here, Y is the dependent variable and $X_i s$ is the independent variable.

Nonlinear regression

Nonlinear regression is a type of regression analysis in which data follows a model and is then represented as a function of mathematics. Simple linear regression relates to two variables (X and Y) with a straight line function, $y = mx + b$, whereas nonlinear regression has to generate a curve. Nonlinear regression uses a regression equation, which is as follows:

$$Y = f(X, \beta) + \varepsilon$$

Let's look at this formula:

- X = A vector of p predictors
- β = A vector of k parameters
- $f(-)$ = A known regression function
- ε = An error term

Nonlinear regression can fit an enormous variety of curves. It uses logarithmic functions, trigonometric functions, exponential functions, and many other fitting methods. This modeling is similar to linear regression modeling because both attempt to graphically control a specific answer from a set of variables. These are more complicated to develop than linear models because the function is generated by means of a series of approximations (iterations) that may result from trial and error. Mathematicians use a variety of established methods, such as the Gauss-Newton and Levenberg-Marquardt methods. The goal of this nonlinear model generated curve line is to make the OLS as small as possible. The smaller the OLS the better the function fits in the dataset's points. It measures how many observations vary from the dataset average.

In the next section, we are going to learn how we can develop and evaluate the regression model using the Python libraries.

Model development and evaluation

In the previous section, we discussed different types of regression theoretically. Now that we've covered the theoretical concepts, it's time to get some practical experience. In this section, we are going to use the scikit-learn library to implement linear regression and evaluate the model. To do this, we will use the famous Boston housing pricing dataset, which is widely used by researchers. We will discuss different model evaluation techniques used in the case of regression.

Let's try to develop some regression models based on the explanation we saw earlier.

Constructing a linear regression model

The first concept that comes to mind of any data science professional when solving any regression problem is to construct a linear regression model. Linear regression is one of the oldest algorithms, but it's still very efficient. We will build a linear regression model in Python using a sample dataset. This dataset is available in scikit-learn as a sample dataset called the Boston housing prices dataset. We will use the `sklearn` library to load the dataset and build the actual model. Let's start by loading and understanding the data:

1. Let's begin by importing all the necessary libraries and creating our dataframe:

```
# Importing the necessary libraries
import pandas as pd
import numpy as np
import matplotlib.pyplot as plt
import seaborn as sns
```

```
from sklearn.datasets import load_boston

sns.set(style="ticks", color_codes=True)
plt.rcParams['figure.figsize'] = (8,5)
plt.rcParams['figure.dpi'] = 150

# loading the data
df =
pd.read_csv("https://raw.githubusercontent.com/PacktPublishing/hand
s-on-exploratory-data-analysis-with-
python/master/Chapter%209/Boston.csv")
```

2. Now, we have the dataset loaded into the `boston` variable. We can look at the keys of the dataframe as follows:

```
print(df.keys())
```

This returns all keys and values as the Python dictionary. The output of the preceding code is as follows:

```
Index(['CRIM', ' ZN ', 'INDUS ', 'CHAS', 'NOX', 'RM', 'AGE', 'DIS',
'RAD', 'TAX', 'PTRATIO', 'LSTAT', 'MEDV'], dtype='object')
```

3. Now that our data is loaded, let's get our DataFrame ready quickly and work ahead:

```
df.head()
# print the columns present in the dataset
print(df.columns)
# print the top 5 rows in the dataset
print(df.head())
```

The output of the preceding code is as follows:

```
Index(['CRIM', ' ZN ', 'INDUS ', 'CHAS', 'NOX', 'RM', 'AGE', 'DIS', 'RAD',
       'TAX', 'PTRATIO', 'LSTAT', 'MEDV'],
      dtype='object')
      CRIM     ZN   INDUS   CHAS    NOX  ...  RAD  TAX  PTRATIO  LSTAT  MEDV
0  0.00632  18.0    2.31      0  0.538  ...    1  296     15.3   4.98  24.0
1  0.02731   0.0    7.07      0  0.469  ...    2  242     17.8   9.14  21.6
2  0.02729   0.0    7.07      0  0.469  ...    2  242     17.8   4.03  34.7
3  0.03237   0.0    2.18      0  0.458  ...    3  222     18.7   2.94  33.4
4  0.06905   0.0    2.18      0  0.458  ...    3  222     18.7   5.33  36.2

[5 rows x 13 columns]
```

Figure 9.1: The first five rows of the DataFrame

The column MEDV is the target variable and, it will be used as the target variable while building the model. The target variable (y) is separate from the feature variable (x).

4. In the new overall dataframe, let's check if we have any missing values:

```
df.isna().sum()
```

Take a look at the following output:

```
CRIM 0
ZN 0
INDUS 0
CHAS 0
NOX 0
RM 0
AGE 0
DIS 0
RAD 0
TAX 0
PTRATIO 0
LSTAT 0
MEDV 0
dtype: int64
```

Particularly in the case of regression, it is important to make sure that our data does not have any missing values because regression won't work if the data has missing values.

Correlation analysis is a crucial part of building any model. We have to understand the distribution of the data and how the independent variables correlate with the dependent variable.

5. Let's plot a heatmap describing the correlation between the columns in the dataset:

```
#plotting heatmap for overall data set
sns.heatmap(df.corr(), square=True, cmap='RdYlGn')
```

The output plot looks like this:

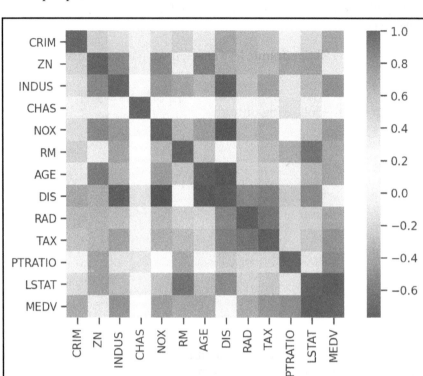

Figure 9.2: Correlation matrix generated from the preceding code snippet

Since we want to build a linear regression model, let's look for a few independent variables that have a significant correlation with MEDV. From the preceding heatmap, RM (the average number of rooms per dwelling) has a positive correlation with MEDV (the median value of owner-occupied homes in $1,000s), so we will take RM as a feature (X) and MEDV as a predictor (y) for our linear regression model.

6. We can use the lmplot method from seaborn to see the relationship between RM and MEDV. Check out the following snippet:

```
sns.lmplot(x = 'RM', y = 'MEDV', data = df)
```

The output of the preceding code is as follows:

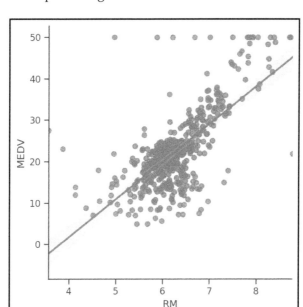

Figure 9.3: Lmplot illustrating the relationship between the RM and MEDV columns

The preceding screenshot shows a strong correlation between these two variables. However, there are some outliers that we can easily spot from the graph. Next, let's create grounds for model development.

Scikit-learn needs to create features and target variables in arrays, so be careful when assigning columns to X and y:

```
# Preparing the data
X = df[['RM']]
y = df[['MEDV']]
```

And now we need to split our data into train and test sets. Sklearn provides methods through which we can split our original dataset into train and test datasets. As we already know, the reason behind the regression model development is to get a formula for predicting output in the future. But how can we be sure about the accuracy of the model's prediction? A logical technique for measuring the model's accuracy is to divide the number of correct predictions, by the total number of observations for the test.

For this task, we must have a new dataset with already known output predictions. The most commonly used technique for this during model development is called the train/test split of the dataset. Here, you divide the dataset into a training dataset and a testing dataset. We train, or fit, the model to the training dataset and then compute the accuracy by making predictions on the test (labeled or predicted) dataset.

7. This is done using the `train_test_split()` function available in `sklearn.model_selection`:

```
# Splitting the dataset into train and test sets
from sklearn.model_selection import train_test_split
X_train, X_test, y_train, y_test = train_test_split(X, y, test_size
= 0.3, random_state = 10)
```

`X` is our independent variable here, and `Y` is our target (output) variable. In `train_test_split`, `test_size` indicates the size of the test dataset. `test_size` is the proportion of our data that is used for the test dataset. Here, we passed a value of `0.3` for `test_size`, which means that our data is now divided into 70% training data and 30% test data. Lastly, `random_state` sets the seed for the random number generator, which splits the data. The `train_test_split()` function will return four arrays: the training data, the testing data, the training outputs, and the testing outputs.

8. Now the final step is training the linear regression model. From the extremely powerful `sklearn` library, we import the `LinearRegression()` function to fit our training dataset to the model. When we run `LinearRegression().fit()`, the function automatically calculates the OLS, which we discussed earlier, and generates an appropriate line function:

```
#Training a Linear Regression Model
from sklearn.linear_model import LinearRegression
regressor = LinearRegression()

# Fitting the training data to our model
regressor.fit(X_train, y_train)
```

Now, we have a model called `regressor` that is fully trained on the training dataset. The next step is to evaluate how well the model predicts the target variable correctly.

Model evaluation

Our linear regression model has now been successfully trained. Remember that we separated some data from our dataset for testing, which we intend to use to find the accuracy of the model. We will be using that to assess the efficiency of our model. R^2-statistics is a common method of measuring the accuracy of regression models:

1. R^2 can be determined using our test dataset in the `LinearRegression.score()` method:

```
#check prediction score/accuracy
regressor.score(X_test, y_test)
```

The output of this `score()` function is as follows:

```
0.5383003344910231
```

The `score(y_test, y_pred)` method predicts the Y values for an input set, X, and compares them against the true Y values. The value of R^2 is generally between 0 and 1. The closer the value of R^2 to 1, the more accurate the model is. Here, the R^2 score is $0.53 \approx 53\%$ accuracy, which is okay. With more than one independent variable, we will improve the performance of our model, which we will be looking at next.

2. Before that, let's predict the *y* values with our model and evaluate it more. And a target variables `DataFrame` is also built:

```
# predict the y values
y_pred=regressor.predict(X_test)
# a data frame with actual and predicted values of y
evaluate = pd.DataFrame({'Actual': y_test.values.flatten(),
'Predicted': y_pred.flatten()})
evaluate.head(10)
```

The target variables `DataFrame` is as follows:

	Actual	Predicted
0	28.4	25.153909
1	31.1	26.773693
2	23.5	22.284072
3	26.6	27.997335
4	19.6	14.484456
5	14.3	23.569336
6	50.0	32.839084
7	14.3	16.535597
8	20.7	19.026896
9	37.6	37.689635

Figure 9.4: The first 10 entries showing the actual values and the predicted values

The preceding screenshot shows the difference between the actual values and the predicted values. We can see them if we plot them:

```
evaluate.head(10).plot(kind = 'bar')
```

The output of the preceding code is as follows:

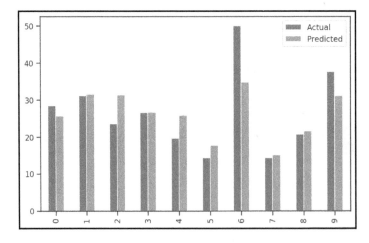

Figure 9.5: Stacked bar plot showing the actual values and the predicted values

Much easier to understand, right? Note that most of the predicted values are lower than the actual values.

Computing accuracy

Sklearn provides metrics that help us evaluate our models with multiple formulas. The three main metrics used to evaluate models are mean absolute error, mean squared error, and R^2 score.

Let's quickly try these methods:

```
# Scoring the model
from sklearn.metrics import r2_score,
mean_squared_error,mean_absolute_error

# R2 Score
print(f"R2 score: {r2_score(y_test, y_pred)}")

# Mean Absolute Error (MAE)
print(f"MSE score: {mean_absolute_error(y_test, y_pred)}")

# Mean Squared Error (MSE)
print(f"MSE score: {mean_squared_error(y_test, y_pred)}")
```

The output of the preceding code is as follows:

```
R2 score: 0.5383003344910231
MSE score: 4.750294229575126
MSE score: 45.0773394247183
```

Note that we are not evaluating the accuracies we got in the preceding output. In any machine learning scenario, we try to improve accuracy by performing several optimization techniques.

Understanding accuracy

We have used the scikit-learn library to train a regression model. In addition to that, we have used the trained model to predict some data, and then we computed the accuracy. For example, examine *Figure 9.5*. The first entry says the actual value is 28.4 but our trained regression model predicted it to be 25.153909. Hence, we have a discrepancy of 28.4 - 25.153909 = 3.246091. Let's try to understand how these discrepancies are understood. Let x_i be the actual value and $\hat{x}_i$ be the value predicted by the model for any sample i.

The error is given by the following formula:

$$\epsilon_i = x_i - \hat{x}_i$$

For any sample `i`, we can get the difference between the prediction and the actual value. We could compute the mean error by just summing the errors, but since some errors are negative and some are positive it is likely that they will cancel each other out. Then, the question remains, how can we know how accurately our trained model performed on all the datasets? This is where we use the concept of squared error. You should know that the square of positive and negative numbers is always positive. Hence, they have no chance to cancel each other out. So, we can represent the squared error with the following equation:

$$\text{Squared Error (SE)} = \sum_i^n \epsilon_i^2$$

Once we know how to compute the squared error, we can compute the mean squared error. That would be easy, right? Of course, so to compute the mean squared error, we can use the following formula:

$$\text{Mean Squared Error (MSE)} = \frac{1}{n} \times SE$$

Now, if we take the root of the mean squared error, we get another accuracy measure called the **root mean squared error** (**RMSE**). The equation now becomes this:

$$\text{Root Mean Squared Error (RMSE)} = \sqrt{MSE}$$

Another type of accuracy measure that is widely used is called the **relative mean squared error** (**rMSE**). Don't get it confused with RMSE. The formula for computing rMSE is as follows:

$$rMSE = \frac{n-1}{n} \frac{\sum_i^n \epsilon_i^2}{\sum_i^n (x_i - E(x)^2)} = \frac{MSE}{Var(x)}$$

In the preceding equation, *E(x)* is referred to as the expected value of x. In addition to rMSE, we have used the R^2 method. The formula for computing R^2 is as follows:

$$R^2 = 1 - rMSE$$

One more type of accuracy measure that is often seen in data science is the absolute error. As the name suggests, it takes the absolute value and computes the sum. The formula for measuring absolute error is as follows:

$$\text{Absolute error (AE)} = \sum_i^n \sqrt{\epsilon_i^2} = \sum_i^n |\epsilon_i|$$

Finally, one more type of error that can be used in addition to absolute error is the mean absolute error. The formula for computing mean absolute error is as follows:

$$\text{Mean Absolute Error(MAE)} = \frac{1}{n} \times AE$$

Was that too many? It was. However, if you check the equations closely, you will see that they are very closely related. Try to focus on the name, which explains what the accuracy measure does. Now, whenever you see any data science model using these accuracy measures, it will make much more sense, won't it?

Congratulations on learning about accuracy measures. In the next section, let's dig more into multiple linear regression, and we will try to use these accuracy measures.

Implementing a multiple linear regression model

When a dependent variable relies on several independent variables, the relationship can be captured using multiple linear regression. Multiple linear regression can be viewed as an extension of simple linear regression. When it comes to implementing multiple linear regression using sklearn, there is not much difference between simple and multiple linear regression:

1. Simply include the extra columns in the X variable and run the code. So, let's include the additional columns for the X variable and follow the same code.

2. Remember, a two-dimensional linear regression model is a straight line; it is a plane in three dimensions, and a hyperplane in over three dimensions:

```
# Preparing the data
X = df[['LSTAT','CRIM','NOX','TAX','PTRATIO','CHAS','DIS']]
y = df[['MEDV']]

# Splitting the dataset into train and test sets
from sklearn.model_selection import train_test_split
X_train, X_test, y_train, y_test = train_test_split(X, y, test_size
= 0.3, random_state = 10)
```

```
# Fitting the training data to our model
regressor.fit(X_train, y_train)

#score of this model
regressor.score(X_test, y_test)
```

The output of this `score()` function is as follows:

```
0.6446942534265363
```

3. Let's predict the y values with our model and evaluate it:

```
# predict the y values
y_pred=regressor.predict(X_test)
# a data frame with actual and predicted values of y
evaluate = pd.DataFrame({'Actual': y_test.values.flatten(),
'Predicted': y_pred.flatten()})
evaluate.head(10)
```

The target variables `DataFrame` is as follows:

	Actual	Predicted
0	28.4	27.445779
1	31.1	31.364849
2	23.5	30.681874
3	26.6	22.143726
4	19.6	23.063037
5	14.3	16.421246
6	50.0	36.733894
7	14.3	15.887917
8	20.7	25.718492
9	37.6	32.816198

Figure 9.6: The first 10 entries showing the actual values and the predicted values

4. Let's make another multiple linear regression model with fewer features:

```
# Preparing the data
X = df[['LSTAT','CRIM','NOX','TAX','PTRATIO']]
y = df[['MEDV']]

# Splitting the dataset into train and test sets
from sklearn.model_selection import train_test_split
X_train, X_test, y_train, y_test = train_test_split(X, y, test_size
= 0.3, random_state = 10)

# Fitting the training data to our model
regressor.fit(X_train, y_train)

#score of this model
regressor.score(X_test, y_test)
```

The output of this `score()` function is as follows:

```
0.5798770784084717
```

The accuracy of this model is 57%. The table below shows the actual and predicted value for the target variable MEDV for this built model is as follows:

	Actual	Predicted
0	28.4	25.512908
1	31.1	31.496427
2	23.5	31.260496
3	26.6	26.553401
4	19.6	25.826407
5	14.3	17.589252
6	50.0	34.913399
7	14.3	15.165121
8	20.7	21.605243
9	37.6	31.078599

Figure 9.7: The first 10 entries showing the actual values and the predicted values

As you can see, changing the features in X will make a change in the accuracy of the model. So you must analyze the correlation among the features carefully and then use them to build the model with greater accuracy.

Summary

In this chapter, we discussed two important concepts: hypothesis testing and regression analysis. In hypothesis testing, we learned about the hypothesis, its basic principles, and different types of hypothesis testing, and we used two different Python libraries (statsmodels and SciPy) to create different hypothesis tests. Moreover, we discussed p-hacking, which is one of the most commonly encountered challenges during hypothetical testing. Next, we discussed different types of regression, and we used scikit-learn to build, test, and evaluate some regression models.

In the next chapter, we are going to discuss model development and evaluation in more detail. We will be discussing several other types of models that we can use besides regression.

Further reading

- Regression Analysis with Python, by *Luca Massaron, Alberto Boschetti, Packt Publishing*, February 29, 2016
- *Statistics for Machine Learning*, by *Pratap Dangeti, Packt Publishing*, July 20, 2017
- *Statistics for Data Science*, by *James D. Miller, Packt Publishing*, November 17, 2017
- *Data Science Algorithms in a Week - Second Edition*, by *Dávid Natingga, Packt Publishing*, October 31, 2018
- *Machine Learning with scikit-learn Quick Start Guide*, by *Kevin Jolly, Packt Publishing*, October 30, 2018

10
Model Development and Evaluation

We have discussed several **Exploratory Data Analysis** (**EDA**) techniques so far. The reason we performed EDA was to prepare our dataset and make sense of it so that it can be used for predictive and analytical purposes. By predictive and analytical, we mean to create and evaluate **Machine Learning** (**ML**) models. In this chapter, we are going to lay the groundwork for data science, understand different types of models that can be built, and how can they be evaluated.

In this chapter, we will cover the following topics:

- Types of machine learning
- Understanding supervised learning
- Understanding unsupervised learning
- Understanding reinforcement learning
- Unified machine learning workflow

Technical requirements

In this chapter, we are going to use a few clustering algorithms. The dataset we'll be using in this chapter can be found at `https://github.com/sureshHARDIYA/phd-resources/blob/master/Data/Review%20Paper/acm/preprocessed.xlsx?raw=true`.

We are also going to use some modules from the scikit-learn library, including `MiniBatchKMeans`, `TfidfVectorizer`, `PCA`, and `TSNE`.

Types of machine learning

Machine learning (ML) is a field of computer science that deals with the creation of algorithms that can discover patterns by themselves without being explicitly programmed. There are different types of ML algorithms, and these are categorized into three different categories, as shown in the following diagram:

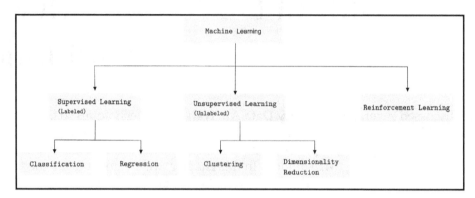

As shown in the preceding diagram, there are three different categories of ML algorithms:

- Supervised learning
- Unsupervised learning
- Reinforcement learning

We will discuss each of these algorithms in brief in the following sections.

Understanding supervised learning

The primary objective of supervised learning is to generalize a model from **labeled training data.** Once a model has been trained, it allows users to make predictions about unseen future data. Here, by **labeled training data**, we mean the training examples know the associated output labels. Hence, it is referred to as supervised learning. The learning process can be thought of as a teacher supervising the entire process. In such a learning process, we know the correct answer initially, and the students learn enough iteratively over time and try to answer unseen questions. The errors in the answers are corrected by the teacher. The process of learning stops when we can ensure the performance of the student has reached an acceptable level.

In supervised learning, we have input variables (x_i) and output variables (Y_i). With this, we can learn a function, f, as shown by the following equation:

$$Y_i = f(x_i)$$

The objective is to learn a general mapping function, f, so that the function can predict the output variable, Y, for any new input data, x. Supervised learning algorithms can be categorized into two groups, as follows:

- Regression
- Classification

Let's take a brief look at these.

Regression

A regression problem has an output variable or dependent variable. This is a real value, such as weight, age, or any other real numbers. We discussed regression in detail in Chapter 9, *Hypothesis Testing and Regression*, including the different types of regression (simple linear regression, multiple linear regression, and non-linear regression), and used the Boston Housing dataset to perform regression analysis.

Since we discussed regression problems in Chapter 9, *Hypothesis Testing and Regression*, we are going to move on and learn more about the classification problem.

Classification

A classification problem has the output variable in the form of a category value; for example, **red** or **white wines; young, adult, or old**. For classification problems, there are different types of classification algorithms.

Some of the most popular ones are as follows:

- Linear classifier: Naive Bayes classifier, logistic regression, linear SVM
- Nearest neighbor
- Decision tree classifier

- Support vector machines
- Random Forest classifier
- Neural network classifiers
- Boosted trees classifier

Having listed the most popular classification algorithms, we must point out that going through each of these classifications algorithms is beyond the scope of this book. However, our main intention here is to point you in the right direction. We suggest that you check out the *Further reading* sections of this book for more details regarding the respective topics.

A proof of concept regarding how these classifiers can be implemented in Python with the Red and White wine dataset can be found in `Chapter 11`, *EDA on Wine Quality Data Analysis*. We will discuss different evaluation techniques that can be used for classification purposes in that chapter too.

Understanding unsupervised learning

Unsupervised machine learning deals with unlabeled data. This type of learning can discover all kinds of unknown patterns in the data and can facilitate useful categorization. Consider a scenario where patients use an online web application to learn about a disease, learn about their symptoms, and manage their illness. Such web applications that provide psychoeducation about certain diseases are referred to as **Internet-Delivered Treatments (IDT)**. Imagine several thousand patients accessing the website at different timestamps of the day, learning about their illness, and all their activities are being logged into our database. When we analyze these log files and plot them using a scatter plot, we find a large group of patients who are accessing the website in the afternoon and a large chunk accessing the website in the evening. Some other patients also follow random login patterns. This scenario illustrates two distinct clusters of patients: one active in the afternoon and one active in the evening. This typical scenario is an example of a clustering task.

There are several types of unsupervised learning algorithms that we can use. However, two major unsupervised learning tasks are **clustering** and **dimensionality reductions**. In the next section, we will discuss more regarding the different applications of unsupervised learning algorithms.

Applications of unsupervised learning

There are several applications of unsupervised learning algorithms. Let's take a look at a few here:

- **Clustering**: These types of algorithms allow us to categorize the dataset into several similar groups, referred to as a cluster. Each cluster represents a group of similar points.
- **Association mining**: These types of unsupervised learning algorithms allow us to find frequently occurring items in our dataset.
- **Anomaly detection**: These types of unsupervised learning algorithms help us to determine unusual data points in any existing dataset.
- **Dimensionality reduction**: These techniques are commonly used in data processing in order to reduce the number of features in a dataset. This is one of the most important tasks to perform in unsupervised learning.

Clustering using MiniBatch K-means clustering

In this section, we are going to use one of the unsupervised learning algorithms, that is, clustering. To be specific, we are going to cluster texts based on an algorithm named MiniBatch K-means clustering algorithm. Let's get some context regarding this.

Whenever a researcher starts working on any particular domain, they perform various literature reviews to comprehend the state of the art in any particular domain. Such a study is referred to as a review paper. When writing such review papers, you set up a set of search keywords and execute the search in many research paper indexing databases, such as scholar.google.com (https://scholar.google.com/). After performing the search in several databases, you will have a list of relevant articles that you want to study. In this case, we have performed the search and the lists of relevant articles have been provided in the form of an Excel sheet. Note that each row in the Excel file contains some metadata about the related paper.

You can find out more about the MiniBatch K-means clustering algorithm by looking at the official documentation of the sklearn library: https://scikit-learn.org/stable/modules/generated/sklearn.cluster.MiniBatchKMeans.html.

Having understood the context, let's load the dataset into our notebook. This should be no mystery to us by now:

1. Let's load the Excel file:

```
import pandas as pd
import numpy as np
import matplotlib.pyplot as plt
import matplotlib.cm as cm
import seaborn as sns

sns.set()
plt.rcParams['figure.figsize'] = (14, 7)

df =
pd.read_excel("https://github.com/sureshHARDIYA/phd-resources/blob/
master/Data/Review%20Paper/acm/preprocessed.xlsx?raw=true")
```

2. Next, let's check the first 10 entries to understand what the data looks like:

```
df.head(10)
```

The output of the preceding code is as follows:

	Unnamed: 0	Abstract	Author	Doi	Journal	Title	Year
0	786	NaN	Rachel D. Williams	NaN	American Society for Information Science	"we're not allowed": public librarians' perspe...	2016
1	885	NaN	Ghassan F. Bati	NaN	Association for Computing Machinery	"trust us": mobile phone use patterns can pred...	2018
2	1083	NaN	Alex Leavitt	NaN	Association for Computing Machinery	"this is a throwaway account": temporary techn...	2015
3	1004	NaN	Yngve Dahl	NaN	Association for Computing Machinery	"there are no secrets here!": professional sta...	2012
4	899	NaN	Max Van Kleek	NaN	Association for Computing Machinery	"the crowd keeps me in shape": social psycholo...	2013
5	1282	NaN	Tawfiq Ammari	NaN	Association for Computing Machinery	"thanks for your interest in our facebook grou...	2016
6	434	NaN	Kathleen O'Leary	NaN	Association for Computing Machinery	"suddenly, we got to become therapists for eac...	2018
7	1168	NaN	Cara Wilson	NaN	Association for Computing Machinery	"put yourself in the picture": designing for f...	2016
8	1238	NaN	Sarah Martindale	NaN	Association for Computing Machinery	"proof in the pudding": designing iot plants t...	2017
9	1272	NaN	Margaret C. Jack	NaN	Association for Computing Machinery	"privacy is not a concept, but a way of dealin...	2019

As we can see, there are several columns. We are only interested in the title of the research paper. Therefore, we'll only focus on the Title column.

Extracting keywords

The next step is to extract the keywords from the title. There are several ways we can extract keywords. Here, we are going to use the `TfidfVectorizer` utility method provided by the `sklearn.feature_extraction` module. Let's get started:

1. To use the library, we need to import the essential libraries:

```
from sklearn.feature_extraction.text import TfidfVectorizer
from sklearn.cluster import MiniBatchKMeans
from sklearn.decomposition import PCA
from sklearn.manifold import TSNE
```

2. Next, let's learn how to extract the keywords:

```
tfidf = TfidfVectorizer(
    min_df = 5,
    max_df = 0.95,
    max_features = 8000,
    stop_words = 'english'
)
tfidf.fit(df.Title)
text = tfidf.transform(df.Title)
```

 You can find out more about TfidfVectorizer by reading the official documentation: `https://scikit-learn.org/stable/modules/generated/sklearn.feature_extraction.text.TfidfVectorizer.html`.

In the preceding code, we are converting the title into TF-IDF features. We are removing the stop words from the title.

 You can read more about stop words at `https://nlp.stanford.edu/IR-book/html/htmledition/dropping-common-terms-stop-words-1.html`.

If you understood the concept of clustering, you probably already understand one of the biggest challenges surrounding the clustering; that is, determining how many clusters there are is optimal. There are some algorithms that can help us in determining the best number of clusters. One such algorithm is the elbow method (`https://www.scikit yb.org/en/latest/api/cluster/elbow.html`).

Let's create a function that takes the text and the maximum number of clusters and plot them on a graph. The code for doing so is as follows:

```
def generate_optimal_clusters(data, max_k):
    iters = range(2, max_k+1, 2)
    sse = []
    for k in iters:
        sse.append(MiniBatchKMeans(n_clusters=k, init_size=1024,
batch_size=2048, random_state=20).fit(data).inertia_)
        print('Fitting {} clusters'.format(k))
    f, ax = plt.subplots(1, 1)
    ax.plot(iters, sse, marker='o')
    ax.set_xlabel('Cluster Centers')
    ax.set_xticks(iters)
    ax.set_xticklabels(iters)
    ax.set_ylabel('SSE')
    ax.set_title('SSE by Cluster Center Plot')
generate_optimal_clusters(text, 20)
```

Note the following points regarding the preceding function:

- It takes two arguments, the text and the maximum number of clusters. In this case, we assume that the maximum number of clusters is 20.
- Next, inside the function, we call the `fit()` method on the `MiniBatchKMeans` cluster for a range from 2, to the maximum number of clusters allowed (2 to 20).
- For each cluster, we calculate the **sum of squared error** (**SSE**) plot on the graph.

The output of the preceding code is as follows:

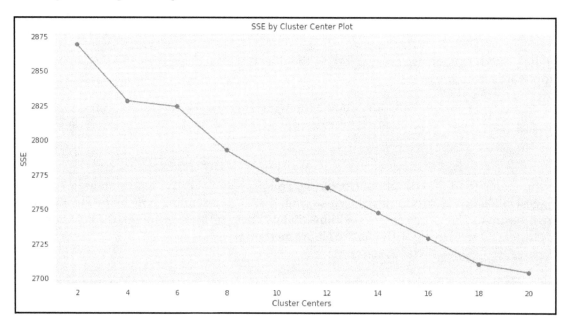

As shown in the preceding plot, the elbow changes at 4. According to the elbow theory, the plot creates an elbow at the optimal cluster number. Hence, the best cluster, in this case, is 4.

Plotting clusters

Now, let's plot the clusters on the graph. We will start plotting using **Principal Component Analysis** (**PCA**) since it is good at capturing the global structure of the data. Then, we will use **t-Distributed Stochastic Neighbor Embedding** (**TSNE**) to plot the graph as it is good at capturing the relationship with the neighbors. Let's get started:

1. Let's start by creating the model again:

```
clusters = MiniBatchKMeans(n_clusters=4, init_size=1024,
batch_size=2048, random_state=20).fit_predict(text)
```

2. Let's plot both graphs. First, we will plot using the PCA technique and then using the TSNE technique. Use the following code to do so:

```
max_label = max(clusters)
max_items = np.random.choice(range(text.shape[0]), size=3000,
replace=True)
pca =
PCA(n_components=2).fit_transform(text[max_items,:].todense())
tsne =
TSNE().fit_transform(PCA(n_components=50).fit_transform(text[max_it
ems,:].todense()))

idx = np.random.choice(range(pca.shape[0]), size=300, replace=True)
label_subset = clusters[max_items]
label_subset = [cm.hsv(i/max_label) for i in label_subset[idx]]

f, ax = plt.subplots(1, 2, figsize=(14, 6))
ax[0].scatter(pca[idx, 0], pca[idx, 1], c=label_subset)
ax[0].set_title('Generated PCA Cluster Plot')

ax[1].scatter(tsne[idx, 0], tsne[idx, 1], c=label_subset)
ax[1].set_title('Generated TSNE Cluster Plot')
```

The output of the preceding code is as follows:

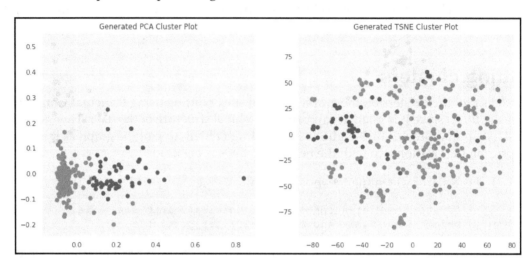

Each color represents one kind of cluster. In the preceding code, we sampled down the features to capture just 3,000 documents for faster processing and plotted them using a scatter plot. For PCA, we reduced the dimensions to 50.

 You can learn more about TSNE from the official website: `https://scikit-learn.org/stable/modules/generated/sklearn.manifold.TSNE.html`.

Note that it is very difficult to find out which keywords were found in each type of cluster. To visualize this better, we need to plot the word cloud from each cluster.

Word cloud

In order to see the top few keywords that belong to each cluster, we need to create a function that provides us with the top 50 words from each of the clusters and plot the word cloud.

Check the function, as follows:

```
from wordcloud import WordCloud

fig, ax = plt.subplots(4, sharex=True, figsize=(15,10*4))

plt.rcParams["axes.grid"] = False
```

```
def high_frequency_keywords(data, clusters, labels, n_terms):
    df = pd.DataFrame(data.todense()).groupby(clusters).mean()
    for i,r in df.iterrows():
        words = ','.join([labels[t] for t in np.argsort(r)[-n_terms:]])
        print('Cluster {} \n'.format(i))
        print(words)
        wordcloud = WordCloud(max_font_size=40, collocations=False, colormap
= 'Reds', background_color = 'white').generate(words)
        ax[i].imshow(wordcloud, interpolation='bilinear')
        ax[i].set_title('Cluster {} '.format(i), fontsize = 20)
        ax[i].axis('off')
high_frequency_keywords(text, clusters, tfidf.get_feature_names(), 50)
```

The output of the preceding code is split into two. Let's take a look at the text output:

```
Cluster 0
bipolar,patient,framework,evaluation,risk,older,internet,healthcare,activit
y,approach,online,anxiety,research,digital,children,assessment,clinical,dem
entia,adaptive,cognitive,intervention,disorders,technology,learning,psychia
tric,community,interventions,management,therapy,review,adults,use,support,d
esigning,schizophrenia,stress,data,people,analysis,care,self,mobile,disorde
r,using,patients,design,study,treatment,based,depression

Cluster 1
cessation,brief,comparing,single,disorder,people,adults,symptoms,risk,clini
cal,women,prevention,reduce,improve,training,use,results,online,personalize
d,internet,cluster,alcohol,anxiety,feedback,efficacy,patients,health,mental
,therapy,primary,help,self,program,care,effects,cognitive,pilot,treatment,d
epression,tailored,effectiveness,web,based,randomised,study,intervention,pr
otocol,randomized,controlled,trial

Cluster 2
qualitative,physical,digital,implementation,self,medical,management,patient
,adults,designing,life,quality,work,development,systems,data,related,childr
en,persons,support,online,analysis,assessment,information,intervention,vete
rans,service,design,patients,problems,behavioral,using,research,systematic,
disorders,use,interventions,primary,treatment,based,study,services,review,s
evere,people,community,illness,care,mental,health

Cluster 3
modeling,implications,ethical,emotion,behavioral,dementia,based,young,desig
ning,homeless,dynamics,group,experiences,robot,predicting,mobile,game,depre
ssion,understanding,physical,people,challenges,therapy,study,patients,manag
ement,technology,impact,technologies,self,anxiety,use,skills,interaction,ne
tworking,personal,disclosure,sites,data,networks,disclosures,using,design,o
nline,network,support,mental,health,media,social
```

Note that it printed four different clusters and 50 frequently occurring words in each cluster. It is easy to see the keywords that belong to each of the clusters and decide if clustering was done correctly or not. To present these words correctly, we generated a word cloud.

The word cloud is as follows:

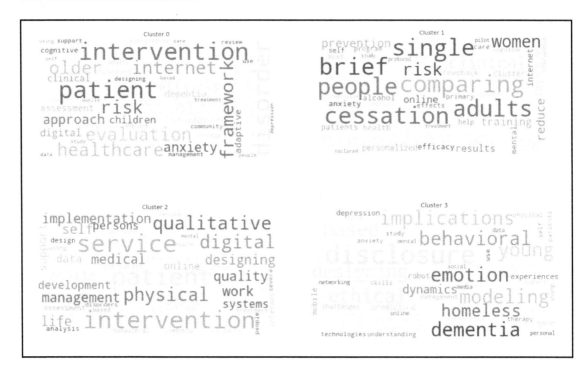

As we can see, there are four clusters. Each cluster shows the most related word. For example, cluster 0 shows a lot of words related to healthcare, intervention, framework, digital health, and so on. By doing this, it is easier to see the relationship between the keywords.

In the next section, we are going to discuss reinforcement learning.

Understanding reinforcement learning

In reinforcement learning, an agent changes its states to maximize its goals. There are four distinct concepts here: agent, state, action, and reward. Let's take a look at these in more detail:

- **Agent:** This is the program we train. It chooses actions over time from its action space within the environment for a specified task.
- **State:** This is the observation that's received by the agent from its environment and represents the agent's current situation.
- **Action:** This is a choice that's made by an agent from its action space. The action changes the state of the agent.
- **Reward**: This is the resultant feedback regarding the agent's action and describes how the agent ought to behave.

Each of these concepts has been illustrated in the following diagram:

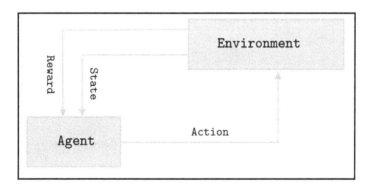

As shown in the preceding diagram, reinforcement learning involves an agent, an environment, a set of actions, a set of states, and a reward system. The agent interacts with the environment and modifies its state. Based on this modification, it gets rewards or penalties for its input. The goal of the agent is to maximize the reward over time.

Difference between supervised and reinforcement learning

A supervised learning algorithm is used when we have a labeled training dataset. Reinforcement learning is used in a scenario where an agent interacts with an environment to observe a basic behavior and change its state to maximize its rewards or goal.

Other differences between them have been given in the following table:

Criteria	Supervised Learning	Reinforcement Learning
Example	Digit recognition.	Chess game.
Works on	Given labeled dataset.	Interacting with the given environment.
Decision	A decision is made on the input given at the beginning.	Here, the algorithm helps make a decision linearly.

One of the essential features of RL is that the agent's action may not affect the immediate state of the environment that it is working in, but it can affect the subsequent states. Hence, the algorithm might not learn in the initial state but can learn after a few states are changed.

Applications of reinforcement learning

There are several use cases of RL algorithms.

Some of the most essential use cases are as follows:

- **Text mining:** Several researchers and companies have started to use the RL-based text generation model to produce highly readable text summaries from long text.
- **Robotics**: Several deep RL-based algorithms are used in the field of robotics engineering to enhance the performance of robotics based on the reward system.
- **Healthcare**: Several studies show that RL can be used in healthcare to optimize medication dosage and treatment policies.
- **Trading**: Several RL-based models are used in trading businesses to optimize trading outcomes.

Unified machine learning workflow

The choice of what machine learning algorithm to use always depends on the type of data you have. If you have a labeled dataset, then your obvious choice will be to select one of the supervised machine learning techniques. Moreover, if your labeled dataset contains real values in the target variable, then you will opt for regression algorithms. Finally, if your labeled dataset contains a categorical variable in the target variable, then you will opt for the classification algorithm. In any case, the algorithm you choose always depends on the type of dataset you have.

In a similar fashion, if your dataset does not contain any target variables, then the obvious choice is unsupervised algorithms. In this section, we are going to look at the unified approach to machine learning.

The machine learning workflow can be divided into several stages:

- Data preprocessing
- Data preparation
- Training sets and corpus creation
- Model creation and training
- Model evaluation
- Best model selection and evaluation
- Model deployment

The entire workflow of the machine learning algorithm can be seen in the following diagram:

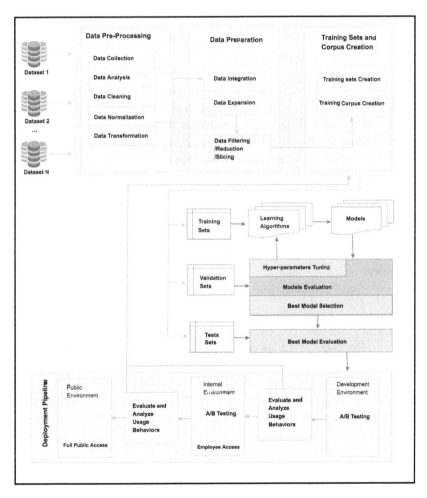

As depicted in the preceding diagram, the first step in any machine learning workflow is data preprocessing. We'll briefly explain each stage in the following sections.

Data preprocessing

Data preprocessing involves several steps, including data collection, data analysis, data cleaning, data normalization, and data transformation. The first step in data preprocessing is data collection. Let's take a look.

Data collection

In **data science**, the most important thing is data. The data holds the ground truth about any events, phenomena, or experiments that are going on around us. Once we've processed the data, we get information. Once we've processed this information, we can derive knowledge from it. Hence, the most prominent stage in knowledge extraction is how relevant the data that's being captured is. There are different types of data, including **structured data**, **unstructured data**, and **semi-structured data**. Structured data maintains a uniform structure in all the observations, similar to relational database tables. Unstructured data does not maintain any particular structure. Semi-structured data maintains some structure in the observation. **JavaScript Object Notation (JSON)** is one of the most popular ways to store semi-structured data.

The process of collecting data in any company depends on the kind of project and the type of information that needs to be studied. The different types of datasets range from text data, file, database, sensors data, and many other **Internet of Things (IoT)** data. However, when learning about a machine learning workflow, most students prefer to avoid the data collection phase and use open source data from places such as Kaggle and the UCI Machine Learning Repository.

Data analysis

This is one of the preliminary analysis phases where we perform exploratory data analysis to understand the dataset. We discussed several techniques that we can perform to do this in Chapter 3, *EDA with Personal Email Analysis*. This step tells us about the type of data we have at hand, the target variable, how many rows and columns we have in the data, the data types of each column, how many missing rows we have, what the data distribution looks like, and so on.

Data cleaning, normalization, and transformation

We discussed data cleaning, normalization, and data transformation in detail in Chapter 4, *Data Transformation*. We discussed how we can rescale the dataset, how we can convert the dataset into a standard dataset, how we can binarize data, and how we can perform one-hot encoding and label encoding.

After all these three steps, our missing data will have been taken care of in terms of noisy data being filtered and inconsistent data being removed.

Data preparation

Sometimes, the dataset we have is not always in the right shape for it to be consumed by machine learning algorithms. In such conditions, data preparation is one of the most essential things we can do. We need to integrate data from several sources, perform slicing and grouping, and aggregate them into the correct format and structure. This step is referred to as data preparation.

We discussed this process in detail in Chapter 6, *Grouping Datasets*. It is essential to note that some books consider data preprocessing and data preparation as the same step as there are several overlapping operations.

Training sets and corpus creation

After the data preparation step, the resulting dataset is used as a training corpus. Generally, the training corpus is split into three chunks: a training set, a validation set, and a testing set.

The **training set** is the chunk of data that you use to train one or more machine learning algorithms. The **validation set** is the chunk of data that you use to validate the trained model. Finally, the **testing set** is the chunk of data that you use to assess the performance of a fully trained classifier.

Model creation and training

Once we have split the dataset into three chunks, we can start the training process. We use the training set to construct the machine learning model. Then, we use the validation set to validate the model. Once the model has been trained, we use the test set to find the final performance of the model.

Model evaluation

Based on the performance of the test data, we can create a **confusion matrix**. This matrix contains four different parameters: true positive, true negative, false positive, and false negative. Consider the following confusion matrix:

	Predicted: Positive	Predicted: Negative
Actual: Positive	True Positive (TP)	False Negative (FN)
Actual: Negative	False Positive (FP)	True Negative (TN)

This matrix shows four distinct parameters:

- **True positives**: The model predicts TRUE when the actual value is TRUE.
- **True negatives**: The model predicts FALSE when the actual value is FALSE.
- **False-positives**: The model predicts TRUE when the actual value is FALSE. This is also referred to as a Type I Error.
- **False-negatives**: The model predicts FALSE when the actual value is TRUE. This is also referred to as a Type II Error.

Once we know about the confusion matrix, we can compute several accuracies of the model, including precision, negative predicate value, sensitivity, specificity, and accuracy. Let's take a look at each of them, one by one, and learn how they can be computed.

The **precision** is the ratio of true positive and the sum of a true positive and false positive. The formula is as follows:

$$precision = \frac{TP}{(TP + FP)}$$

The formula for the **Negative Predictive Value (NPV)** is as follows:

$$NAV = \frac{TN}{(TN + FN)}$$

Similarity, the formula for **sensitivity** is as follows:

$$sensitivity = \frac{TP}{(TP + FN)}$$

The formula for specificity is as follows:

$$specificity = \frac{TN}{(TN + FP)}$$

Finally, the accuracy of the model is given by the formula as:

$$accuracy = \frac{TP + TN}{(TP + TN + FP + FN)}$$

Let's take a look at an example. Consider we built a supervised classification algorithm that looks at the picture of a window and classifies it as dirty or not dirty. The final confusion matrix is as follows:

	Predicted: Dirty	Predicted: Not dirty
Actual: Dirty	TP = 90	FN = 40
Actual: Not dirty	FP = 10	TN = 60

Now, let's compute the accuracy measures for this case:

- Precision = TP / (TP + FP) = 90 /(90 + 10) = 90%. This means 90% of the pictures that were classified as dirty were actually dirty.
- Sensitivity = TP / (TP + FN) = 90/(90 + 40) = 69.23%. This means 69.23% of the dirty windows were correctly classified and excluded from all non-dirty windows.
- Specificity = TN / (TN + FP) = 60 / (10 + 60) = 85.71%. This means that 85.71% of the non-dirty windows were accurately classified and excluded from the dirty windows.
- Accuracy = (TP + TN)/(TP + TN + FP + FN) = 75%. This means 75% of the samples were correctly classified.

Another commonly used accuracy model that you will encounter is the **F1 Score**. It is given by the following equation:

$$\text{F1 Score} = 2 \times \frac{precision \times recall}{precision + recall}$$

As we can see, the F1 score is a weighted average of the recall and precision. There are too many accuracy measures, right? This can be intimidating at the beginning, but you will get used to it over time.

Best model selection and evaluation

Model selection is an essential step in the machine learning algorithm workflow. However, model selection carries different meanings in different contexts:

- **Context 1**: In the machine learning workflow context, **model selection is the process of selecting the best machine learning algorithms**, such as logistic regression, SVM, decision tree, Random Forest classifier, and so on.
- **Context 2**: Similarly, the model selection phase also refers to the process of choosing between different **hyperparameters** for any selected machine learning algorithm.

In general, model selection is the method of choosing one best machine learning algorithm from a list of possible candidate algorithms for a given training dataset. There are different model selection techniques. In a normal scenario, we split the training corpus into a training set, a validation set, and a testing set. Then, we fit several candidate models on the training set, evaluate the models using the validation set, and report the performance of the model on the testing set. However, this scenario of model selection only works when we have a sufficiently large training corpus.

However, in many cases, the amount of data for training and testing is limited. In such a case, the model selection becomes difficult. In such a case, we can use two different techniques: **probabilistic measure** and **resampling method**. We suggest that you go through the *Further reading* section of this chapter if you wish to understand these model selection techniques.

Model deployment

Once you've got the best model based on your dataset and the model has been fully trained, it is time to deploy it. Showing how a model can be fully deployed into a working environment is beyond the scope of this book. You can find sufficient resources that will point you in the right direction in the *Further reading* section.

The main idea regarding model deployment is to use the trained model in a real working environment. Once deployed, it should go through A/B user testing so that you know how it will work in a real scenario. Once it has been fully tested, the API can be made available to the public.

Summary

In this chapter, we laid some of the groundwork for data science, understood different types of models that can be built, and how they can be evaluated. First, we discussed several supervised learning algorithms, including regression and classification. Then, we discussed the unsupervised learning algorithm, including clustering and using text data to cluster them into different clusters using the MiniBatchKMeans algorithm. Finally, we briefly discussed reinforcement learning.

In the next chapter, we are going to use all the techniques we have learned so far to perform EDA on the Wine Quality dataset. Moreover, we will be using supervised learning algorithms to classify wine quality.

Further reading

- *Supervised Machine Learning with Python, Taylor Smith, Packt Publishing*
- *Large Scale Machine Learning with Python, Bastiaan Sjardin, Luca Massaron, Et al., Packt Publishing*
- *Advanced Machine Learning with Python, John Hearty, Packt Publishing*
- *Hands-On Unsupervised Learning with Python, Giuseppe Bonaccorso, Packt Publishing*
- *Mastering Machine Learning for Penetration Testing, Chiheb Chebbi, Packt Publishing*
- *Hands-On Data Science and Python Machine Learning, Frank Kane, Packt Publishing*
- *Building Machine Learning Systems with Python - Third Edition, Luis Pedro Coelho, Willi Richert, Et al., Packt Publishing*

EDA on Wine Quality Data Analysis

11

We have discussed a plethora of tools and techniques regarding **Exploratory Data Analysis (EDA)** so far, including how we can import datasets from different sources and how to remove outliers from the dataset, perform data analysis on the dataset, and generate illustrative visualization from such a dataset. In addition to this, we have discussed how we can apply advanced data analysis such as the correlation between variables, regression analysis, and time series analysis, and build advanced models based on such datasets. In this chapter, we are going to apply all of these techniques to the Wine Quality dataset.

The main topics discussed in this chapter include the following:

- Disclosing the wine quality dataset
- Analyzing red wine
- Analyzing white wine
- Model development and evaluation
- Further reading

Technical requirements

The entire code base for this chapter can be found in the GitHub repository shared with this book inside the CH012 folder. The dataset used in this chapter can be downloaded from the UCI website (https://archive.ics.uci.edu/ml/datasets/wine+quality), which is open source for end users.

We assume that you have been following the previous chapters and have ample knowledge about the required Python libraries.

Disclosing the wine quality dataset

The Wine Quality dataset contains information about various physicochemical properties of wines. The entire dataset is grouped into two categories: red wine and white wine. Each wine has a quality label associated with it. The label is in the range of 0 to 10. In the next section, we are going to download and load the dataset into Python and perform an initial analysis to disclose what is inside it.

Loading the dataset

As mentioned in the *Technical requirements* section, the dataset can be download from the UCI website directly. Now, let's use the pandas pd.read_csv() method to load the dataset into the Python environment. By now, this operation should be relatively easy and intuitive:

1. We start by loading the pandas library and create two different dataframes, namely, df_red for holding the red wine dataset and df_white for holding the white wine dataset:

```
import pandas as pd

df_red =
pd.read_csv("https://archive.ics.uci.edu/ml/machine-learning-databa
ses/wine-quality/winequality-red.csv", delimiter=";")
df_white =
pd.read_csv("https://archive.ics.uci.edu/ml/machine-learning-databa
ses/wine-quality/winequality-white.csv", delimiter=";")
```

2. We have two dataframes created. Let's check the name of the available columns:

```
df_red.columns
```

Furthermore, the output of the preceding code is given here:

```
Index(['fixed acidity', 'volatile acidity', 'citric acid',
'residual sugar',
       'chlorides', 'free sulfur dioxide', 'total sulfur dioxide',
'density',
       'pH', 'sulphates', 'alcohol', 'quality'],
       dtype='object')
```

As shown in this output, the dataset contains the following columns:

- Fixed acidity: It indicates the amount of tartaric acid in wine and is measured in g/dm^3.
- Volatile acidity: It indicates the amount of acetic acid in the wine. It is measured in g/dm^3.
- Citric acid: It indicates the amount of citric acid in the wine. It is also measured in g/dm^3.
- Residual sugar: It indicates the amount of sugar left in the wine after the fermentation process is done. It is also measured in g/dm^3.
- Free sulfur dioxide: It measures the amount of sulfur dioxide (SO_2) in free form. It is also measured in g/dm^3.
- Total sulfur dioxide: It measures the total amount of SO_2 in the wine. This chemical works as an antioxidant and antimicrobial agent.
- Density: It indicates the density of the wine and is measured in g/dm^3.
- pH: It indicates the pH value of the wine. The range of value is between 0 to 14.0, which indicates very high acidity, and 14 indicates basic acidity.
- Sulphates: It indicates the amount of potassium sulphate in the wine. It is also measured in g/dm^3.
- Alcohol: It indicates the alcohol content in the wine.
- Quality: It indicates the quality of the wine, which is ranged from 1 to 10. Here, the higher the value is, the better the wine.

Having discussed different columns in the dataset, let's now see some basic statistics of the data in the next section.

Descriptive statistics

Let's see some sample data from the red wine dataframe. Remember, we can use different methods to see the data from a dataframe, including `pd.head()`, `pd.tail()`, and `pd.iloc()`:

1. Here, I am going to check the entries between the 100th and 110th rows:

    ```
    df_red.iloc[100:110]
    ```

    The output of the preceding code is given here:

	fixed acidity	volatile acidity	citric acid	residual sugar	chlorides	free sulfur dioxide	total sulfur dioxide	density	pH	sulphates	alcohol	quality
100	8.3	0.610	0.30	2.1	0.084	11.0	50.0	0.9972	3.40	0.61	10.2	6
101	7.8	0.500	0.30	1.9	0.075	8.0	22.0	0.9959	3.31	0.56	10.4	6
102	8.1	0.545	0.18	1.9	0.080	13.0	35.0	0.9972	3.30	0.59	9.0	6
103	8.1	0.575	0.22	2.1	0.077	12.0	65.0	0.9967	3.29	0.51	9.2	5
104	7.2	0.490	0.24	2.2	0.070	5.0	36.0	0.9960	3.33	0.48	9.4	5
105	8.1	0.575	0.22	2.1	0.077	12.0	65.0	0.9967	3.29	0.51	9.2	5
106	7.8	0.410	0.68	1.7	0.467	18.0	69.0	0.9973	3.08	1.31	9.3	5
107	6.2	0.630	0.31	1.7	0.088	15.0	64.0	0.9969	3.46	0.79	9.3	5
108	8.0	0.330	0.53	2.5	0.091	18.0	80.0	0.9976	3.37	0.80	9.6	6
109	8.1	0.785	0.52	2.0	0.122	37.0	153.0	0.9969	3.21	0.69	9.3	5

Figure 12.1 - Display the entries from the 100th to 110th rows from the red wine dataframe

2. In addition to this, we can see the datatypes for each column. Let's use the snippet given here:

    ```
    df_red.dtypes
    ```

    The output of the preceding code is as follows:

    ```
    fixed acidity float64
    volatile acidity float64
    citric acid float64
    residual sugar float64
    chlorides float64
    free sulfur dioxide float64
    total sulfur dioxide float64
    density float64
    pH float64
    sulphates float64
    alcohol float64
    quality int64
    dtype: object
    ```

As shown in the preceding output, most of the columns are in `float64` format, except the `quality` column, which is `int64`.

3. We can also describe the dataframe to get more descriptive information. Do you remember the name of the method to do so? Of course, we use the `pd.describe()` method. Check out the snippet:

```
df_red.describe()
```

The output of the preceding code is given here:

	fixed acidity	volatile acidity	citric acid	residual sugar	chlorides	free sulfur dioxide	total sulfur dioxide	density	pH	sulphates	alcohol	quality
count	1599.000000	1599.000000	1599.000000	1599.000000	1599.000000	1599.000000	1599.000000	1599.000000	1599.000000	1599.000000	1599.000000	1599.000000
mean	8.319637	0.527821	0.270976	2.538806	0.087467	15.874922	46.467792	0.996747	3.311113	0.658149	10.422983	5.636023
std	1.741096	0.179060	0.194801	1.409928	0.047065	10.460157	32.895324	0.001887	0.154386	0.169507	1.065668	0.807569
min	4.600000	0.120000	0.000000	0.900000	0.012000	1.000000	6.000000	0.990070	2.740000	0.330000	8.400000	3.000000
25%	7.100000	0.390000	0.090000	1.900000	0.070000	7.000000	22.000000	0.995600	3.210000	0.550000	9.500000	5.000000
50%	7.900000	0.520000	0.260000	2.200000	0.079000	14.000000	38.000000	0.996750	3.310000	0.620000	10.200000	6.000000
75%	9.200000	0.640000	0.420000	2.600000	0.090000	21.000000	62.000000	0.997835	3.400000	0.730000	11.100000	6.000000
max	15.900000	1.580000	1.000000	15.500000	0.611000	72.000000	289.000000	1.003690	4.010000	2.000000	14.900000	8.000000

Figure 12.2 - Output of the described method

Note that *Figure 12.2*, which is the output of the `pd.describe()` method, indicates that each column has the same number of entries, 1,599, which is shown in the row count. By now, each row and column value should make sense. If you are still confused, we would highly recommend revising `Chapter 5`, *Descriptive Statistics*.

Data wrangling

Well, *Figure 12.2* shows that each column has the same number of items, indicating there are no missing values.

We can verify that by using the `pd.info()` method shown here:

```
df_red.info()
```

The output of the preceding code is given:

```
<class 'pandas.core.frame.DataFrame'>
RangeIndex: 1599 entries, 0 to 1598
Data columns (total 12 columns):
fixed acidity 1599 non-null float64
volatile acidity 1599 non-null float64
citric acid 1599 non-null float64
residual sugar 1599 non-null float64
```

```
chlorides 1599 non-null float64
free sulfur dioxide 1599 non-null float64
total sulfur dioxide 1599 non-null float64
density 1599 non-null float64
pH 1599 non-null float64
sulphates 1599 non-null float64
alcohol 1599 non-null float64
quality 1599 non-null int64
dtypes: float64(11), int64(1)
memory usage: 150.0 KB
```

As shown in the preceding output, none of the columns have a null value. Since there are no null entries, we don't need to deal with the missing values. Assuming there were some, then we would take care of them using techniques we outlined in Chapter 4, *Data Transformation*.

 We can also access the data quality and missing values using the ways shown in Chapter 4, *Data Transformation*. We can use the pandas method, df_red.isnull().sum().

Knowing that there is no need for further data transformation steps, let's just go over the data analysis of the red wine in the next section.

Analyzing red wine

In this section, we will continue analyzing the red wine dataset. First, we will start by exploring the most correlated columns. Second, we will compare two different columns and observe their columns.

Let's first start with the quality column:

```
import seaborn as sns

sns.set(rc={'figure.figsize': (14, 8)})
sns.countplot(df_red['quality'])
```

The output of the preceding code is given here:

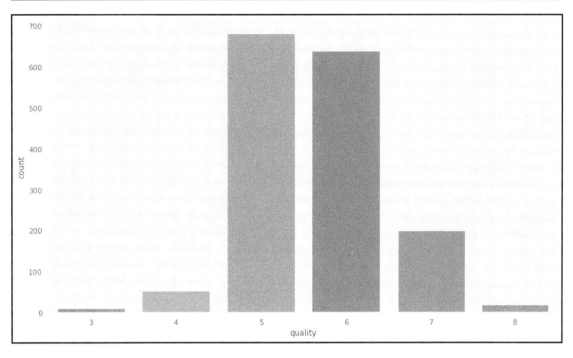

Figure 12.3 - The output indicates that the majority of wine is of medium quality

That was not difficult, was it? As I always argue, one of the most important aspects when you have a graph, is to be able to interpret the results. If you check *Figure 12.3*, you can see that the majority of the red wine belongs to the group with quality labels 3 and 4, followed by the labels 5 and 6, and some of the red wine belongs to the group with label 7, and so on.

Finding correlated columns

Let's next find out which of the columns from the red wine database are highly correlated. If you recall, we discussed different types of correlation in Chapter 7, *Correlation*. Just so you grasp the intention behind the correlation, I highly recommend going through Chapter 7, *Correlation*, just to revamp your memory. Having said that, let's continue with finding highly correlated columns:

1. We can continue using the seaborn.pairplot() method, as shown here:

```
sns.pairplot(df_red)
```

And you should get a highly comprehensive graph, as shown in the screenshot:

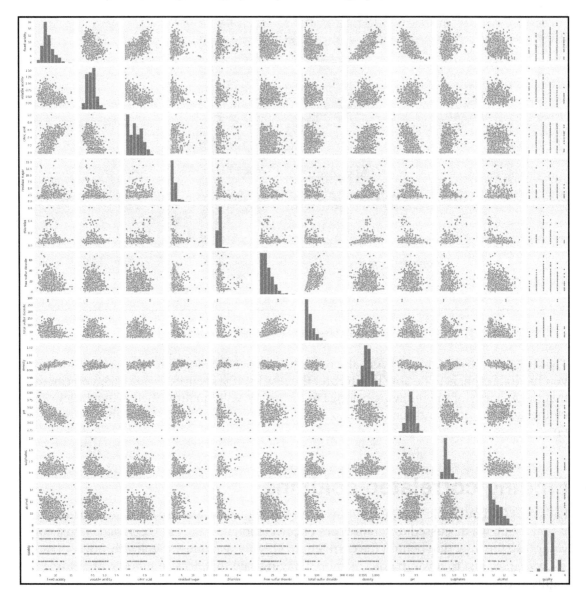

Figure 12.4 - Correlation between different columns of the red wine dataframe

The preceding screenshot shows scattered plots for every possible combination pair of columns. The graph illustrates some positive correlation between fixed acidity and density. There is a negative correlation of acidity with pH. Similarly, there is a negative correlation between alcohol percentage and density. Moreover, you can exactly see which columns have a positive or negative correlation with other columns. However, since there are no numbers of the `pairplot` graph, it might be a bit biased to interpret the results. For example, examine the correlation between the columns for the fixed acidity and the volatile acidity. The graph might be somehow symmetric. However, you might argue there are some sparse points on the right side of the graph so there's lightly negative correlation. Here, my point is, without any specific quantifiable number, it is hard to tell. This is the reason why we can use the `sns.heatmap()` method to quantify the correlation.

2. We can generate the `heatmap` graph, as shown here:

```
sns.heatmap(df_red.corr(), annot=True, fmt='.2f', linewidths=2)
```

And the output it generates is as follows:

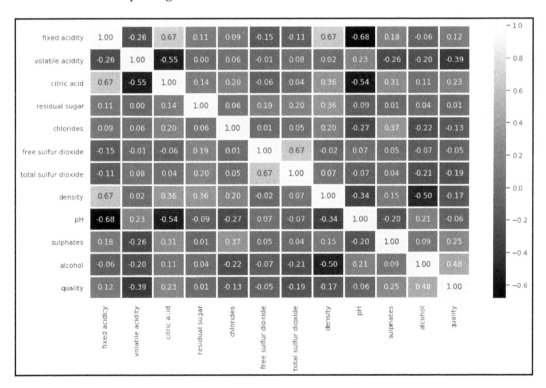

Figure 12.5 - Heatmap showing the correlation between different columns

Figure 12.5 depicts the correlation between different columns. Since we are focusing on the quality column, the quality column has a positive correlation with alcohol, sulfates, residual sugar, citric acid, and fixed acidity. Since there are numbers, it is easy to see which columns are positively correlated and which columns are negatively correlated.

Look at *Figure 12.5* and see whether you can draw the following conclusions:

- Alcohol is positively correlated with the quality of the red wine.
- Alcohol has a weak positive correlation with the pH value.
- Citric acid and density have a strong positive correlation with fixed acidity.
- pH has a negative correlation with density, fixed acidity, citric acid, and sulfates.

There are several conclusions we can draw from the heatmap in *Figure 12.5*. Moreover, it is essential we realize the significance of the correlation and how it can benefit us in deciding feature sets during data science model development.

 A column has a perfect positive correlation with itself. For example, the quality of wine has a positive correlation with itself. This is the reason why all of the diagonal elements have a positive correlation of 1.

We can further dive into individual columns and check their distribution. Say, for example, we want to see how alcohol concentration is distributed with respect to the quality of the red wine. First, let's plot the distribution plot, as shown here:

```
sns.distplot(df_red['alcohol'])
```

The output of the preceding code is as follows:

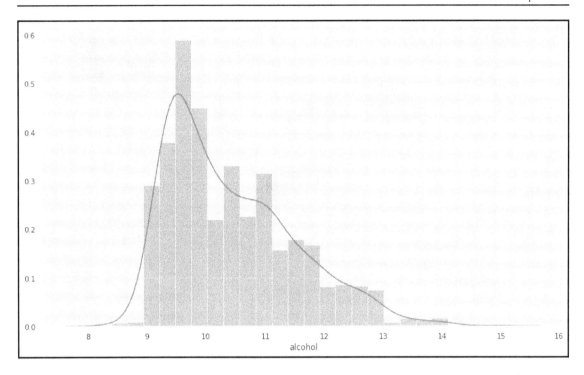

Figure 12.6 - Alcohol distribution graph

From *Figure 12.6*, we can see that alcohol distribution is positively skewed with the quality of the red wine. We can verify this using the `skew` method from scipy.stats. Check the snippet given here:

```
from scipy.stats import skew
skew(df_red['alcohol'])
```

And the output of the preceding code is as follows:

```
0.8600210646566755
```

The output verifies that alcohol is positively skewed. That gives deeper insight into the alcohol column.

Note that we can verify each column and try to see their skewness, distribution, and correlation with respect to the other column. This is generally essential as we are going through the process of feature engineering.

Alcohol versus quality

Let's see how the quality of wine varies with respect to alcohol concentration. This can be done using the box plot. Check the code snippet given here:

```
sns.boxplot(x='quality', y='alcohol', data = df_red)
```

And the output of the preceding code is as follows:

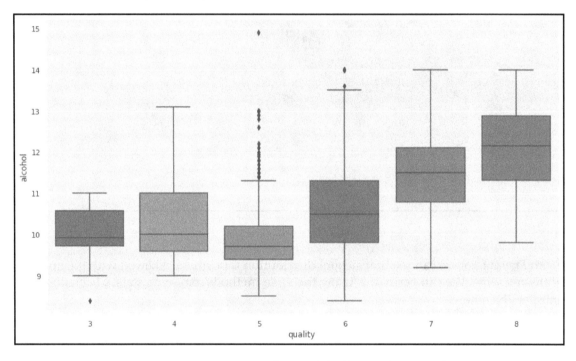

Figure 12.7 - A box plot showing the variation of the quality of wine with respect to alcohol concentration

Note the box in *Figure 12.7* showing some dots outside of the graph. Those are outliers. Most of the outliers as shown in *Figure 12.7* are around wine with quality 5 and 6. We can remove the outliers by passing an argument, showoutliers=False, as shown in the following code:

```
sns.boxplot(x='quality', y='alcohol', data = df_red, showfliers=False)
```

And the output of the code is much cleaner, as shown here:

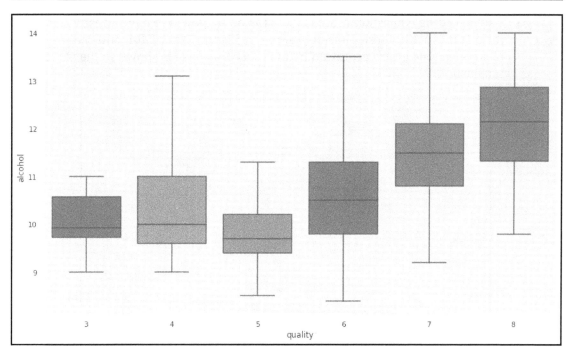

Figure 12.8 -A box plot showing the variation of the quality of wine with respect to alcohol concentration without outliers

Note that, from *Figure 12.8*, it seems that as the quality of wine increases, so does the alcohol concentration. That would make sense, right? The higher the alcohol concentration is, the higher the quality of the wine.

Alcohol versus pH

Next, let's also see the correlation between the alcohol `column` and pH values. From *Figure 12.5*, we already know they are weakly positively correlated. Let's verify the results in this section:

1. First, let's see the joint plot:

```
sns.jointplot(x='alcohol',y='pH',data=df_red, kind='reg')
```

The preceding code should not be new to you by now. We have already discussed the significance of these plots in `Chapter 2`, *Visual Aids in EDA,* and `Chapter 7`, *Correlation*. The graph produced by the preceding code is shown in the screenshot:

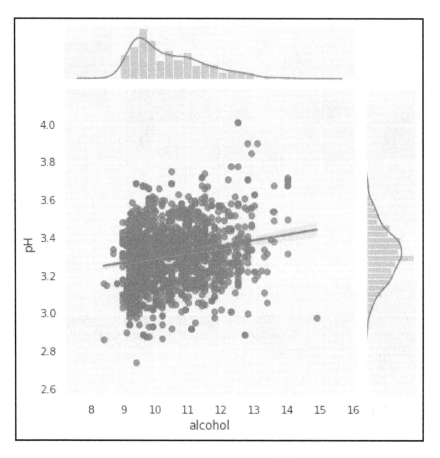

Figure 12.9 - Joint plot illustrating the correlation between alcohol concentration and the pH values

This screenshot shows that alcohol is weakly positively related to the pH values. Moreover, the regression line is depicted in the screenshot, illustrating the correlation between them.

2. We can quantify the correlation using Pearson regression from `scipy.stats`, as shown here:

```
from scipy.stats import pearsonr

def get_correlation(column1, column2, df):
    pearson_corr, p_value = pearsonr(df[column1], df[column2])
    print("Correlation between {} and {} is {}".format(column1,
column2, pearson_corr))
    print("P-value of this correlation is {}".format(p_value))
```

3. And we can use the preceding method to see the correlation between any two columns. Let's see the correlation between `alcohol` and `pH`:

```
get_correlation('alcohol','pH', df_red)
```

The output of the preceding code is given as follows:

```
Correlation between alcohol and pH is 0.20563250850549825
P-value of this correlation is 9.96449774146556e-17
```

Note that, this is approximately the same value that is shown in *Figure 12.5*. Now you know different ways in which you can check how strongly or weakly two or more columns are related.

In the next section, we are going to analyze the white wine dataframe and compare it with the red wine.

Analyzing white wine

In this section, we are going to analyze white wine and compare it with the red wine analysis from the previous section. Let's start by loading the white wine dataframe:

```
df_white =
pd.read_csv("https://archive.ics.uci.edu/ml/machine-learning-databases/wine
-quality/winequality-white.csv", delimiter=";")
```

This code loads the white wine dataset into the `df_white` dataframe.

Red wine versus white wine

Our output class is the `quality` column. Based on that column, we can try to find the average quality of each wine as follows:

```
print("white mean = ",df_white["quality"].mean())
print("red mean =",df_red["quality"].mean())
```

And the output of the code is as follows:

```
white mean = 5.87790935075541
red mean = 5.6360225140712945
```

As the output says, the average white wine quality is 5.877 and that of red wine is 5.63. The columns in both dataframes are the same.

Adding a new attribute

Let's add a new attribute, `wine_category`, to both dataframes. Do you recall how we did that?

Of course, check the example code given as follows:

```
df_white['wine_category'] = 'white'
df_red['wine_category'] = 'red'
```

That was easy, right? Next, let's see what are the unique values of the column quality in both types of wines:

```
print('RED WINE: List of "quality"', sorted(df_red['quality'].unique()))
print('WHITE WINE: List of "quality"',
sorted(df_white['quality'].unique()))
```

The output of the preceding code is given as follows:

```
RED WINE: List of "quality" [3, 4, 5, 6, 7, 8]
WHITE WINE: List of "quality" [3, 4, 5, 6, 7, 8, 9]
```

Note that both the red and the white wines have the same unique values for the quality column.

Converting into a categorical column

Although the quality column is numerical, here, we are interested in taking quality as the class. To make it clear, let's convert numerical values into categorical values in this subsection.

To do so, we need a set of rules. Let's define a set of rules:

$$\text{quality\_label} = \begin{cases} low & \text{if value} \leq 5 \\ medium & \text{if } 5 < value \leq 7 \\ high & \text{if value} > 7 \end{cases}$$

That sounds doable, right? Of course, it is. Let's check the code, given as follows:

```
df_red['quality_label'] = df_red['quality'].apply(lambda value: ('low' if
value <= 5 else 'medium') if value <= 7 else 'high')
df_red['quality_label'] = pd.Categorical(df_red['quality_label'],
categories=['low', 'medium', 'high'])

df_white['quality_label'] = df_white['quality'].apply(lambda value: ('low'
if value <= 5 else 'medium') if value <= 7 else 'high')
df_white['quality_label'] = pd.Categorical(df_white['quality_label'],
categories=['low', 'medium', 'high'])
```

The preceding code should be self-explanatory by now. We just used the `pandas.apply()` method to check the value in the `quality` columns. Based on their values, if they are less than or equal to five, we categorized them as low-quality wine. Similarly, if the value of the `quality` column is greater than 5 and less than or equal to 7, we classified them as medium-quality wine. Finally, any rows with a `quality` column containing a value greater than 7 were classified as high-quality wine.

Let's count the number of values in each category of wine:

```
print(df_white['quality_label'].value_counts())
df_red['quality_label'].value_counts()
```

And the output of the preceding code is given as follows:

```
medium 3078
low 1640
high 180
Name: quality_label, dtype: int64

medium 837
low 744
```

```
high 18
Name: quality_label, dtype: int64
```

The top one is for white wine and the lower one is red wine. It is pretty obvious from the preceding output that most of the wines are of medium quality in both cases.

Concatenating dataframes

Let's perform a combined exploration of both types of dataframes. Do you remember how we can merge dataframes? If not, I highly recommend pausing here and quickly skimming through Chapter 6, *Grouping Datasets*:

1. Let's see how we can concatenate both dataframes:

   ```
   df_wines = pd.concat([df_red, df_white])
   ```

2. Let's also re-shuffle the rows so that it randomizes the data points:

   ```
   df_wines = df_wines.sample(frac=1.0,
   random_state=42).reset_index(drop=True)
   ```

   Note that the drop=True argument resets the indexes to the default integer index.

3. Next, we would like to check the first few columns to see whether all of the rows are correctly merged:

   ```
   df_wines.head()
   ```

   The output of the preceding code is given as follows:

	fixed acidity	volatile acidity	citric acid	residual sugar	chlorides	free sulfur dioxide	total sulfur dioxide	density	pH	sulphates	alcohol	quality	wine_category	quality_label
0	7.0	0.17	0.74	12.8	0.045	24.0	126.0	0.99420	3.26	0.38	12.2	8	white	high
1	7.7	0.64	0.21	2.2	0.077	32.0	133.0	0.99560	3.27	0.45	9.9	5	red	low
2	6.8	0.39	0.34	7.4	0.020	38.0	133.0	0.99212	3.18	0.44	12.0	7	white	medium
3	6.3	0.28	0.47	11.2	0.040	61.0	183.0	0.99592	3.12	0.51	9.5	6	white	medium
4	7.4	0.35	0.20	13.9	0.054	63.0	229.0	0.99888	3.11	0.50	8.9	6	white	medium
5	7.2	0.53	0.14	2.1	0.064	15.0	29.0	0.99323	3.35	0.61	12.1	6	red	medium
6	7.5	0.27	0.31	17.7	0.051	33.0	173.0	0.99900	3.09	0.64	10.2	5	white	low
7	6.8	0.11	0.27	8.6	0.044	45.0	104.0	0.99454	3.20	0.37	9.9	6	white	medium
8	9.0	0.44	0.49	2.4	0.078	26.0	121.0	0.99780	3.23	0.58	9.2	5	red	low
9	7.1	0.23	0.30	2.6	0.034	62.0	148.0	0.99121	3.03	0.56	11.3	7	white	medium

Figure 12.10 - Output of the df.head(10) code snippet shown earlier

Note that in *Figure 12.10*, we have correctly populated the columns, wine_category and quality_label.

Grouping columns

We have already discussed several ways in which we can group columns and rows using the pandas dataframe in Chapter 6, *Grouping Dataset*. In this section, we will use the same technique to group different columns together:

1. Let's use the combined dataframe and group them using the columns, alcohol, density, pH, and quality.
2. Next, we can apply the pd.describe() method to get the most frequently used descriptive statistics:

```
subset_attr = ['alcohol', 'density', 'pH', 'quality']

low = round(df_wines[df_wines['quality_label'] ==
'low'][subset_attr].describe(), 2)
medium = round(df_wines[df_wines['quality_label'] ==
'medium'][subset_attr].describe(), 2)
high = round(df_wines[df_wines['quality_label'] ==
'high'][subset_attr].describe(), 2)

pd.concat([low, medium, high], axis=1,
          keys=['    Low Quality Wine',
                '    Medium Quality Wine',
                '    High Quality Wine'])
```

In the preceding code snippet, first, we created a subset of attributes that we are interested in. Then, we created three different dataframes for low-quality wine, medium-quality wine, and high-quality wine. Finally, we concatenated them. The output of the preceding code is given here:

	Low Quality Wine				Medium Quality Wine				High Quality Wine			
	alcohol	density	pH	quality	alcohol	density	pH	quality	alcohol	density	pH	quality
count	2384.00	2384.00	2384.00	2384.00	3915.00	3915.00	3915.00	3915.00	198.00	198.00	198.00	198.00
mean	9.87	1.00	3.21	4.88	10.81	0.99	3.22	6.28	11.69	0.99	3.23	8.03
std	0.84	0.00	0.16	0.36	1.20	0.00	0.16	0.45	1.27	0.00	0.16	0.16
min	8.00	0.99	2.74	3.00	8.40	0.99	2.72	6.00	8.50	0.99	2.88	8.00
25%	9.30	0.99	3.11	5.00	9.80	0.99	3.11	6.00	11.00	0.99	3.13	8.00
50%	9.60	1.00	3.20	5.00	10.80	0.99	3.21	6.00	12.00	0.00	3.23	8.00
75%	10.40	1.00	3.31	5.00	11.70	1.00	3.33	7.00	12.60	0.99	3.33	8.00
max	14.90	1.00	3.90	5.00	14.20	1.04	4.01	7.00	14.00	1.00	3.72	9.00

Figure 12.11 - Output of grouping the columns and performing the describe operation

As shown in the preceding screenshot, we have grouped the dataset into three distinct groups: low-quality wine, medium-quality wine, and high-quality wine. Each group shows three different attributes: alcohol, density, and pH value. Using the concatenation method to group the columns based on certain conditions can be very handy during the data analysis phase.

In the next section, we are going to discuss the univariate analysis for the wine quality dataset.

Univariate analysis

We have already discussed univariate, bivariate, and multivariate analysis in Chapter 7, *Correlation*. Let's revise and see how much you remember.

The simplest way to visualize the numeric data and their distribution is by using a histogram. Let's plot the histogram here; we start by importing the required matplotlib.pyplot library:

```
import matplotlib.pyplot as plt
from mpl_toolkits.mplot3d import Axes3D
%matplotlib inline
```

Next, we draw the histogram, as shown:

```
fig = df_wines.hist(bins=15, color='fuchsia', edgecolor='darkmagenta',
linewidth=1.0, xlabelsize=10, ylabelsize=10, xrot=45, yrot=0,
figsize=(10,9), grid=False)

plt.tight_layout(rect=(0, 0, 1.5, 1.5))
```

Note that we have used the tight_layout() method to keep the graph combined.

 You can get the list of all matplotlib color codes from the official website, at https://matplotlib.org/examples/color/named_colors.html.

The output of the preceding code is given as follows:

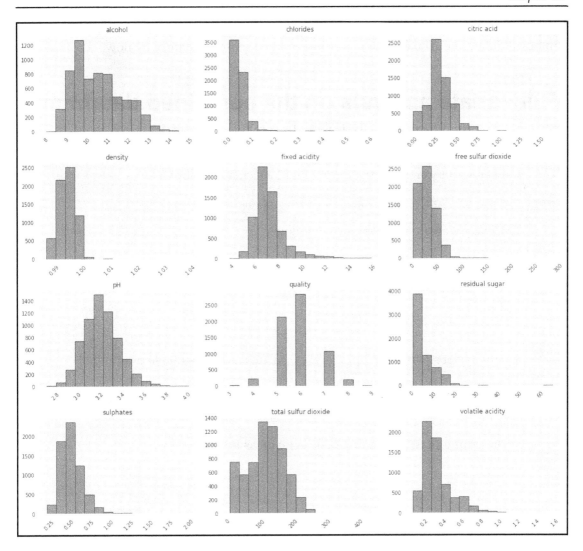

Figure 12.12 - Output of the univariate analysis

The preceding screenshot shows each of the variables/columns and their distribution in the combined dataframe. The resulting graph should be self-explanatory by now.

Multivariate analysis on the combined dataframe

Let's perform the multivariate analysis with the combined dataset. We are going to use the same heatmap diagram to perform multivariate analysis:

1. Let's start by creating the figure. First, we create a subplot:

```
fig, (ax) = plt.subplots(1, 1, figsize=(14,8))
```

2. Next, we create the heatmap, as follows:

```
hm = sns.heatmap(df_wines.corr(),
                 ax=ax,
                   cmap="bwr",
                   annot=True,
                   fmt='.2f',
                   linewidths=.05)
```

3. Finally, let's plot the subplot and populate it with a suitable title:

```
fig.subplots_adjust(top=0.93)
fig.suptitle('Combined Wine Attributes and their Correlation
Heatmap', fontsize=14, fontweight='bold')
```

The output of the preceding code is given as follows:

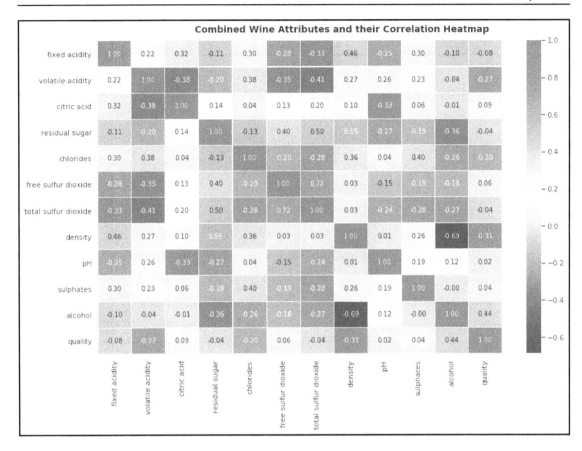

Figure 12.13 - A heatmap illustrating correlation between several columns

Note the preceding screenshot is similar to *Figure 12.5* and should be interpreted in the same way. The only difference, in this case, is that we have performed multivariate analysis on the combined dataframe.

Discrete categorical attributes

We have one discrete categorical column in our dataframe, `wine_category`.

Let's visualize it using a count plot using the `seaborn` library:

```
fig = plt.figure(figsize=(16, 8))

sns.countplot(data=df_wines, x="quality", hue="wine_category")
```

The output of the preceding code is given as follows:

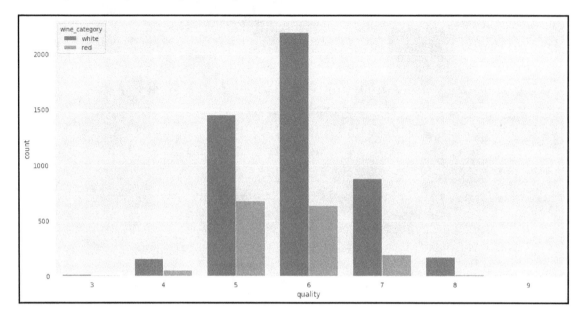

Figure 12.14 - Visualizing the discrete categorical dataset

Figure 12.14 shows different categories of wine [3, 4, 5, 6, 7, 8, 9] and their frequency distributions over a nice count plot. It is a clearer illustration for end stakeholders.

3-D visualization

Generally, we start with one-dimensional visualization and move to further dimensions. Having seen 2-D visualization earlier, let's add one more dimension and plot 3-D charts. We will use the `matplotlib.pyplot` method to do so:

1. Let's start first by creating the axes:

```
fig = plt.figure(figsize=(16, 12))
ax = fig.add_subplot(111, projection='3d')
```

2. Then, add the columns to the axes:

```
xscale = df_wines['residual sugar']
yscale = df_wines['free sulfur dioxide']
zscale = df_wines['total sulfur dioxide']
ax.scatter(xscale, yscale, zscale, s=50, alpha=0.6, edgecolors='w')
```

Here, we are interested in looking into the residual sugar, free sulfur dioxide, and total sulfur dioxide columns.

3. Finally, let's add the labels to all of the axes:

```
ax.set_xlabel('Residual Sugar')
ax.set_ylabel('free sulfur dioxide')
ax.set_zlabel('Total sulfur dioxide')

plt.show()
```

The output of the preceding code is given as follows:

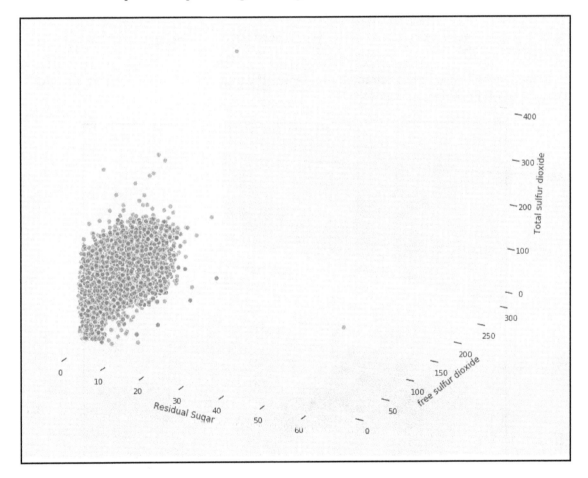

Figure 12.14 - 3-D plot illustrating the correlation between three different columns

Figure 12.14 shows that three variables show a positive correlation with respect to one another. In the preceding example, we used the Matplotlib library. We can also use the `seaborn` library to plot three different variables. Check the code snippet given here:

```
fig = plt.figure(figsize=(16, 12))

plt.scatter(x = df_wines['fixed acidity'],
            y = df_wines['free sulfur dioxide'],
            s = df_wines['total sulfur dioxide'] * 2,
            alpha=0.4,
            edgecolors='w')

plt.xlabel('Fixed Acidity')
plt.ylabel('free sulfur dioxide')
plt.title('Wine free sulfur dioxide Content - Fixed Acidity - total sulfur
dioxide', y=1.05)
```

Note that we have used the `s` parameter to denote the third variable (total sulfur dioxide). The output of the code is as follows:

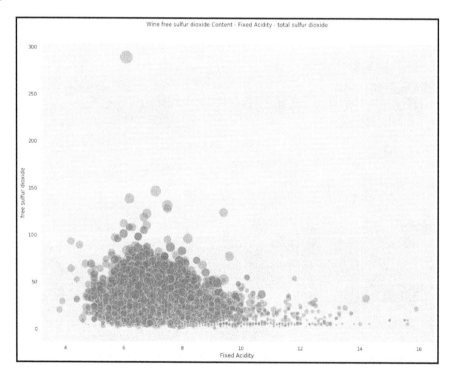

Figure 12.16 - Plot illustrating three different variables as shown in the preceding code

Note that in *Figure 12.16,* the size of the circles denotes the third variable. In this case, the larger the radius of the circle is, the higher the value of residual sugar. So, if you look carefully, you will notice most of the higher circles are located between the *x* axis with values of 4 and 10 and with the *y* axis with values between 25 and 150.

In the next section, we are going to develop different types of models and apply some classical **Machine Learning** (**ML**) algorithms and evaluate their performances.

Model development and evaluation

In this section, we are going to develop different types of classical ML models and evaluate their performances. We have already discussed in detail the development of models and their evaluation in `Chapter 9`, *Hypothesis Testing and Regression* and `Chapter 10`, *Model Development and Evaluation*. Here, we will dive directly into implementation.

We are going to use different types of following algorithms and evaluate their performances:

- Logistic regression
- Support vector machine
- K-nearest neighbor classifier
- Random forest classifier
- Decision tree classifier
- Gradient boosting classifier
- Gaussian Naive Bayes classifier

While going over each classifier in depth is out of the scope of this chapter and book, our aim here is to present how we can continue developing ML algorithms after performing EDA operations on certain databases:

1. Let's first import the required libraries:

```
from sklearn.linear_model import LogisticRegression
from sklearn.svm import LinearSVC, SVC
from sklearn.neighbors import KNeighborsClassifier
from sklearn.ensemble import
RandomForestClassifier,GradientBoostingClassifier,AdaBoostClassifie
r
from sklearn.tree import DecisionTreeClassifier
from sklearn.naive_bayes import GaussianNB
from sklearn.model_selection import train_test_split,cross_validate
from sklearn.preprocessing import
```

```
MinMaxScaler,StandardScaler,LabelEncoder
from sklearn.metrics import
accuracy_score,precision_score,recall_score,f1_score
```

Note that we are going to use the combined dataframe. Next, we are going to encode the categorical values for the `quality_label` column. We will encode the values so that all of the low values will be changed to 0, the medium values will be changed to 1, and the high values will be changed to 2.

2. Let's perform the encoding:

```
label_quality = LabelEncoder()

df_wines['quality_label'] =
label_quality.fit_transform(df_wines['quality_label'])
```

That was not difficult, right? We just utilized the `LabelEncoder` utility function provided by the `sklearn` preprocessing functionality.

3. Now, let's split our dataset into a training set and test set. We will use 70% of the dataset as the training set and the remaining 30% as the test set:

```
x_train,x_test,y_train,y_test=train_test_split(df_wines.drop(['qual
ity','wine_category'],axis=1),df_wines['quality_label'],test_size=0
.30,random_state=42)
```

We used the `train_test_split()` method provided by the `sklearn` library. Note the following things in the preceding category:

- In the preceding code, we no longer need the `quality` and `wine_category` columns, so we drop them.
- Next, we take 30% of the data as the test set. We can do that by simply passing the `test_size = 0.30` argument.

4. Next, we create the model. Note that we could build the model individually for each of the algorithms we listed above. Instead, here we are going to list them and loop over each of them and compute the accuracy. Check the code snippet given as follows:

```
models=[LogisticRegression(),
        LinearSVC(),
        SVC(kernel='rbf'),
        KNeighborsClassifier(),
        RandomForestClassifier(),
        DecisionTreeClassifier(),
        GradientBoostingClassifier(),
```

```
                    GaussianNB()]

        model_names=['LogisticRegression','LinearSVM','rbfSVM',
        'KNearestNeighbors', 'RandomForestClassifier', 'DecisionTree',
        'GradientBoostingClassifier', 'GaussianNB']
```

5. Next, we will loop over each model, create a model, and then evaluate the accuracy. Check the code snippet given as follows:

```
acc=[]
eval_acc={}

for model in range(len(models)):
    classification_model=models[model]
    classification_model.fit(x_train,y_train)
    pred=classification_model.predict(x_test)
    acc.append(accuracy_score(pred,y_test))
eval_acc={'Modelling Algorithm':model_names,'Accuracy':acc}
eval_acc
```

The output of the preceding code is given here:

```
{'Accuracy': [0.9687179487179487,
  0.9733333333333334,
  0.6051282051282051,
  0.6912820512820513,
  1.0,
  1.0,
  1.0,
  1.0],
 'Modelling Algorithm': ['LogisticRegression',
  'LinearSVM',
  'rbfSVM',
  'KNearestNeighbors',
  'RandomForestClassifier',
  'DecisionTree',
  'GradientBoostingClassifier',
  'GaussianNB']}
```

6. Let's create a dataframe of the accuracy and show it in a bar chart:

```
acc_table=pd.DataFrame(eval_acc)
acc_table = acc_table.sort_values(by='Accuracy', ascending=[False])
acc_table
```

The output of the preceding code is given as follows:

	Modelling Algorithm	Accuracy
4	RandomForestClassifier	1.000000
5	DecisionTree	1.000000
6	GradientBoostingClassifier	1.000000
7	GaussianNB	1.000000
1	LinearSVM	0.983590
0	LogisticRegression	0.968718
3	KNearestNeighbors	0.691282
2	rbfSVM	0.605128

Figure 12.17 - Accuracy dataframe of different algorithms

Note that converting quality into a categorical dataset gave us higher accuracy. Most of the algorithms gave 100% accuracy as shown in the previous screenshot.

7. Let's create a bar plot:

```
sns.barplot(y='Modelling Algorithm',x='Accuracy',data=acc_table)
```

The output of the preceding code is given as follows:

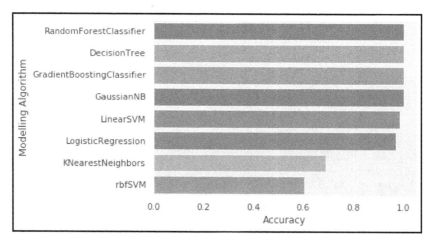

Figure 12.18 - Different types of algorithms and their accuracies

Note that, as shown in the screenshot, the random forest, the decision tree, the gradient boosting classifier, and the Gaussian Naive Bayes classifier all gave 100% accuracy.

Great! Congratulations, you have successfully completed the main project. Please note that all of the code, snippets, and methods illustrated in this book have been given to provide minimal ways in which a particular problem can be solved. There is always a way in which you can perform deeper analysis. We motivate you to go through the *Further reading* sections on each chapter to get advanced knowledge about the particular domain.

Summary

In this chapter, we used the Wine Quality dataset provided by UCI to perform EDA. We discussed how we can perform EDA techniques such as data loading, data wrangling, data transformation, correlation between variables, regression analysis, and building classical ML models based on the datasets.

This is the final chapter in this book. As mentioned earlier, the explanation of the theory, codes, and illustrations provided in this book have been given to provide you with a base knowledge set. We assume that after reading this book, you will gain sufficient insights, techniques, and skills to take it to the next level.

Further reading

- *Supervised Machine Learning with Python, Taylor Smith, Packt Publishing,* May 26, 2019
- *Large Scale Machine Learning with Python, Bastiaan Sjardin, Luca Massaron, et al., Packt Publishing,* August 2, 2016
- *Advanced Machine Learning with Python, John Hearty, Packt Publishing,* July 27, 2016
- *Hands-On Unsupervised Learning with Python, Giuseppe Bonaccorso, Packt Publishing,* February 28, 2019
- *Mastering Machine Learning for Penetration Testing, Chiheb Chebbi, Packt Publishing,* June 26, 2018
- *Hands-On Data Science and Python Machine Learning, Frank Kane, Packt Publishing,* July 30, 2017
- *Building Machine Learning Systems with Python – Third Edition, Luis Pedro Coelho, Willi Richert, et al., Packt Publishing,* July 30, 2018
- The wine quality dataset is attributed to *P. Cortez, A. Cerdeira, F. Almeida, T. Matos,* and *J. Reis. Modeling wine preferences by data mining from physicochemical properties.* In Decision Support Systems, Elsevier, 47(4):547-553, 2009.

Appendix

As mentioned previously, data preprocessing and data transformation are two of the most essential processes in data mining and other data science approaches. During the data processing stage, our data is often in the form of a string. Most of the datasets found on the internet are string-based. Hence, string manipulation techniques are an essential part of **exploratory data analysis (EDA)**.

In this appendix chapter, we are going to learn about the following topics:

- String manipulation
- Using pandas vectorized string functions
- Using regular expressions

String manipulation

By string manipulation, we mean how you can create strings, access characters in those strings, slice the strings, and delete or update characters in the strings and other string operators. In the following sections, we are going to see all these steps, one by one.

Creating strings

We can create strings in Python in three different ways:

- Using a single quote
- Using a double quote
- Using a triple quote.

Have a look at the following example:

```
String1 = 'Creating a String with single Quotes.'
String2 = "Creating a String with double Quotes."
String3 = '''Creating a String with triple Quotes.'''
print(String1)
print(String2)
print(String3)
```

The output of all three `print` statements is the same. They create a string, as intended.

Accessing characters in Python

Python provides an indexing mechanism to access any character from any string. The index of any string starts with 0. We can also access any character from the back of any string, using a negative index value. For example, -1 indicates the last character of the string, -2 refers to the second-to-last character, and so on. Note that if we try accessing any index that is not within the limit of the string, Python alerts us with a `TypeError`.

Here's the Python code used to access the characters of a string:

```
# characters of String
String = "Exploratory Data Analysis"

# Printing First character
print("\nFirst character of String is: ")
print(String[0])

# Printing Last character
print("\nLast character of String is: ")
print(String[-1])
```

The output of each code block is displayed with an inline comment, which makes it easier to comprehend.

String slicing

To access a range of characters in a string, a slicing method is used. Slicing in a string is done using a slicing operator (`:`). Here's a program that demonstrates string slicing:

```
# Creating a String
String = "Exploratory Data Analysis"

# Outputs: Slicing characters from 3-12:loratory
print("\nSlicing characters from 3-12: ")
print(String[3:12])

# Outputs:Slicing characters between 3rd and 2nd last character: loratory
Data Analys
print("\nSlicing characters between " + "3rd and 2nd last character: ")
print(String[3:-2])
```

The output of each code block is displayed with an inline comment, which makes it easier to comprehend.

Deleting/updating from a string

Python does not support string mutation. That is to say, it does not allow any characters from a string to be deleted or updated. If we attempt to do so, it raises an error. However, the deletion of the entire string is possible with the use of the built-in `del` keyword. The main reason for getting an error in the case of a string update is that strings are immutable. In the following code block, let's create a string, and try to update some characters in it, as follows:

```
# Updation of a character

String = "Exploratory Data Analysis"

String[2] = 'p'
print("\nUpdating character at 2nd Index: ")
print(String)
```

The preceding code should give you an error.

Escape sequencing in Python

A string already comes with the single (`'`) and double (`' '`) quotes incorporated within its syntax. Hence, if we need to print a single or a double quote within a string, it causes a `SyntaxError`. To avoid such an error, the quotes—whether they are single or double quotes—must be escaped. This phenomenon is called an escape sequence. An escape sequence begins with a backslash (`\`) and can be understood differently. If we intend to use a single quote or a double quote as a string, then it must be escaped by appending a backslash before it. Let's see it in action.

We will show the following example for all three cases (a single quote, a double quote, and a triple quote):

```
String = '''I'm a "Data Scientist"'''

# Initial String
print("Initial String with use of Triple Quotes: ")
print(String)

# Escaping Single Quote
String = 'I\'m a "Data Scientist"'
print("\nEscaping Single Quote: ")
print(String)

# Escaping Double Quotes
```

```
String = "I'm a \"Data Scientist\""
print("\nEscaping Double Quotes: ")
print(String)
```

In computer science, we often need to provide a path to some files or datasets on different occasions. This is the same when working with data science. The first step is to load the dataset. To do so, we have to provide a link or path to the file by using a double slash, in order to escape the double slash. We then print the paths with escape sequences, as shown in the following example:

```
String = "C:\\Python\\DataScience\\"
print("\nEscaping Backslashes: ")
print(String)
```

The preceding code generates the following output:

```
Escaping Backslashes:
C:\Python\DataScience\
```

Note the use of the double slash in the code—this provides a single slash as the output. This is why escaping is a very useful mechanism.

Formatting strings

We can use the `format()` method to format a string in Python. This method is very flexible and powerful when displaying output in any particular format. The `format()` method holds curly braces `{}` as placeholders that can be replaced by any particular arguments according to a specific order. Have a look at these next examples.

Let's first see an example for a default order:

```
# Default order
String1 = "{} {} {}".format('Exploratory ', 'Data ', 'Analysis')
print("Print String in default order: ")
print(String1)
```

The output of the preceding code is as follows:

```
Print String in default order:
Exploratory Data Analysis
```

In addition to this default order, we can use positional formatting. For example, you have a string such as `('Exploratory', 'Data', 'Analysis')`, and we want to display a `('Data', 'Exploratory', 'Analysis')` string. We can do this by using positional formatting, as shown in the following example:

```
# Positional Formatting
String1 = "{1} {0} {2}".format('Exploratory', 'Data', 'Analysis')
print("\nPrint String in Positional order: ")
print(String1)
```

We can also format any string by using keywords. For example, have a look at the following code:

```
# Keyword Formatting
String1 = "{l} {f} {g}".format(g = 'Exploratory', f = 'Data', l =
'Analysis')
print("\nPrint String in order of Keywords: ")
print(String1)
```

The output of the preceding code is as follows:

```
Print String in order of Keywords:
Analysis Data Exploratory
```

Next, we are going to look at how we can load a text dataset and perform preprocessing operations.

Using pandas vectorized string functions

For string formatting, it would be better to use a dataset that's a little messier. We will use the dataset that I collected during my Ph.D. research study when writing a review paper. It can be found here: https://raw.githubusercontent.com/sureshHARDIYA/phd-resources/master/Data/Review%20Paper/preprocessed.csv.

1. Let's load this text article and then display the first eight entries. Let's start by loading the data and checking its structure and a few of the comments, as follows:

```
import numpy as np
import pandas as pd
import os
```

2. Next, let's read the text file and display the last 10 items, as follows:

```
text =
pd.read_csv("https://raw.githubusercontent.com/sureshHARDIYA/phd-re
sources/master/Data/Review%20Paper/preprocessed.csv")
text = text["TITLE"]
print (text.shape)
print( text.tail(10))
```

3. The output of the preceding code can be seen in the following screenshot:

```
⎀  (705,)
    695                    alpha lipoic acid for dementia
    696        almitrine-raubasine combination for dementia
    697      agomelatine versus other antidepressive agent...
    698      aerobic exercise to improve cognitive functio...
    699      advance treatment directives for people with ...
    700      adjuvant therapy with antidepressants for the...
    701                        acupuncture for schizophrenia
    702                      acetyl-1-carnitine for dementia
    703    acetylsalicylic acid (aspirin) for schizophrenia
    704      acetylcholinesterase inhibitors for schizophr...
    Name: TITLE, dtype: object
```

Figure 1: This is the output of the preceding code

Pandas extends built-in functions that operate on an entire series of strings. In the next section, we are going to use the same dataset with pandas string functions.

Using string functions with a pandas DataFrame

Let's use built-in functions with a pandas DataFrame. We will continue to use the same dataset that was imported in the previous section. Most of the string manipulation functions in Python work with the pandas vectorized string methods.

Here is a list of pandas string functions that reflect Python string methods:

len()	lower()	translate()	islower()
ljust()	upper()	startswith()	isupper()
rjust()	find()	endswith()	isnumeric()
center()	rfind()	isalnum()	isdecimal()
zfill()	index()	isalpha()	split()
strip()	rindex()	isdigit()	rsplit()
rstrip()	capitalize()	isspace()	partition()
lstrip()	swapcase()	istitle()	rpartition()

Figure 2 - List of vectorized string functions in pandas

Let's practice the following use cases:

1. Extract the first sentence from the `text` column of the DataFrame and convert it into lowercase characters, as follows:

```
text[0].lower()
```

2. Convert all the comments in the `text` column to lowercase and display the first eight entries, as follows:

```
text.str.lower().head(8)
```

3. Extract the first sentence and convert it into uppercase characters, as follows:

```
text[0].upper()
```

4. Get the length of each comment in the text field and display the first eight entries, as follows:

```
text.str.len().head(8)
```

5. Combine all the comments into a single string and display the first 500 characters, as follows:

```
text.str.cat()[0:500]
```

   It is wise to verify that all the comments are concatenated together. Can you think of any use cases where we probably need to combine all the comments together into a single string? Well, how about—say—we want to see the most frequent words chosen by all users when commenting.

6. Slice each string in a series and return the result in an elementwise fashion with `series.str.slice()`, as shown in the following code snippet:

```
text.str.slice(0, 10).head(8)
```

7. Replace the occurrences of a given substring with a different substring using `str.replace()`, as shown in the following code snippet:

```
text.str.replace("Wolves", "Fox").head(8)
```

In the preceding example, all the cases of `Wolves` would be replaced with `Fox`. This acts as a *search and replace* functionality that you can find in many content management systems and editors.

While working with text data, we frequently test whether character strings contain a certain substring or pattern of characters. Let's search for only those comments that mention Andrew Wiggins. We'd need to match all posts that mention him and avoid matching posts that don't mention him.

Use `series.str.contains()` to get a series of true/false values, indicating whether each string contains a given substring, as follows:

```
# Get first 10 comments about Andrew Wiggins
selected_comments = text.str.lower().str.contains("wigg|drew")

text[selected_comments].head(10)
```

Just for information, let's calculate the ratio of comments that mention Andrew Wiggins, as follows:

```
len(text[selected_comments])/len(text)
```

And the output is 0.06649063850216035. As you can see, `6.6%` of comments make mention of Andrew Wiggins. This is the output of the string pattern argument we supplied to `str.contains()`.

Posts about Andrew Wiggins could use any number of different names to refer to him—Wiggins, Andrew, Wigg, Drew—so we needed something that is a little more flexible than a single substring to match all the posts we're interested in. The pattern we supplied is a simple example of a regular expression.

Using regular expressions

A regular expression, or regex, is a sequence of characters and special metacharacters used to match a set of character strings. Regular expressions allow you to be more expressive with string-matching operations than just providing a simple substring. You can think of it as a *pattern* that you want to match with strings of different lengths, made up of different characters.

In the `str.contains()` method, we supplied the regular expression, `wigg|drew`. In this case, the vertical bar `|` is a metacharacter that acts as the OR operator, so this regular expression matches any string that contains the substring `wigg` or `drew`.

Metacharacters let you change how you make matches. When you provide a regular expression that contains no metacharacters, it simply matches the exact substring. For instance, `Wiggins` would only match strings containing the exact substring, `Wiggins`.

Here is a list of basic metacharacters, and what they do:

- ".": The period is a metacharacter that matches any character other than a newline, as illustrated in the following code block:

```
# Match any substring ending in ill
my_words = pd.Series(["abaa","cabb","Abaa","sabb","dcbb"])

my_words.str.contains(".abb")
```

- "[ ]": Square brackets specify a set of characters to match. Look at the following example snippet and compare your output with the notebook given with this chapter:

```
my_words.str.contains("[Aa]abb")
```

- "^": Outside of square brackets, the caret symbol searches for matches at the beginning of a string, as illustrated in the following code block:

```
Sentence_series= pd.Series(["Where did he go", "He went to the shop", "he is good"])

Sentence_series.str.contains("^(He|he)")
```

- "( )": Parentheses in regular expressions are used for grouping and to enforce the proper order of operations, just as they are used in math and logical expressions. In the preceding examples, the parentheses let us group the OR expressions so that the "^" and "$" symbols operate on the entire OR statement.
- "*": An asterisk matches 0 or more copies of the preceding character.
- "?": A question mark matches 0 or 1 copy of the preceding character.
- "+": A plus sign matches 1 or more copies of the preceding character.
- "{ }": Curly braces match a preceding character for a specified number of repetitions:
  - "{m}": The preceding element is matched m times.
  - "{m, }": The preceding element is matched m times or more.
  - "{m,n}": The preceding element is matched between m and n times.

Regular expressions include several special character sets that allow us to quickly specify certain common character types. They include the following:

- [a-z]: Match any lowercase letter.
- [A-Z]: Match any uppercase letter.

- [0-9]: Match any digit.
- [a-zA-Z0-9]: Match any letter or digit.
- Adding the "^" symbol inside the square brackets matches any characters *not* in the set:
    - [^a-z]: Match any character that is not a lowercase letter.
    - [^A-Z]: Match any character that is not an uppercase letter.
    - [^0-9]: Match any character that is not a digit.
    - [^a-zA-Z0-9]: Match any character that is not a letter or digit.
- Python regular expressions also include a shorthand for specifying common sequences:
    - \d: Match any digit.
    - \D: Match any non-digit.
    - \w: Match a word character.
    - \W: Match a non-word character.
    - \s: Match whitespace (spaces, tabs, newlines, and so on.).
    - \S: Match non-whitespace.

Remember—we did escape sequencing while string formatting. Likewise, you must escape with "" in a metacharacter when you want to match the metacharacter symbol itself.

For instance, if you want to match periods, you can't use "." because it is a metacharacter that matches anything. Instead, you'd use . to escape the period's metacharacter behavior and match the period itself. This is illustrated in the following code block:

```
# Match a single period and then a space

Word_series3 = pd.Series(["Mr. SK","Dr. Deepak","Miss\Mrs Gaire."])

Word_series3.str.contains("\. ")
```

If you want to match the escape character \ itself, you either have to use four backslashes "\" or encode the string as a raw string in the form r"mystring" and then use double backslashes. Raw strings are an alternate string representation in Python that simplifies some oddities in performing regular expressions on normal strings, as illustrated in the following code snippet:

```
# Match strings containing a backslash
Word_series3.str.contains(r"\\")
```

While dealing with special string characters in regular expressions, a raw string is often used because it avoids issues that may arise with those special characters.

Regular expressions are commonly used to match the patterns of phone numbers, email addresses, and web addresses in between the text. Pandas has several string functions that accept regular expression patterns and perform the operation. We are now familiar with these functions: `series.str.contains()` and `series.str.replace()`.

Now, let's use some more functions in our dataset of comments.

Use `series.str.count()` to count the occurrences of a pattern in each string, as follows:

```
text.str.count(r"[Ww]olves").head(8)
```

Use `series.str.findall()` to get each matched substring and return the result as a list, as follows:

```
text.str.findall(r"[Ww]olves").head(8)
```

There are endless ways in which a string can be manipulated. We chose to illustrate the most basic ways in order to make it simple for you to understand.

Further reading

- *Python Text Processing with NLTK 2.0 Cookbook, Jacob Perkins, Packt Publishing, November 9, 2010.*
- *NLTK Essentials, Nitin Hardeniya, Packt Publishing, July 26, 2015.*
- *Hands-On Natural Language Processing with Python, Rajesh Arumugam, Rajalingappaa Shanmugamani, Packt Publishing, July 17, 2018.*
- *Data Analysis with Python, David Taieb, Packt Publishing, December 31, 2018.*

Other Books You May Enjoy

If you enjoyed this book, you may be interested in these other books by Packt:

Python Feature Engineering Cookbook
Soledad Galli

ISBN: 978-1-78980-631-1

- Simplify your feature engineering pipelines with powerful Python packages
- Get to grips with imputing missing values
- Encode categorical variables with a wide set of techniques
- Extract insights from text quickly and effortlessly
- Develop features from transactional data and time series data
- Derive new features by combining existing variables
- Understand how to transform, discretize, and scale your variables
- Create informative variables from date and time

Hands-On Data Analysis with Pandas
Stefanie Molin

ISBN: 978-1-78961-532-6

- Understand how data analysts and scientists gather and analyze data
- Perform data analysis and data wrangling using Python
- Combine, group, and aggregate data from multiple sources
- Create data visualizations with pandas, matplotlib, and seaborn
- Apply machine learning (ML) algorithms to identify patterns and make predictions
- Use Python data science libraries to analyze real-world datasets
- Use pandas to solve common data representation and analysis problems
- Build Python scripts, modules, and packages for reusable analysis code

Leave a review - let other readers know what you think

Please share your thoughts on this book with others by leaving a review on the site that you bought it from. If you purchased the book from Amazon, please leave us an honest review on this book's Amazon page. This is vital so that other potential readers can see and use your unbiased opinion to make purchasing decisions, we can understand what our customers think about our products, and our authors can see your feedback on the title that they have worked with Packt to create. It will only take a few minutes of your time, but is valuable to other potential customers, our authors, and Packt. Thank you!

Index

171
  subnet of columns, selecting 168, 169

H

histogram 62, 63, 64, 65
hypothesis testing
  about 238
  average reading time, checking 241
  normalization 238
  performing, statsmodels library used 240
  standard normalization 238
  T-test 242, 243
  types 242

I

independent variable 45
Internet-Delivered Treatments (IDT) 264
interval scales 20

J

JavaScript Object Notation (JSON) 276

K

KNIME
  about 22
  URL 22
kurtosis 157
kurtosis, types
  about 158, 159
  leptokurtic 158
  mesokurtic 158
  platykurtic 158

L

labeled training data 262
labels 17
libraries
  exploring 69
Likert scale 19
line chart
  about 38, 39
  creating 40, 41
linear regression model
  accuracy 255, 257

accuracy, computing 255
constructing 247, 249, 252
evaluating 253, 255
lollipop chart 65, 66, 67

M

machine learning (ML)
  about 262
  categories 262
  supervised learning 262
  unsupervised learning 264
mathematical operations
  with NaN values 118, 119
Matplotlib 35
measure of central tendency
  about 147
  mean/average 147
  median 148
  mode 148, 150, 151, 152, 153
measure of dispersion
  about 20, 153
  kurtosis 157
  percentiles, calculating 159
  quartiles 160
  skewness 156, 157
  standard deviation 153
  variance 154
measure of variability 153
measurement scales
  about 17
  interval scales 20
  nominal scales 17
  ordinal scales 19
  ratio scales 20
median item 19
MiniBatch K-means clustering
  keywords, extracting 267, 268
  reference link 265
  used, for clustering 265
  used, for plotting clusters 269, 270
  word cloud, plotting 270, 272
missing values
  dropping 116
  dropping, by columns 117, 118
  filling 119, 120

interpolating 122
model development 309, 311, 312
model evaluation 309, 311, 312
multiple linear regression 246
multiple linear regression model
  implementing 257, 259, 260
multivariate analysis
  about 201, 203, 204, 205
  discussing, with Titanic dataset 206, 207, 208,
  209, 210, 212, 213

N

NaN values
  in pandas objects 114, 115
negative correlation 194
Negative Predictive Value (NPV) 278
negative skewness 156
numerical data
  about 15
  continuous data 15
  discrete data 15

O

Open Power System Data
  using, for TSA 222
ordinal scales 19
Ordinary Least Squares (OLS) 246
outcome variable 244

P

p-hacking 243
pandas library
  reference link 29
pandas
  about 29, 30, 31, 32, 33, 34
  documentation, reference link 41
parameters, hypothesis testing
  alternative hypothesis 239
  level of significance 239
  null hypothesis 239
  p-values 239
  Type I error and Type II error 239
parameters, scatter plot
  reference link 51
percentiles

calculating 159
pie chart 55, 56, 57, 58
pivot tables 180, 182, 183, 184
Ploty
  about 69
  URL 69
Poisson point process 144
polar chart 60, 61, 62
polytomous variable 17
positive correlation 194
positive skewness 156
precision 278
predictor 244
Principal Component Analysis (PCA) 269
probabilistic measure 280
probability density function (PDF) 141
probability distribution 141
probability function 141
probability mass function (PMF) 141
Python
  about 22
  URL 22

Q

qualitative data 18
qualitative datasets 16
quantitative data 15
quartiles
  about 160
  visualizing 161, 162, 163

R

R programming language
  about 22
  URL 22
random sampling
  with replacement 132
  without replacement 131
rare engine-location 201
ratio scales 20
red wine dataset
  analyzing 288, 289
  correlated columns, finding 289, 291, 292, 293
  correlation, between column alcohol and pH
    values 295, 297

www.ingramcontent.com/pod-product-compliance
Lightning Source LLC
Chambersburg PA
CBHW080617060326
40690CB00021B/4726